CARE STANDARDS MANUAL

AUSTRALIA
Law Book Co.
Sydney

CANADA and USA
Carswell
Toronto

HONG KONG
Sweet & Maxwell Asia

NEW ZEALAND
Brookers
Wellington

SINGAPORE and MALAYSIA
Sweet & Maxwell Asia
Singapore and Kuala Lumpur

CARE STANDARDS MANUAL

The regulation of establishments and agencies providing services to adults

by

Richard M. Jones M.A., Solicitor

President, Institute of Mental Health Act Practitioners
Consultant in Mental Health and Community Care Law,
Morgan Cole, Solicitors

THOMSON

™

SWEET & MAXWELL

Published in 2004 by
Sweet & Maxwell Ltd of
100 Avenue Road, Swiss Cottage,
London NW3 3PF
www.sweetandmaxwell.co.uk
Typeset, printed and bound in Great Britain by
Hobbs The Printers Ltd, Southampton

No natural forests were destroyed to
make this product: only farmed
timber was used and re-planted.

ISBN 0 421 691409

**A catalogue record for this book is
available from the British Library**

PREFACE

The Better Regulation Task Force, which was set up by the Chancellor of the Duchy of Lancaster in September 1997 to advise the present Government on improving the quality of government regulation, identified five principles of good regulation:

- **Transparency**, meaning that: policy objectives, including the need for regulation, are clearly defined and effectively communicated to all those concerned; regulations are simple and clear, and come with guidance in plain English; those being regulated understand their obligations and know what to expect from the enforcing authorities.
- **Accountability**, meaning that: regulators are accountable to government, citizens and Parliament; proposals are published and all those affected consulted before decisions are taken; there is a well-publicised, accessible, fair and efficient appeals procedure.
- **Targeting**, meaning that: the approach taken is aimed at the problem and not scatter-gun or universal; a goals approach is used where possible to allow for future flexibility; those being regulated must be left some freedom to decide how to achieve these goals; regulations are reviewed from time to time to test whether they are still necessary and effective; if not, they should be modified or eliminated.
- **Consistency**, meaning that: new regulations are consistent with existing regulations; regulations are compatible with EU and international trade and competition policy; there is even enforcement by the relevant authorities.
- **Proportionality**, meaning that: alternatives to regulation are fully considered; the impact on all those affected by the regulation is identified, establishing the right balance between risk and cost; no needless demands are made on those regulated; any enforcement action is in proportion to the seriousness of the offence.

The report of the Task Force on long-term care for the elderly concluded that the existing regulatory arrangements failed on all these principles. Has the regulatory regime established under the Care Standards Act 2000, referred to throughout this work as "the Act", improved matters? There have clearly been some significant improvements, for example, the new Care Standards Tribunal is well on its way to meeting the requirement for a "well-publicised, accessible and fair and efficient appeals procedure" and the National Care Standards Commission (the "NCSC") made a considerable investment in improving communication with both the regulated and the general public. However, major concerns about the way that regulation is working remain and these will require the urgent attenton of the new regulatory bodies, the Commission for Healthcare Audit and Inspection, which is to be known as the Healthcare Commission, and the Commission for Social Care Inspection. The concerns relate to the principles of transparency, targeting and proportionality.

There is a significant distinction in the Act between regulations, which are made by Parliament under the authority of s.22 of the Act, and the statements of national minimum standards, which are published by the Minister under the authority of s.23 of the Act. The principal difference between the regulations and the standards is that the former are binding on establishments and agencies, while the latter are not. This difference, which is of crucial importance to the regulated, was not fully appreciated by the NCSC and this led to the regulated being confused about their obligations and being uncertain about "what to expect from the enforcing authorities". It is clearly essential for the regulators to understand the nature of the legislation which they are required to operate.

With regard to targeting, there is both anecdotal evidence and evidence from the decisions of the Care Standards Tribunal with regard to the regulation of care homes that the NCSC followed its predecessors by focusing its regulatory attentions on process rather than outcome issues. The NCSC appeared to have adopted a crude "tick box" culture which assumes that if a regulatory box is ticked this will necessarily have a positive outcome for the service user, and that if a regulatory box is not ticked this will have a negative outcome for the service user. If they are to succeed in the objective of truly protecting the interests of service users, the regulators will need to develop a model of regulation which focuses on the quality of life that the service user enjoys rather than on a strict adherence to the very substantial raft of bureaucratic requirements that now confront the regulated. The extent to which the current regulatory regime places demands on the regulated can be gauged from the following extract of a letter that a doctor wrote to *The Times* on March 17, 2004:

"In order to comply with the requirements of the NCSC, the private hospital at which I have been working part-time for the past six years now requires that I present to the general manager, at a face to face meeting, the following documentation: positive proof of identification with a photograph (*i.e.* passport); double proof of current home address (utility bill, bank statement); birth certificate; documentary evidence of relevant professional qualifications, accreditations and specialist experience; a current professional indemnity certificate; evidence of continuing professional development or continuing medical education; an up to date copy of my CV; and an enhanced disclosure certificate from the Criminal Records Bureau, which I am required to pay for, and which has to be up-dated every three years."

The doctor ended his letter by remarking that strangely, for a consultant radiologist, he was not required to submit an eye-test result! The new regulators should consider whether it would be appropriate for them to join forces to announce a review of regulatory requirements with a view to testing out the targeting princple that they are "still necessary and effective".

The final area of concern relates to the occasional inability of the NCSC to adopt a proportionate approach to enforcing the Act. An example of this failing can be found in the case of *Joyce v NCSC* where the Care Standards Tribunal considered an appeal against the decision of the NCSC to cancel Mrs Joyce's registration in respect of a care home. The NCSC had taken action because of the failure of Mrs Joyce to appoint an individual to manage the care home, thereby breaching the Care Homes Regulations 2001. Although the tribunal found that there had been a breach of the regulations, the appeal was allowed because the lack of a registered manager had not "significantly or materially affected services users" and "closure would have a disproportionate effect upon the public, health agencies, social care agencies, the users currently at the home, potential future users, owners and staff". When contemplating regulatory action, the regulators should bear in mind that the purpose of enforcement action is to protect the interests of actual and potential service users and that any action taken should be "in proportion to the seriousness of the offence".

I have attempted to describe the law as in force on June 8, 2004.

Richard Jones
Morgan Cole
Bradley Court
Park Place
Cardiff CF10 3DP

CONTENTS

Part 4—Regulations and National Minimum Standards

Part 5—Inspections

Part 6—Offences

Part 7—Care Standards Tribunal

Annex A—Interpretation

Annex B—Department of Health Guidance

Table of Cases

Table of Cases

Table of Cases

Table of Cases

Table of Statutes

Table of Statutory Instruments

Table of Statutory Instruments

PART 1

DEFINITIONS OF ESTABLISHMENTS AND AGENCIES

This Part sets out the statutory definitions of the establishments and agencies that are **1–001** required to be registered under the Act. Although the focus of this Manual is on establishments and agencies that care for adults, all of the definitions are reproduced for the sake of completeness.

The approach that has been taken to the regulation of independent hospitals is that all non-NHS hospitals, including those who provide services to NHS patients will be regulated under the Act (s.2(2)). Primary private care premises are also brought within the regulatory framework by virtue of being categorised as independent clinics: see s.2(4) and reg.4 of the Private and Voluntary Health Care (England) Regulations 2001 (SI 2001/3698). Doctors who provide private treatment to patients but who do not operate from a registerable establishment are required to register as independent medical agencies (s.2(5)). Occupational medical schemes are exempted from registration by reg.5 of the 2001 Regulations.

The definition of "care home", which contains no reference to the age of service users, must be read in conjunction with s.121(9) of the Act which states that an establishment is not a care home unless the care provided "includes assistance with bodily functions where such assistance is required". The meaning of the phrase "bodily functions" has been considered by the Court of Appeal in *R. v National Insurance Commissioner Ex p. Secretary of State for Social Services* and by the House of Lords in *Wooding v Secretary of State for Social Services*. These cases are considered in Annex A. Regulation 3 of the Care Homes Regulations 2001 (SI 2001/3965) excludes certain establishments from the definition of a care home. A care home can care for a patient who has been granted leave of absence under s.17 of the Mental Health Act 1983 without having to be registered an independent hospital (s.2(3)(b), (6)).

Domiciliary care agencies, which arrange for the provision of personal care to people in **1–002** their own homes, are brought with the regulatory framework for the first time. An organisation that only provides practical care, such as assistance with shopping and housework, is not required to be registered. Registration is also not required if the provider of the personal care is working alone: see reg.3 of the Domiciliary Care Agencies Regulations 2002 (SI 2002/3214).

The Act transfers responsibility for the registration of nurses agencies from local authorities to the Commission for Social Care Inspection. An NHS Trust which supplies nurses to work solely for other NHS Trusts is not required to be registered: see reg.3 of the Nurses Agencies Regulations 2002 (SI 2002/3212). Section 111 of the Act brings nurses agencies within the scope of the Employment Agencies Act 1973 and regulations made under that Act.

Section 42 of the Act enables regulations to be made to extend the registration requirements to social care services that are not mentioned in the definition sections.

Children's homes

1–003   **1.**—(1) Subsections (2) to (6) have effect for the purposes of this Act.

(2) An establishment is a children's home (subject to the following provisions of this section) if it provides care and accommodation wholly or mainly for children.

(3) An establishment is not a children's home merely because a child is cared for and accommodated there by a parent or relative of his or by a foster parent.

(4) An establishment is not a children's home if it is—

(a) a health service hospital;

(b) an independent hospital or an independent clinic; or

(c) a residential family centre,

or if it is of a description excepted by regulations.

(5) Subject to subsection (6), an establishment is not a children's home if it is a school.

(6) A school is a children's home at any time if at that time accommodation is provided for children at the school and either—

(a) in each year that fell within the period of two years ending at that time, accommodation was provided for children, either at the school or under arrangements made by the proprietor of the school, for more than 295 days; or

(b) it is intended to provide accommodation for children, either at the school or under arrangements made by the proprietor of the school, for more than 295 days in any year;

and in this subsection "year" means a period of twelve months.

But accommodation shall not for the purposes of paragraph (a) be regarded as provided to children for a number of days unless there is at least one child to whom it is provided for that number of days; and paragraph (b) shall be construed accordingly.

(7) For the purposes of this section a person is a foster parent in relation to a child if—

(a) he is a local authority foster parent in relation to the child;

(b) he is a foster parent with whom a child has been placed by a voluntary organisation under section 59(1)(a) of the 1989 Act; or

(c) he fosters the child privately.

DEFINITIONS

1–004   child: s.121(1).
health service hospital: s.121(1).
independent clinic: s.2(4).
independent hospital: s.2(2)(3).
parent: s.121(1).
relative: s.121(1).
residential family centre: s.4(2).

school: s.121(1).

GENERAL NOTE

Children's homes are subject to regulation under the Act. This section defines a chil- **1–005**
dren's home as an establishment which provides care and accommodation wholly or
mainly for children. According to the Explanatory Notes (para.25) this definition "will
catch community homes, voluntary homes and registered children's homes (including
small private homes) as defined in the Children Act 1989, and homes for disabled children". It also covers certain boarding schools (subss.(5), (6)) and Youth Treatment
Centres established under s.82(5) of the 1989 Act. Interim arrangements for the registration
of small private children's homes are contained in s.40. Subsections (3) to (6) exclude certain establishments from the definition.

SUBS.(2)

Children's home: An establishment cannot be both a care home and a children's home **1–006**
(s.3(3)(c)). However, a care home can accommodate children and a children's home can
accommodate adults. A child can therefore continue to be accommodated in the home
after reaching adulthood.

Accommodation: The fact that this section is concerned with children's "homes" must
mean that the term accommodation excludes accommodation that is not provided
overnight.

SUBS.(3)

The 1989 Act exempts from regulation children's homes that accommodate three or less **1–007**
children. As this Act closes this loophole in s.30, it was necessary to ensure that "establishments" that are providing care for children in a domestic environment are not subject to
registration.

Merely: A children's home can accommodate and care for children of the description contained in this provision.

Foster parent: This is defined in subs.(7).

SUBS.(4)

Description excepted by regulations: Regulation 3 of the Children's Homes Regulations **1–008**
2001 states:

"(1) For the purposes of the Act, establishments of the following descriptions are excepted from being a children's home—

(a) any institution within the further education sector as defined by section 91(3) of the
    Further and Higher Education Act 1992;
(b) subject to paragraph (2), any establishment providing accommodation for children
    for less than 28 days in any twelve month period in relation to any one child, for
    the purposes of—
    (i) a holiday; or
    (ii) recreational, sporting, cultural or educational activities;
(c) subject to paragraph (2), any premises at which a person provides day care within the
    meaning of Part XA of the 1989 Act for less than 28 days in any twelve month period
    in relation to any one child;
(d) subject to paragraph (2), any establishment providing accommodation for children
    aged 16 and over—
    (i) to enable them to undergo training or apprenticeship;
    (ii) for the purposes of a holiday; or
    (iii) for recreational, sporting, cultural or educational purposes;
(e) any approved bail hostel or approved probation hostel; and

(f) any institution provided for young offenders under or by virtue of section 43(1) of the Prison Act 1952.

(2) The exceptions in paragraphs (1)(b), (c) and (d) do not apply to any establishment or premises in which the children who are accommodated are wholly or mainly of a description falling within section 3(2) of the Act.

(3) For the purposes of calculating the period of 28 days mentioned in paragraph (1)(c), no account is to be taken of any period of 24 hours during which at least 9 hours are spent by a child in the care of his parent or relative, and day care is not provided for him during that time."

SUBS.(6)

1–009 As originally drafted this provision only applied to independent boarding schools. These schools are required to be registered as children's homes under s.62(6) of the 1989 Act. As the Government recognised during the passage of the Bill that there was no good reason why children in either voluntary or state sector schools should not benefit from the protection of registration, this provision was amended to extend the requirement to register to all categories of boarding school.

Concern was expressed during the Bill's passage that a boarding school which provided holiday camps during the school holidays would be required to register as a children's home. This was not the Government's intention and the clause was amended to put beyond doubt that an individual child has to be accommodated for more than 295 days before the boarding school is required to register as a children's home. These schools, which are also required to be registered under education legislation, are likely to cater for children with disabilities or children whose parents are overseas or foreign children. Welfare provision for children who are pupils of independent schools that are not required to be registered under this Act is contained in s.87 of the 1989 Act.

The fact that a teacher lives with his or her children in a family setting on the school site does not, of itself, render the school registerable as a children's home because of the exclusion contained in subs.(3).

Independent hospitals, etc.

1–010 **2.**—(1) Subsections (2) to (6) apply for the purposes of this Act.

(2) A hospital which is not a health service hospital is an independent hospital.

(3) "Hospital" (except in the expression health service hospital) means—

(a) an establishment—

(i) the main purpose of which is to provide medical or psychiatric treatment for illness or mental disorder or palliative care; or

(ii) in which (whether or not other services are also provided) any of the listed services are provided;

(b) any other establishment in which treatment or nursing (or both) are provided for persons liable to be detained under the Mental Health Act 1983.

(4) "Independent clinic" means an establishment of a prescribed kind (not being a hospital) in which services are provided by medical practitioners (whether or not any services are also provided for the purposes of the establishment elsewhere).

But an establishment in which, or for the purposes of which, services are provided by medical practitioners in pursuance of the National Health Service Act 1977 is not an independent clinic.

(5) "Independent medical agency" means an undertaking (not being an independent clinic [or an independent hospital]) which consists of or includes the provision of services by medical practitioners.

But if any of the services are provided for the purposes of an independent clinic, or by medical practitioners in pursuance of the National Health Service Act 1977, it is not an independent medical agency.

(6) References to a person liable to be detained under the Mental Health Act 1983 do not include a person absent in pursuance of leave granted under section 17 of that Act.

(7) In this section "listed services" means—

(a) medical treatment under anaesthesia or sedation;

(b) dental treatment under general anaesthesia;

(c) obstetric services and, in connection with childbirth, medical services;

(d) termination of pregnancies;

(e) cosmetic surgery

   [(a) other than—
   (i) ear and body piercing;
   (ii) tattooing;
   (iii) the subcutaneous injection of a substance or substances into the skin for cosmetic purposes; and
   (iv) the removal of hair roots or small blemishes on the skin by the application of heat using an electric current.];

(f) treatment using prescribed techniques or prescribed technology.

(8) Regulations may—

(a) except any description of establishment from the definitions in subsections (2) to (4);

(b) except any description of undertaking from the definition in subsection (5);

(c) modify the definition in subsection (7).

AMENDMENTS
The words in square brackets in subs.(5) were inserted by the Health and Social Care **1–011** (Community Health and Standards) Act 2003, s.106.
   The words in square brackets in subs.(7)(e) were added by the Private and Voluntary Health Care (England) Regulations 2001 (SI 2001/3968), reg.3(4).

DEFINITIONS
   health service hospital: s.121(1). **1–012**
   illness: s.121(1).
   medical: s.121(1).
   mental disorder: s.121(1).
   prescribed: s.121(1).

treatment: s.121(1).
undertaking: s.121(1).

GENERAL NOTE

1–013   This section sets out the range of independent healthcare services that are to be regulated under this Act. NHS hospitals are excluded (subs.(2)) because:

> "the independent healthcare provisions of the Bill are built on the fundamental principle that it will not be the [National Care Standards Commission's] task to be concerned with NHS Services. Providers of NHS Services will come under the separate arrangements specifically introduced to provide quality assurance in the NHS. Therefore, clinics that provide any NHS service will come under the NHS arrangements, and not under the [Commission]" (*per* the Parliamentary Under-Secretary of State, Lord Hunt of Kings Heath (*Hansard*, HL, Vol.611, col.646).

Hospitals established by Royal Charter or special Act of Parliament and premises used by GPs solely for private work come within the scope of this section. However, most premises used by dentists, by members of professions supplementary to medicine and by complementary medicine practitioners will not be registerable, unless a listed service (see subs.(7)) is being provided, or unless dental treatment is being provided under general anaesthesia. Premises that provide long-term nursing care, but not medical services, which were previously registered as "nursing homes" under the Registered Homes Act 1984, are now registerable as "care homes" (see s.3). Hospital premises cannot also be registered as a care home (s.3(3)(c)).

1–014   The legal test of whether an establishment is an independent hospital was considered by the tribunal in *Raphael Medical Centre (Neurological Rehabilitation) and another v NCSC* [2002] 54, 55 N.C. The tribunal held that:

(1) The test is an objective test, and the regulator responsible for registration must concentrate on the functions of the establishment.

(2) The regulator must look to the "main purpose" of the establishment. There may be subsidiary, ancillary purposes, even purposes not wholly connected with the main purpose, but it is the "main purpose" that determines whether the establishment is an independent hospital (*Glasgow Corporation v Johnstone and others* [1965] A.C. 609, HL applied).

(3) As the test is objective, what the establishment calls itself or holds itself out as is not the key factor. It is of course relevant to see what the establishment says it does, but this by itself is not sufficient.

(4) In considering the provision of medical treatment, the fact that there are medically qualified staff who are not employed on full-time contracts does not by itself prevent registration as an independent hospital. Context is paramount in this connection, and whereas a large number of beds may require full-time contracts, there may be situations where part-time and/or on call medical staff are more appropriate.

(5) With one rider, the tribunal adopted the following submission made on behalf of the NCSC about the definition of medical treatment:

(a) Treatment is not the same as care and would normally mean an active intervention (which may be surgical or non-surgical) to deal with illness.
(b) The question of whether treatment is medical depends upon whether it is an aspect of the science of medicine.

(c) Relevant factors in determining this include the qualifications of those who provide the treatment in question and the extent of involvement from registered medical practitioners.
(d) Treatment, which is normally provided by those who are not medically qualified, will not normally be medical treatment. The degree of direction of a qualified medical practitioner will, however, be a relevant factor.
(e) If decisions of the nature, extent and manner of any treatment require the knowledge of a registered medical practitioner, then this will be relevant.

The rider that the tribunal added to these submissions is that "treatment" should be given a purposive meaning so as to accurately reflect the fact that much of medicine today is administered by multi-professional specialist teams.

Subs.(2)
The effect of this provision is that all non-NHS hospitals, including those who provide services to NHS patients, will be regulated. **1–015**

Subs.(3)
The Explanatory Notes (para.28) state that the definition of independent hospital: **1–016**

"will encompass all those hospitals and mental nursing homes registered to take detained patients which are currently regulated under Part II of the Registered Homes Act 1984 and other private and voluntary hospitals which are currently not regulated—for example those run by bodies established by Royal Charter or by special Act of Parliament."

The Government resisted amendments to include within the definition of independent hospital "private patient units within a health service hospital". *Per* Lord Hunt of Kings Heath:

"I believe the amendments to be misconceived. They assume that NHS paybeds need to be subject to regulation because otherwise they would be subject to no control. That is not the case. NHS paybeds, including those in dedicated units, are the responsibility of the NHS hospital where they are sited. They will be subject to clinical governance and all the other controls that apply to the NHS. The amendments would mean that even though a perfectly good system of management and clinical governance covered the whole hospital, certain parts of the hospital would be subject to another regulatory regime. That would be duplicatory and wasteful of time and effort. It would also distract the National Care Standards Commission inspectors from their key task of improving regulation of the currently poorly regulated private sector into inspecting parts of the NHS where perfectly good systems of clinical governance are in place" (*Hansard*, HL, Vol.608, col.411).

Para.(a)
The main purpose: The establishment could have multiple functions: see the *Raphael* **1–017** *Medical Centre* case, noted above. An establishment which has within its boundaries premises that are used to provide medical treatment and premises that are used to provide care, would need to be separately registered as both an independent hospital and a care home.
    In addition to providing services within the hospital building, the independent hospital could be providing outreach services in the home of a discharged patient.
    Psychiatric: This would include establishments that treat patients suffering from alcoholism and/or dependence on drugs (which are mental disorders) but not establishments that assist those who merely misuse alcohol or drugs. It also includes establishments who treat patients with recognised eating disorders. "Clinics" that help people to slim, as opposed to treating people for obesity, are not included. Establishments that only or mainly provide

counselling services would not be come within the definition of independent hospital. They would come within the definition of care home if they also provided accommodation, together with nursing or personal care for one or more of the categories set out in s.3(2).

An establishment that provides personal or nursing care for elderly people with dementia would be registrable as a care home as its main purpose is to provide nursing or care, not psychiatric treatment.

Treatment: See the *Raphael Medical Centre* case, noted above.

Palliative care: The fact that an establishment provides some palliative care in addition to "treatment" does not prevent registration as an independent hospital. However, an establishment that provides some palliative care in addition to "care" should be registered as a care home as long as the provision of palliative care is not its main purpose: see the note on subs.(7).

In the *Raphael Medical Centre* case, noted above, the tribunal was "broadly sympathetic" to the submission by counsel that palliative care "would seem to be the active care of patients the primary aim of which is not to cure illness, injury or mental disorder but to control and alleviate their symptoms (including pain), to improve the psychological, social and spiritual aspects of the patient, and to provide the best quality of life to the patient."

Listed services: See subs.(7). An establishment that provides a listed service must be registered as an "independent hospital". Unlike "independent clinics" and "independent medical agencies", which will only treat private patients, the patients being treated can either be private patients or NHS patients.

PARA.(B)

1–018 *Liable to be detained under the Mental Health Act 1983:* This term covers persons who are actually detained in the hospital and includes patients who have been made subject to hospital orders by a court under Part III of the 1983 Act. It does not include patients who are being cared for in an establishment subsequent to having been granted leave of absence under s.17 of the 1983 Act (subs.(6)). Such patients can be accommodated in care homes.

Patients who are detained in a registered establishments under the 1983 Act may be discharged from the power detaining them by the Secretary of State and, if the patient is being maintained by the NHS, by the NHS trust or Health Authority that is maintaining the patient (s.23(3) of the 1983 Act). To assist them in the exercise of this power, s.24(3),(4) of the 1983 Act provides these bodies with a power to visit and examine the patient and to require the production of relevant documents..

SUBS.(4)

1–019 This provision brings private primary care premises within the regulatory framework. Clinics that treat NHS patients as well as private patients are excluded. If a doctor operates two separate clinics on different premises and in one treats NHS patients and in the other private patients, the latter would need to be registered under this provision.

Prescribed kind: See the Private and Voluntary Health Care (England) Regulations 2001 (SI 2001/3968), reg.4.

Not being a hospital: If a private doctor provides treatment under anaesthesia or sedation, which is a "listed service" under subs.(7), he would need to be registered as an "independent hospital" rather than as an "independent clinic".

Elsewhere: For example in the patient's home.

SUBS.(5)

1–020 This provision was introduced by the Government because of concern expressed by Lord Clement-Jones "about the quality of care provided to private patients by call-out doctors, who were contacted by phoning an advertised number" (*Hansard*, HL, Vol.611, col.645). It covers doctors who provide treatment to private patients but who do not operate from establishments that could be registered. Hence the use of the term "undertaking" rather than "establishment".

An undertaking which provides medical services solely under arrangements made on behalf of patients by their employer or another person are exempted from registration (Private and Voluntary Health Care (England) Regulations 2001 (SI 2001/3968), reg.5).

SUBS.(6)

The fact that an establishment cares for patients who are on leave of absence from the hos- **1–021** pital where they are liable to be detained under the Mental Health Act 1983 (c.20) does not trigger a requirement to register as an independent hospital under subs.(3)(b).

SUBS.(7)

Palliative care was removed from the definition of listed services as originally drafted **1–022** because the Government recognised that "because a care home might provide some pallia- tive care to patients who are terminally ill, as drafted the Bill would require such a care home to be registered as an independent hospital. We recognise that that would be totally inappropriate" (*per* Lord Hunt of Kings Heath, *Hansard*, HL, Vol.615, col.935).

PARA.(A)

Sedation: It is submitted that this term refers the use of medication to induce the nervous **1–023** system to calm.

PARA.(B)

Dental treatment: It was recommended in "A Conscious Decision" (Department of **1–024** Health, July 2000) that after December 31, 2001 general anaesthesia for dental treatment should only be administered in a hospital setting with critical care facilities. Interim gui- dance was given by the Department in a letter dated February 15, 2001 and in a letter dated May 31, 2001 headed "General Anaesthesia for Dental treatment in a Hospital Setting with Critical Care Facilities", the Chief Dental Officer stated that from January 1, 2002 "it is intended to confine the administration of general anaesthesia for dental treat- ment to a hospital setting with critical care facilities". The letter went on to provide guidance on the meaning of the terms "hospital setting" and "critical care facilities". The guidance contained in the Chief Dental Officer's letter was applied by the Care Standards Tribunal in *Appiah-Anane v NCSC* [2002] 0096 N.C.

PARA.(C)

Obstetric services: Maternity homes run by midwives come within this definition. **1–025**

PARA.(E)

Cosmetic surgery: The National Care Standards Commission published a report to the **1–026** Chief Medical Officer for England on the findings of inspections of 22 private cosmetic surgery establishments in central London during March/April 2003.

PARA.(F)

Prescribed techniques or prescribed technology: See the Private and Voluntary Health Care **1–027** (England) Regulations 2001 (SI 2001/3968), reg.3.

SUBS.(8)
PARA.(A)

Regulations: See SI 2001/3968, above, reg.3(3). **1–028**

PARA.(B)

Regulations: See SI 2001/3968, above, reg.5. **1–029**

PARA.(C)

Regulations: See SI 2001/3968, above, reg.3(1)(2). **1–030**

Care homes

1–031   **3.**—(1) For the purposes of this Act, an establishment is a care home if it provides accommodation, together with nursing or personal care, for any of the following persons.

(2) They are—

(a) persons who are or have been ill;

(b) persons who have or have had a mental disorder;

(c) persons who are disabled or infirm;

(d) persons who are or have been dependent on alcohol or drugs.

(3) But an establishment is not a care home if it is—

(a) a hospital;

(b) an independent clinic; or

(c) a children's home,

or if it is of a description excepted by regulations.

DEFINITIONS

1–032   children's home: s.1.
disabled: s.121(2).
illness: s.121(1).
independent clinic: s.2.
mental disorder: s.121(1).
personal care: s.121(3).

GENERAL NOTE

1–033   The definition of care home in this section is intended to include residential care homes and nursing homes, as defined in the Registered Homes Act 1984. It includes residential care homes run by NHS bodies, "as the provision of residential (as against nursing) homes is not a core NHS function" (Explanatory Notes, para.33), but excludes hospitals, children's homes and independent clinics as they are separately provided for. It also includes local authority residential homes provided under Pt III of the National Assistance Act 1948 (c.29). The requirement contained in the 1984 Act for residential care homes to provide residents with board is removed. The Minister explained that board had been excluded from the definition because some homes were currently escaping the requirement to register by, for example, making residents pay for their meals rather than include food in the overall contract price (*Hansard*, HL, Vol.608, col.444).

Although the definition in this section is broad:

". . . that is not to say that a single care home will be able to take any type of client whatever his or her needs. We do not believe that would be at all appropriate. As I have said, people will have different needs and require different types of care. The needs of the young adult with a physical disability will be different from those of an older person with Alzheimer's disease. Obviously different types of care home will be needed to accommodate them. Homes will be registered to provide certain types of care only, which will be specified in the registration certificates . . .

People applying for registration will be required to give certain information in their applications. That will include the type of care that they wish to provide as well as the numbers of people they wish to accommodate, their age range, and so on. The commission may then grant the application either unconditionally or subject to such conditions as it thinks fit, provided, of course, that the establishment meets the relevant regulations and standards. In the case of a care home, the commission will alway impose registration conditions relating to the category of care that the homes may provide, the maximum number of residents it may accommodate and their age range. Those will be the minimum conditions of registration placed on all care homes." (*per* Lord Hunt of Kings Heath, *Hansard*, Vol.608, col.491).

The fact that for other purposes, another court has held that the establishment in not a **1–034** care home does not permit the owner to escape from the regulating procedures laid down in this Act (*Hunter v Cumbria County Council*, CO 1574/00, October 3, 2000, DC).

A statement of national minimum standards for care homes for older people and for care homes for younger adults have been published by the Secretary of State under s.23(1).

Guidance on continuing NHS health care in light of the judgment of the Court of Appeal in *R. v North and East Devon Health Authority Ex p. Coughlan* [2000] 2 W.L.R. 622 is to be found in Circular No.LAC (2001) 18: HSC 2001/015. *Coughlan* is authority for the proposition that a care home can amount to a "home" for the purposes of Art.8 of the European Convention on Human Rights.

SUPPORTED HOUSING SCHEMES

Since the Act came into force, there has been concern about the application of the defi- **1–035** nition of care home to housing schemes that are described as either very sheltered housing, extra care housing or supported housing. Common features of these arrangements are that the users live in their own self-contained dwelling, are usually granted tenancies and are provided with support services, which can include the provision of personal care.

Where domiciliary care is being provided in a person's own home, the body providing the personal care would be likely to require registration as a domiciliary care agency. Registration as a care home in this situation is not required even if a significant amount of personal care is being provided by the agency. This would be the case even if the agency and the landlord were organisationally linked, if the tenant had a genuine choice as to the identity of the care provider. As a rule of thumb, a non-owner-occupier can be said to be living in their own home for the purposes of the Act if that person has the right to deny entry to a care worker without such action prejudicing his or her security of housing tenure. This is the case irrespective of whether the person is living alone or in accommodation that is shared with others.

In *Alternative Futures Ltd v NCSC* [2002] 101–111 N.C., the tribunal was concerned with the dividing line between a care home and supported housing in the context of an application under s.15 of the Act for deregistration of a care home. Paragraph 106 of the decision sets out the requirements of the consultation process with service users that must precede the application:

"For us, the consultation process emphasising the choices available is of the utmost significance. It is necessary to have evidence that the service users should sign by themselves, or where appropriate by advocates and relatives, assured tenancy agreements following full consultation with each of them and their relatives and advocates. It is also necessary that the service users and/or their relatives and advocates should be consulted on the proposal to deregister and positively want their status to be changed to that of tenants in the new scheme. There should be a choice of care provider as part of the process of choice, although we acknowledge that this may be difficult in practice. These considerations should be set against the requirement in our view that there should be a full community care assessment undertaken by the commissioning body in which needs and options are fully discussed with the service users and their carers. There should be a detailed service plan drawn up in consultation with each service user. Service users must be able to exercise a choice over what care is provided and which carer provides the care and it should be made clear to the service user that their relatives and advocates that they may bar entry to a carer in the exercise of their tenancy rights. Thus, service user choice is essential in the delivery of care services and if a tenant does not want the existing provider to provide the care, alternative suitable provision would have to be made available following discussions with the service user concerned and other interested parties."

1–036   The tribunal further stated that on an application to deregister the major emphasis must be placed on "real and significant choice of the service user" (para.60), that in reaching a decision on whether an application to deregister is to be granted, there must be "clear evidence of a change of substance to bring the accommodation outside the statutory definition" (para.57) and that if a service user's lack of capacity were to form any part it the registration authority's or the tribunal's decision to refuse cancellation of registration, then the assessment of must be undertaken by a suitably qualified independent person (paras 48, 96).

The tribunal said that the existence of a valid tenancy agreement is "not by itself conclusive" of the question whether an establishment does or does not fall within the definition of care home (para.56). If such an agreement is in place and the establishment is registered as a care home, the rights conveyed under the agreement must be consistent with the requirements of the Care Homes Regulations 2001, especially the management requirements. As this is unlikely to be the case, the existence of a valid tenancy agreement will, in practice, prevent the tenant's home from coming within the definition of a care home.

Guidance on "Supported Housing and Care Homes", which was published by the Department of Health in August 2002, is reproduced in Annex B.

SUBS.(1)

1–037   *Establishment:* This term is not defined. In *Bogdal v Kingston upon Hull City Council* [1998] EWHC 156 (Admin), a case under the 1984 Act, Moses J. said at para.39 that "there must be some element of organisation about the premises which would enable it be . . . qualified [as an establishment]". Therefore an ordinary home which does not contain a relevant element of organisation within it cannot be a care home.

Care Home: If an establishment meets the criteria for registration as a care home, it must be registered as a care home irrespective of what it might call itself.

Accommodation: The fact that this section is concerned with care "homes" must mean that the term "accommodation" excludes accommodation that is not provided overnight. In *Cotgreave v Cheshire County Council*, 157 J.P. 85, *The Times*, July 9, 1992, a case under the 1984 Act, the Divisional Court held that people who attended at a residential care home only during the day were not resident there. Establishments that provide personal care for persons in the dependant categories who are on holiday would be registerable because people whose stay in the accommodation is temporary are to be treated as resident there. In *Swindells v Cheshire County Council*, CO/0611/92, *The Times*, February 18, 1993, DC, also a case under the 1984 Act, Staughton J. said:

"The application of the Act cannot, in my judgment, vary according to the intention of the person who is occupying accommodation. Many of the people who are persuaded by relatives to enter residential care homes are not themselves at all sure that they want to stay there very long; and some quite soon form the intention to leave as soon a they can. That is not a matter of importance to the application of the Act. It is the accommodation which has to be residential; and if residential accommodation is provided it does not matter whether the occupier intends to stay for a long or a short time."

1–038   *Together with:* The nursing or personal care must be provided at the establishment. It is submitted that the term "together with" means that there must be some connection between the provider of the accommodation and the provider of the nursing or personal care.

However, registration as a care home may not be required merely because the same provider provides both care and accommodation. Registration would not be required if the service user has a genuine option of choosing an alternative care provider.

Whether the establishment can provide nursing care or personal care or a combination of both is dependant on its registration category (National Care Standards Commission (Registration) Regulations 2001 (SI 2001/3969), reg.8, Sch.7, Pt II).

Nursing care: This is not defined. In April 2003, the Royal College of Nursing published the following definition of nursing: "Nursing is the use of clinical judgment in the provision of care to enable people to improve, maintain, or recover health, to cope with health problems, and to achieve the best possible quality of life, whatever their disease or disability, until death". As clinical judgment can only be exercised by a qualified nurse, it could be argued that "nursing care" means nursing care provided by a registered nurse. Section 49(2) of the Health and Social Care Act 2001, defines "nursing care by a registered nurse" as "any services provided by a registered nurse and involving: (a) the provision of care; or (b) the planning, supervision or delegation of the provision of care, other than any services which, having regard to their nature and the circumstances in which they are provided, do not need to be provided by a registered nurse." It is therefore suggested that "nursing care" in this provision means nursing care provided by, or given under the supervision or direction of a registered nurse. This approach is consistent with reg.8 of the Care Homes Regulations 2001 (SI 2001/3965) which requires a registered nurse to work at a care home which provides nursing and medicines or medical treatment to service users.

Personal care: An establishment is not a care home unless the care provided includes **1–039** assistance with bodily functions, where such assistance is required (s.121(9)). There is no obligation for such assistance to be given ordinarily or regularly. The requirement to provide assistance with bodily functions does not mean that personal care provided by a care home is limited to such assistance, but that this type of assistance must be available and given, when required. The Explanatory Notes (para.34) state that personal care "may include, for instance, assistance with bathing, dressing and eating for people who are unable to do these things without help". The finding of the Registered Homes Tribunal in *Harrison v Cornwall County Council* (Decn. No.146) that the term personal care under the 1984 Act "embraces care in many forms, emotional or psychiatric as well as physical" was approved by the Court of Appeal in *Harrison v Cornwall County Council* ((1991) 90 L.G.R. 81). Personal care under the 1984 Act was found not to extend to "general counselling and support services" in *R. v Allerdale Housing Benefit Review Board Ex p. Doughty* [2000] C.O.D. 462 at para.40.

Personal care is not defined in this Act, although there is provision in s.121(3) to exclude prescribed activities from being categorised as personal care. Personal care should be distinguished from care of a general nature which lacks any personal dimension. The National Minimum Standards for Domiciliary Care state that the "established, ordinary meaning [of personal care] includes four main types of care which are:

• assistance with bodily functions such as feeding, bathing and toileting;

• care falling just short of assistance with bodily functions, but still involving physical and intimate touching including activities such as helping a person get out of a bath and helping them to get dressed;

• non-physical care, such as advice, encouragement and supervision relating to the foregoing, such as prompting a person to take a bath and supervising them during this;

• emotional and psychological support, including the promotion of social functioning, behaviour management, and assistance with cognitive functions."

The Report by the Royal Commission on Long-Term Care (Cm.4192–1) said that personal care:

"would cover all direct care related to:

— personal toilet (washing, bathing, skin care, personal presentation, dressing and undressing and skin care);
— eating and drinking (as opposed to obtaining and preparing food and drink);
— managing urinary and bowel functions (including maintaining continence and managing incontinence);
— managing problems associated with immobility;
— management of prescribed treatment (*e.g.* administration and monitoring medication);
— behaviour management and ensuring personal safety (*e.g.* for those with cognitive impairment—minimising stress and risk)."

Personal care also includes the associated teaching, enabling, psychological support from a knowledgeable professional and skilled professional, and assistance with cognitive functions (*e.g.* reminding, for those with dementia) that are needed either to enable a person to do these things for himself/herself or to enable a relative to do them for him/her" (para.6.44).

Persons: There is no minimum number of residents who have to be accommodated before the home becomes registerable. The residents could include children.

Subs.(2)

1–040   There is no requirement that every resident of the care home needs to come within one or more of the categories set out here.

Although there is no reference to old age in the categories, the *Shorter Oxford English* defines "infirm" as "physically weak or feeble, especially through age".

Para.(b)

1–041   *Mental disorder:* Is defined in s.121(1). This provision and s.2(6) enable a care home to accommodate persons who are on leave of absence from a hospital under the terms of s.17 of the Mental Health Act 1983.

Para.(c)

1–042   *Disabled:* Is defined in s.121(2).

Para.(d)

1–043   This category does not cover the prevention of dependency.

Subs.(3)

1–044   *Hospital:* See s.2(3).

Children: Homes that provide personal care and accommodation for disabled children are to be treated as children's homes (s.1(2)).

Regulations: See the Care Homes Regulations 2001 (SI 2001/3965), reg.3.

Other basic definitions

1–045   **4.**—(1) This section has effect for the purposes of this Act.

(2) "Residential family centre" means, subject to subsection (6), any establishment at which—

(a) accommodation is provided for children and their parents;

(b) the parents' capacity to respond to the children's needs and to safeguard their welfare is monitored or assessed; and

(c) the parents are given such advice, guidance or counselling as is considered necessary.

In this subsection "parent", in relation to a child, includes any person who is looking after him.

(3) "Domiciliary care agency" means, subject to subsection (6), an undertaking which consists of or includes arranging the provision of personal care in their own homes for persons who by reason of illness, infirmity or disability are unable to provide it for themselves without assistance.

(4) "Fostering agency" means, subject to subsection (6)—

(a) an undertaking which consists of or includes discharged functions of local authorities in connection with the placing of children with foster parents; or

(b) a voluntary organisation which places children with foster parents under section 59(1) of the 1989 Act.

(5) "Nurses agency" means, subject to subsection (6), an employment agency or employment business, being (in either case) a business which consists of or includes supplying, or providing services for the purpose of supplying, registered nurses, registered midwives or registered health visitors.

(6) The definitions in subsections (2) to (5) do not include any description of establishment, undertaking or organisation excepted from those definitions by regulations.

(7) "Voluntary adoption agency" means an adoption society within the meaning of the Adoption Act 1976 which is a voluntary organisation within the meaning of that Act.

(8) Below in this Act—

(a) any reference to a description of establishment is a reference to a children's home, [a children's home providing accommodation for the purpose of restricting liberty,] an independent hospital, an independent hospital in which treatment or nursing (or both) are provided for persons liable to be detained under the Mental Health Act 1983, an independent clinic, a care home or a residential family centre;

(b) a reference to any establishment is a reference to an establishment of any of those descriptions.

(9) Below in this Act—

(a) any reference to a description of agency is a reference to an independent medical agency, a domiciliary care agency, a nurses agency, a fostering agency or a voluntary adoption agency;

(b) a reference to any agency is a reference to an agency of any of those descriptions.

AMENDMENT
1–046   The words in square brackets in subs.(8)(a) were inserted by the Health and Social Care (Community Health and Standards) Act 2003, s.107.

DEFINITIONS
1–047   child: s.121(1).
disability: s.121(2).
illness: s.121(1).
personal care: s.120(3).
undertaking: s.121(1)
employment agency: s.121(1).
voluntary organisation: s.121(1).

GENERAL NOTE
1–048   This section defines "residential family centre", "domiciliary care agency", "fostering agency", "nurses agency", "voluntary adoption agency", "establishment" and "agency".

SUBS.(2)
1–049   A residential family centre is a residential establishment where the monitoring and assessment of parents' capacity to respond to their children's needs and to safeguard their welfare is carried out, together the provision of necessary advice, guidance or counselling.

PARA.(A)
1–050   *Provided:* The centres could be operated by local authorities, voluntary organisations or private agencies.
Children and their parents: Both must be accommodated at the establishment. The term "parent" includes those parenting a child without having parental responsibility for that child.

PARA.(B)
1–051   *Parents' capacity:* The parents will be the main carers of their children at the centre.

SUBS.(3)
1–052   Where care workers are independently employed by a service user utilising the direct payments scheme provided for under s.57 of the Health and Social Care Act 2001, there is no registration requirement. However, there is a registration requirement if the care workers are supplied to the service user by an agency: see the note on "an undertaking".
The Select Committee on Health which investigated Elder Abuse commented that the powers of the registration authority in respect of domiciliary care agencies "are confined essentially to the fitness of the agency rather than to standards of the services delivered to the person in their own home. There is, for example, as yet no regulatory requirement for notification of adverse incidents equivalent to that which exists in relation to occurrences in care homes" (2nd Report Session 2003-4, para.158).
Undertaking: Which could comprise a sole proprietor who provides all of the personal care provided to clients.
Personal care: It is the Department of Health's view that only the types of personal care set out in the first two bullet points in the definition of personal care contained in the National Minimum Standards for Domiciliary Care, which is reproduced in the note on "personal care" in s.3(1), will give rise to registration as a domiciliary care agency (Domiciliary care: National Minimum Standards, p.6). Services of a practical nature which would not come within the definition of personal care include helping a person with business and/ or financial matters, undertaking housework, shopping, ensuring that a dwelling is secure, and household maintenance.

An undertaking: Including organisations that supply care staff to service users who will be employed directly by the service user. An undertaking carried on by an individual is exempted from registration if the provisions of reg.3 of the Domiciliary Care Regulations 2003 (SI 2002/3214) are satisfied.

In their own homes: This means the place where the service users live. The agency could provide care workers who live in the service user's home.

Assistance: Either by helping the service user to perform the activity or performing the activity for the service user.

Subs.(4)

This definition includes both independent agencies which provide a fostering agency **1–053** service to local authorities, and voluntary organisations (such as Barnardos) who operate in their own right.

Subs.(5)

Section 111 of this Act ensures that nurses agencies come within the remit of the **1–054** Employment Agencies Act 1973 as well as this Act. Guidance which sets out the arrangements for the transition from licensing by local authorities under the Nurses Agencies Act 1957 to registration under this Act is contained in Department of Health Circular LAC (2002) 20.

There was no requirement for local authorities to inspect under the 1957 Act. The Department of Health originally considered replacing the 1957 Act by simply ensuring that the 1973 Act should govern nurses agencies—as it does all other employment businesses and agencies. The 1973 Act does not involve licensing or routine inspection but the Employment Agencies Standards Inspectorate responds to concerns and complaints about agencies and also does spot checks of agencies that supply staff to work with vulnerable people. The Inspectorate also has enforcement powers over agencies. However, the Government was persuaded during the consultation on this Act that nurses agencies should be registered under this Act, as an additional tier of regulation.

If a nurse supplied by the agency provides personal care to an individual in their own home, registration as a domiciliary care agency may be required.

Subs.(6)

See SI 2002/3214, reg.3, noted above and the Nurses Agencies Regulations 2002 (SI **1–055** 2002/3212), reg.3.

Subss.(8), (9)

The establishment or agency need not be run for profit (s.121(5)). **1–056**

Power to extend the application of Part II

42.—(1) Regulations may provide for the provisions of this Part to apply, with **1–057** such modifications as may be specified in the regulations, to prescribed persons to whom subsection (2) or (3) applies.

(2) This subsection applies to—

(a) local authorities providing services in the exercise of their social services functions; and

(b) persons who provide services which are similar to services which—

(i) may or must be so provided by local authorities; or

(ii) may or must be provided by Health Authorities, Special Health Authorities, NHS trusts or Primary Care Trusts.

(3) This subsection applies to persons who carry on or manage an undertaking (other than an establishment or agency) which consists of or includes supplying, or providing services for the purpose of supplying, individuals mentioned in subsection (4).

(4) The individuals referred to in subsection (3) are those who provide services for the purposes of any of the services mentioned in subsection (2).

[(5) Regulations under subsection (1) made by the Secretary of State may in particular specify whether, for the purposes of the application of this Part to any person, the registration authority is to be the CHAI or the CSCI.]

AMENDMENT

1–058   Subsection (5) was inserted by the Health and Social Care (Community Health and Standards) Act 2003, s.147, Sch.9, Pt 2, para.25.

DEFINITIONS

1–059   agency: s.4(9).
establishment: s.4(8).
local authority: s.121(1).
prescribed: s.121(1).
regulations: s.121(1).
CHAI: s.121(13).
CSCI: s.121(13).

GENERAL NOTE

1–060   This section enables regulations to be made to extend the application of Part 2 of the Act to social care services that are not on the face of the Act. In doing so it introduces a degree of flexibility that was absent from the Registered Homes Act 1984. Flexibility with regard to health care services is provided for in s.2(8)(c).

During the passage of the Bill, the Government announced that it will use its powers under this section "to introduce regulation by the National Care Standards Commission of day centres which provide nursing or personal care. . .[I]t will not be possible to do this from the start of the Commission's life, but we will carry out a review within one year of the Commission being established to decide the details of exactly how and when the regulatory regime will come into force" (*per* Lord Hunt of Kings Heath, *Hansard*, HL, Vol.611, col.650).

SUBS.(3)

1–061   The purpose of this provision, the wording of which was described by the Minister of State as "dense" (Standing Committee G, col.414), is to extend regulatory requirements to businesses that are providing services to individuals who provide services for any of the purposes mentioned in subs.(2).

PART 2

REGISTRATION AUTHORITIES

Delivering the NHS Plan: Next steps on investment, next steps for reform (Cm. 5503) set **2–001** out the Government's intention to create a new Commission for Healthcare Audit and Inspection ("the CHAI") which would have the responsibility for the review and inspection of providers of NHS health care and also for the registration under the Care Standards Act 2000 of independent providers of healthcare in England, and a new Commission for Social Care Inspection ("the CSCI") which would have responsibility for inspecting local authority social services in England and also for the registration under the Act of providers of social care in England. The CHAI is to be known as the Healthcare Commission. The CHAI and the CSCI were established by ss.41 and 42 of the Health and Social Care (Community Health and Standards) Act 2003 respectively. The constitution of each body is governed by Schs 6 and 7 of that Act.

The National Care Standards Commission, the regulatory body which was established under the Act, is abolished by s.44 of the 2003 Act and its functions have been transferred to the new regulatory bodies, the CHAI and the CSCI, by s.102 of that Act as follows:

- The NCSC's functions under Part 2 of the Act have been transferred to the CHAI insofar as they relate to—

  (a) independent hospitals;
  (b) independent clinics; and
  (c) independent medical agencies.

- The NCSC's functions under that Part are transferred to the CSCI insofar as they relate to—

  (d) children's homes;
  (e) care homes;
  (f) residential family centres;
  (g) domiciliary care agencies;
  (h) nurses agencies;
  (i) fostering agencies;
  (j) voluntary adoption agencies; and
  (k) adoption support agencies.

The general duties of CHAI and the CSCI are set out in ss.5A and 5B respectively. The registers of regulated services, which the Commissions are required to keep, must be available for public inspection (s.36). The service of documents by the Commissions is governed by s.37.

The CSCI is required by para.5(2) of Sch.7 to the 2003 Act to appoint a Children's Rights **2–002** Director. The Director, who is an employee of the CSCI, is required to perform the functions set out in reg.3 of the Commission for Social Care Inspection (Children's Rights Director) Regulations 2004 (SI 2004/615). These include the duty to secure, so far as possible, that the CSCI in exercising its functions:

(a) safeguards and promotes the rights and welfare of children who are provided with services under this Act; and

(b) gives proper consideration to the views of children to whom such services are provided and to the views of the parents of such children.

Section 120 of the 2003 Act requires the CHAI and the CSCI to co-operate with each other where this seems appropriate for the "efficient and effective discharge of their respective functions", and to consult with each other in prescribed circumstances. The same section enables each body to delegate the exercise of any of its functions to the other and to pool financial resources in the circumstances prescribed by the Commission for Social Care Inspection (Explanation and Co-operation) Regulations 2004 (SI 2004/555), reg.3 and the Commission for Healthcare Audit and Inspection (Explanation, Statements of Action and Co-operation) Regulations 2004 (SI 2004/557), reg.4. Both bodies are required to prepare and publish a Code of Practice it proposes to follow in relation to confidential personal information (ss.140, 141).

The CHAI and the CSCI have websites at *www.chai.org.uk* and *www.csci.org.uk*

In Wales, the National Assembly for Wales has the responsibility for the delivery of health and social care services. Whilst the CHAI will be an England and Wales body and will carry out functions in Wales in relation to the NHS, the local review of NHS bodies will be made by a new body, the Healthcare Inspectorate Wales. The regulation of agencies and establishment in Wales under the Act will continue to be undertaken by the Care Standards Inspectorate for Wales which has a website at *www.wales.gov.uk/subisocialpolicycarestandards*.

Section 113 (1A) of the Act confers default powers on the Secretary of State "if he is satisfied that—

(a) the CHAI or the CSCI has without reasonable excuse failed to discharge, or properly to discharge, any of its functions under this Act, or

(b) in discharging any of its functions under this Act the CHAI or the CSCI has without reasonable excuse failed to comply with any directions given by him in relation to those functions."

Under s.10 of the Act, the Secretary of State may hold an enquiry into any matter concerning a regulated service.

TRANSITIONAL PROVISIONS

2–003 Transitional provisions relating to the transfer of functions from the NCSC to either the CHAI or the CSCI are contained in art.11 of the Health and Social Care (Community Health and Standards) Act 2003 (Commission for Healthcare Audit and Inspection and Commission for Social Care Inspection) (Transitional and Consequential Provisions) Order 2004 (SI 2004/664) which reads:

"(1) Anything which immediately before 1st April is in the process of being done by or in relation to the NCSC may, if it relates to any function transferred under section 102(1) of the [2003] Act, be continued by or in relation to the transferee.

(2) Anything done (or having effect as if done) by or in relation to the NCSC before 1st April 2004 for the purpose of, or in connection with, any function transferred under section 102(1) of the Act is, so far as is required for continuing its effect, to have effect as if done by, or in relation to, the transferee.

(3) Any reference to the NCSC in any document constituting or relating to anything to which paragraph (1) or (2) applies in relation to a function is, so far as is required for giving effect to those provisions, to be construed as reference to the transferee.

(4) In this article 'transferee', in relation to a function, means the body to which the function is transferred under section 102(1)."

Registration authorities

5.—[(1)] For the purposes of this Act—   **2–004**

(a) the registration authority in relation to England is;

   [(i) the CHAI, in the case of independent hospitals, independent clinics and
         independent medical agencies;
   (ii) the CSCI, in the case of children's homes, care homes, residential fam-
         ily centres, domiciliary care agencies, nurses agencies, fostering
         agencies, voluntary adoption agencies and adoption support agencies;]

(b) the registration authority in relation to Wales is the National Assembly for
     Wales (referred to in this Act as "the Assembly").

[(2) This section is subject to section 36A.]

AMENDMENT

The words in square brackets in subs.(1) were substituted by the Health and Social Care **2–005**
(Community Health and Standards) Act 2003, s.147, Sch.9, Pt 2, para.17.
Subsection (2) was inserted by the Adoption and Children Act 2002, Sch.3, para.105.

GENERAL NOTE

This section, s.6 and Sch.1 provide for the Commission of Health Audit and Inspection **2–006**
and the Commission for Social Care Inspection to be the registration authorities for establishments and agencies. The general functions of the two inspectorates are set out in ss.5A
and 5B. This section also establishes the Assembly as the registration authority in Wales.
Further provisions relating to the Assembly are contained in s.8.
   In "Confidentiality and the Sharing of Information", Journal of Mental Health Law
(2003) 9 at 42, Fenella Morris writes:

"*In Leach v. National Care Standards Commission*, unreported, Master Yoxhall, 30
October 2002, upheld the National Care Standard Commission's refusal to disclose
the source of, ultimately disproved, allegations of abuse and neglect at a residential
care home for the elderly. The claimant sought disclosure in order to bring defamation
proceedings given the damage the allegations had caused to his business. The Court
found that the public interest in the protection of the vulnerable from abuse, and the particular need for independent reporting in respect of those who may not be able to raise the
alarm themselves, outweighed the claimant's interests in disclosure."

Although the Royal Commission on Long-Term Care recommended, at para.7.1, that
registration authorities should be independent of Government and Parliament, and the
Minister of State emphasised that such independence was necessary to "command wide-
spread public confidence and support" (Standing Committee G, col.144), the National
Assembly for Wales decided, after conducting a consultation exercise, that the new regulatory arrangements in Wales should be set up as part of the Assembly rather than as an
Assembly sponsored body. There are obvious conflicts of interests that arise when a single
body has legislative, funding and regulatory responsibilities. The regulatory function of the
Assembly under this Act is undertaken by the Care Standards Inspectorate for Wales which
"will be a division of the Assembly and will be co-joined at senior management level with
the Social Services Inspectorate for Wales under a Chief Inspector" (Health and Social
Services Committee HSS-08-01, para.7).

Subs.(2)

2–007   Section 36A resolves a conflict between this Act, which requires each branch of a voluntary adoption agency to register as a separate agency, and the Adoption and Children Act 2002 which requires every registered adoption society to be an incorporated body. An incorporated body can only be registered as a single body; each branch cannot be registered separately.

[General duties of Commission for Healthcare Audit and Inspection

2–008   **5A.**—(1) The Commission for Healthcare Audit and Inspection (referred to in this Act as "the CHAI") shall have the general duty of keeping the Secretary of State informed about—

(a) the provision in England of independent health services; and

(b) in particular, the availability and quality of the services.

(2) The CHAI shall have the general duty of encouraging improvement in the quality of independent health services provided in England.

(3) The CHAI shall make information about independent health services provided in England available to the public.

(4) When asked to do so by the Secretary of State, the CHAI shall give him advice or information on such matters relating to the provision in England of independent health services as may be specified in his request.

(5) The CHAI may at any time give advice to the Secretary of State on—

(a) any changes which the CHAI thinks should be made, for the purpose of securing improvement in the quality of independent health services provided in England, in the standards set out in statements under section 23;

(b) any other matter connected with the provision in England of such services.

(6) In the exercise of its functions under this Act the CHAI must have particular regard to the need to safeguard and promote the rights and welfare of children.

(7) The Secretary of State may by regulations confer additional functions on the CHAI in relation to the provision in England of independent health services.

(8) In this section "independent health services" means services of the kind provided by persons for whom the CHAI is the registration authority."]

AMENDMENT

2–009   This section was inserted by the Health and Social Care (Community Health and Standards) Act 2003, s.103.

[General duties of Commission for Social Care Inspection

2–010   **5B.**—(1) The Commission for Social Care Inspection (referred to in this Act as "the CSCI") shall have the general duty of keeping the Secretary of State informed about—

(a) the provision in England of registered social care services; and

(b) in particular, the availability and quality of the services.

(2) The CSCI shall have the general duty of encouraging improvement in the quality of registered social care services provided in England.

(3) The CSCI shall make information about registered social care services provided in England available to the public.

(4) When asked to do so by the Secretary of State, the CSCI shall give him advice or information on such matters relating to the provision in England of registered social care services as may be specified in his request.

(5) The CSCI may at any time give advice to the Secretary of State on—

(a) any changes which the CSCI thinks should be made, for the purpose of securing improvement in the quality of registered social care services provided in England, in the standards set out in statements under section 23;

(b) any other matter connected with the provision in England of registered social care services.

(6) In the exercise of its functions under this Act the CSCI must have particular regard to the need to safeguard and promote the rights and welfare of children.

(7) The Secretary of State may by regulations confer additional functions on the CSCI in relation to the provision in England of registered social care services.

(8) In this section, "registered social care services" means services of the kind provided by persons for whom the CSCI is the registration authority."]

AMENDMENT
This section was inserted by the Health and Social Care (Community Health and **2–011** Standards) Act 2003, s.104.

General functions of the Assembly
8.—(1) The Assembly shall have the general duty of encouraging improvement **2–012** in the quality of Part II services provided in Wales.

(2) The Assembly shall make information about Part II services provided in Wales available to the public.

(3) In relation to Part II services provided in Wales, the Assembly shall have any additional function specified in regulations made by the Assembly; but the regulations may only specify a function corresponding to a function which, by virtue of [section 5A or 5B is exercisable by the CHAI or the CSCI] in relation to Part II services provided in England.

(4) The Assembly may charge a reasonable fee determined by it in connection with the exercise of any power conferred on it by or under this Act.

(5) The Assembly may provide training for the purpose of assisting persons to attain standards set out in any statements published by it under section 23.

[(6) The Assembly must have particular regard to the need to safeguard and promote the rights and welfare of children in the exercise of—

(a) its functions exercisable by virtue of section 5(b) and subsections (1) to (3) of this section; and

(b) any other functions exercisable by the Assembly corresponding to functions exercisable by the CSCI in relation to England.]

[(6) In this section, "Part II services" means services of the kind provided by persons registered under Part II, other than the provision of—

(a) medical or psychiatric treatment or

(b) listed services (as defined in section 2).]

AMENDMENTS
2–013   The first subs.(6) was inserted by the Health and Social Care (Community Health and Standards) Act 2003, s.109. The second subs.(6) was inserted by s.147, Sch.9, Pt 2, para.18 of that Act.

DEFINITIONS
2–014   CHAI: s.121(13).
CSCI: s.121(13).

GENERAL NOTE
2–015   This section sets out the responsibilities of the National Assembly for Wales for the regulation of Pt II services.

SUBS.(3)
This provision gives to the Assembly, "the flexibility to confer on itself by regulation additional regulatory functions under Pt II where those functions have been conferred on the National Care Standards Commission in England by the Secretary of State" (*per* the Parliamentary Under-Secretary of State for Wales, Mr David Hanson, Standing Committee G, col.204).

Inquiries
2–017   **10.**—(1) [*Repealed by the Health and Social Care (Community Health and Standards) Act 2003, s.196, Sch.14, Pt 2.*].

(2) The appropriate Minister may cause an inquiry to be held into any matter connected with a service provided in or by an establishment or agency.

(3) Before an inquiry is begun, the person causing the inquiry to be held may direct that it shall be held in private.

(4) Where no direction has been given, the person holding the inquiry may if he thinks fit hold it, or any part of it, in private.

(5) Subsections (2) to (5) of section 250 of the Local Government Act 1972 (powers in relation to local inquiries) shall apply in relation to an inquiry under this section as they apply in relation to a local inquiry under that section; and references in those provisions as so applied to a Minister shall be taken to include references to the Assembly.

(6) Subsections (3) and (4) apply in relation to an inquiry under section 35 of the Government of Wales Act 1998 into any matter relevant to the exercise of—

(a) any functions exercisable by the Assembly by virtue of section 5(b) or 8(3); or

(b) any other functions exercisable by the Assembly corresponding to functions exercisable [by the CHAI or the CSCI under the Act] in relation to England,

as they apply in relation to an inquiry under this section.

(7) The report of the person who held the inquiry shall, unless the Minister who caused the inquiry to be held considers that there are exceptional circumstances which make it inappropriate to publish it, be published in a manner which that Minister considers appropriate.

AMENDMENTS

The words in square brackets in subs.(8)(b) were substituted by the Health and Social **2–018** Care (Community Health and Standards) Act 2003, s.1147, Sch.9, Pt 2, para.19.

DEFINITIONS

agency: s.4(9).   **2–019**
appropriate minister: s.121(1).
establishment: s.4(8).
CHAI: s.121(13)
CSCI: s.121(13).

GENERAL NOTE

This section enables the Secretary of State to hold an inquiry into any matter concerned **2–020** with a regulated service. Inquiries could be held in private (subss.(3)(4)) and the reports of inquiries will have to be published in such a manner as the Minister considers appropriate unless the Minister considers it inappropriate to publish the report because of exceptional circumstances (subs.(7)).

The Secretary of State may cause an inquiry to be held into any matter connected with the exercise by the CHAI or the CSCI of any of their functions (Health and Social Care (Community Health and Standards) Act 2003, ss.134, 135).

The National Assembly for Wales can cause an inquiry to be held into equivalent matters under of s.35 of the Government of Wales Act 1998 which enables the Assembly to "cause an inquiry to be held into any matter relevant to the exercise of its functions." In the context of this Act, this would require the Assembly to investigate its own operations.

SUBS.(2)

Any matter: The Explanatory Notes (para.56) offer the following example: "if a consultant **2–021** surgeon working in a private hospital was found to have unusually high death rates among his patients, the Secretary of State could set up an inquiry to investigate."

SUBS.(5)

This provision enables the person holding the inquiry to issue a summons requiring an **2–022** individual to give evidence or produce any documents in their custody or under their control at a stated time or place. A failure to respond could lead to a fine or imprisonment.

SUBS.(7)

Exceptional circumstances: "We must construe 'exceptional' as an ordinary, familiar **2–023** English adjective, and not as a term of art. It describes a circumstance which is such as to form an exception, which is out of the ordinary course, or unusual, or special, or uncommon. To be exceptional, a circumstance need not be unique, or unprecedented, or very rare; but it cannot be one that is regularly, or routinely, or normally encountered" (*R. v Kelly: Attorney-General's Reference (No.53 of 1998)* [1999] 2 All E.R. 13, *per* Lord Bingham C.J. at 20).

Provision of copies of registers

36.—(1) Subject to subsection (3), the registration authority shall secure that **2–024** copies of any register kept for the purposes of this Part are available at its offices for inspection at all reasonable times by any person.

(2) Subject to subsections (3) and (4), any person who asks the registration authority for a copy of, or of an extract from, a register kept for the purposes of this Part shall be entitled to have one.

(3) Regulations may provide that subsections (1) and (2) shall not apply—

(a) in such circumstances as may be prescribed; or

(b) to such parts of a register as may be prescribed.

(4) A fee determined by the registration authority shall be payable for the copy except—

(a) in prescribed circumstances;

(b) in any other case where the registration authority considers it appropriate to provide the copy free of charge.

DEFINITIONS

2–025   prescribed: s.121(1).
registration authority: s.5.
regulations: s.121(1).

GENERAL NOTE

2–026   The Commissions are required to keep registers of establishments and agencies by the National Care Standards Commission (Registration) Regulations 2001 (SI 2001/3969), reg.8.

SUBS.(3)

2–027   The Minister of State explained the need for this provision:

"We have to be careful, particularly in relation to registered children's homes, that information is only provided to people who have a bona fide or legitimate need to know about the services. Our concern, to put it in a nutshell, is that we do not inadvertently make information on the whereabouts of children's homes and the ages of children accommodated in them available to paedophiles" (Standing Committee G, col.405).

Service of documents

2–028   **37.**—(1) Any notice or other document required under this Part to be served on a person carrying on or managing, or intending to carry on or manage, an establishment or agency may be served on him—

(a) by being delivered personally to him; or

(b) by being sent by post to him in a registered letter or by the recorded delivery service at his proper address.

(2) For the purposes of section 7 of the Interpretation Act 1978 (which defines "service by post") a letter addressed to a person carrying on or managing an establishment or agency enclosing a notice or other document under this Act shall be deemed to be properly addressed if it is addressed to him at the establishment or agency.

(3) Where a notice or other document is served as mentioned in subsection (1)(b), the service shall, unless the contrary is proved, be deemed to have been affected on the third day after the day on which it is sent.

(4) Any notice or other document required to be served on a body corporate or a firm shall be duly served if it is served on the secretary or clerk of that body or a partner of that firm.

(5) For the purposes of this section, and of section 7 of the Interpretation Act 1978 in its application to this section, without prejudice to subsection (2) above, the proper address of a person shall be—

(a) in the case of a secretary or clerk of a body corporate, that of the registered or principal office of that body;

(b) in the case of a partner of a firm, that of the principal office of the firm; and

(c) in any other case, the last known address of the person.

DEFINITIONS

    agency: s.4(9).   **2–029**

    establishment: s.4(8).

GENERAL NOTE

    Under this section documents or notices that are required to be served may be delivered **2–030** personally or sent by registered letter or recorded delivery. A document that is sent by registered letter or recorded delivery is deemed to have been effected on the third day after the day on which it is sent (subs.(3)).

PART 3

REGISTRATION

Any person who carries on or manages an establishment or agency without being registered **3–001** commits an offence (s.11(1)). Where the activities of an agency are carried out from branches, each branch must be registered (s.11(2)). An application for registration must be submitted to the registration authority (s.12(1)). The application must be on a form approved by the registration authority (SI 2001/3969, reg.3), contain prescribed information and be accompanied by the prescribed fee (s.12(2)). Although an individual, company or partnership can be registered to carry on the establishment or agency, only an individual can be registered to be its manager (s.12(3)). The onus is on the registration authority to grant registration if it is satisfied that the applicant satisfies the statutory requirements (s.13(2)). If the registration authority is not so satisfied, it must refuse the application. The registration authority is required to interview the applicant (SI 2001/3969, reg.5). The registration can be either conditional or unconditional (s.13(3)) and if conditions are imposed, they can be varied or removed by the registration authority at any time (s.13(5)). The authority also has the power to impose new conditions (s.13(5)).

The registration authority has the power to cancel the registration of a person on one of the grounds set out in s.14(1). An urgent procedure for cancellation is provided for in s.20. The registered person can apply to the registration authority for his or her registration to be cancelled or for the variation or removal of the conditions of registration (s.15(1)).

Generally speaking, the registration authority must give notice to an applicant or registered person of its intended decision relating to registration (s.17). Such a person has the right to make written representations to the authority within 28 days of service of the notice (s.18). The registration authority is required to give written notice of its decisions (s.19). The notice must contain details of the right of appeal under s.21.

The National Care Standards Commission (Registration) Regulations 2001 (SI 2001/3969) are concerned with the requirements of the registration procedure. The Commission for Healthcare Audit and Inspection (Fees and Frequency of Inspections) Regulations 2004 (SI 2004/661) and the Commission for Social Care Inspection (Fees and Frequency of Inspections) Regulations 2004 (SI 2004/662) set out the fees that are payable on an application for registration and on an application for the variation or removal of a condition of registration. They also prescribe the frequency of inspections by the CHAI and the CSCI.

TRANSITIONAL PROVISIONS
In *Re A Care Home (Guidance Note)* [2002] 32 N.C., the tribunal said that the intention of **3–002** the Care Standards Act (Commencement No.9) England) and Transitional and Savings Provisions) Order 2001 (SI 2001/3852) was that there should be an automatic transfer of registration, and that the service category and the service user categories would reflect the existing provision but be brought up to date to reflect the new terminology of the 2000 Act. The intent and purpose of the transitional regime is to effect the transfer of the regulatory status from the previous regulators to the NCSC without in any way granting either any greater capacity or any lesser capacity on homes.

Requirement to register

3–003   **11.**—(1) Any person who carries on or manages an establishment or agency of any description without being registered under this Part in respect of it (as an establishment or, as the case may be, agency of that description) shall be guilty of an offence.

(2) Where the activities of an agency are carried on from two or more branches, each of those branches shall be treated as a separate agency for the purposes of this Part.

(3) The [references in subsections (1) and (2) to an agency do] not include a reference to a voluntary adoption agency.

(4) The Secretary of State may by regulations make provision about the keeping of registers by [the CHAI or the CSCI] for the purposes of this Part.

(5) A person guilty of an offence under this section shall be liable on summary conviction—

(a) if subsection (6) does not apply, to a fine not exceeding level 5 on the standard scale;

(b) if subsection (6) applies, to imprisonment for a term not exceeding six months, or to a fine not exceeding level 5 on the standard scale, or to both.

(6) This subsection applies if—

(a) the person was registered in respect of the establishment or agency at a time before the commission of the offence but the registration was cancelled before the offence was committed; or

(b) the conviction is a second or subsequent conviction of the offence and the earlier conviction, or one of the earlier convictions, was of an offence in relation to an establishment or agency of the same description.

AMENDMENT

3–004   The words in square brackets in subs.(3) were substituted by the Adoption and Children Act 2002, Sch.3, para.106.

The words in square brackets in subs.(4) were substituted by the Health and Social Care (Community Health and Standards) Act 2003, s.147, Sch.9, Pt 2, para.20.

DEFINITIONS

3–005   agency: s.4(9).
establishment: s.4(8).
regulations: s.121(1).
voluntary adoption agency: s.4(7).
CHAI: s.121(13).
CSCI: s.121(13).

GENERAL NOTE

3–006   Under this section any person who carries on or manages an establishment or agency (but not a voluntary adoption agency (subs.(3))) must be registered. If an agency operates from two or more branches, each branch is treated as a separate agency for the purposes of registration (subs.(2)). It is an offence to contravene this requirement. Conviction will result in a fine not exceeding level 5, and, in certain circumstances, to a term of imprisonment not exceeding six months (subss.(5), (6)).

Person: It is the person that is registered and not the establishment or agency (s.12(1)). **3–008**
The person can carry on or manage more than one establishment or agency (s.12(4)).

Carries on: The person who carries on the establishment or agency is the person who is
accountable for the operation of the business. He or she "will be carrying on the [establish-
ment or agency] in the sense that he or she will have control or direction of the
[establishment or agency]" (*R. v Humberside County Council Ex p. Bogdal* (1992) 11
B.M.L.R. 46, *per* Brooke J. at 54). In a decision under the 1984 Act, the Registered
Homes Tribunal held that the person carrying on the establishment could include a person
who is concerned with financial and administrative arrangements through being a partner in
the business of running the establishment, even though he or she was not involved in the
day to day care of service users (*McMillan v Lancashire County Council* (Decn.
No.35)). The person who carries on the establishment need not necessarily own the buildings in which the business is carried on. A corporation can own the establishment or agency
(Interpretation Act 1978, s.5, Sch.1). If a company is incorporated for the purpose of making profits for its shareholders then prima facie any gainful use to which it puts its assets
amounts to the carrying on of a business (*American Leaf Blending C. Sdn Bhd v
Director-General of Inland Revenue* [1978] 3 All E.R. 1185, PC). Re-registration is not
required where there is a change of name or management of a company already registered
under this Act, although the registration authority should be informed of the change (Care
Homes Regulations 2001, reg.39(e)). A partnership can be registered as such: there is no
need for each individual partner to be registered. The partnership must appoint a manager
(*ibid.*, reg.8(1)(b)(i)).

Manages: The manager, who will have day-to-day control of the running of the establish- **3–009**
ment or agency, must be an individual; also see the note on s.12(3). The circumstances
which require the appointment of a manager are set out in the Care Homes Regulations
2001 (SI 2001/3965), reg.8.

The term "manager" is not defined in this Act. In *Varcoe v Devon County Council*
(Decn. No.48), the Registered Homes Tribunal was concerned with the interpretation of
this term under the 1984 Act. The tribunal said:

> "We are conscious of the fact that the parties to this appeal were hoping that we should
> be able to give some guidance as to the meaning of 'manager' . . .; we do not feel able to
> do this. Each case must be decided on its merits looking in particular at the functions of
> the proposed manager, the hours spent on the premises, the employment structure of the
> home and in the light of those and other facts giving the word manager its normal every-
> day meaning making a decision as to whether that person is 'the manager' or not."

Beldam L.J., speaking in *Jones v Director of Public Prosecutions, The Times,* June 4,
1992, D.C., said that exercising control was a requirement of "managing".

There is no provision in this Act to provide for the provisional registration of a manager
who has been appointed to replace a manager who has relinquished his or her position without notice. This is a most unsatisfactory situation. It is submitted that the registration
authority should be immediately informed of the appointment and that the manager, who
is committing an offence under this provision in the absence of being registered, should
submit an application for registration at the earliest opportunity.

Establishment: If more than one category of establishment is carried on in the same building, each category must be separately registered.

An establishment can comprise a number of separate buildings located on the same site.
In *Harrison v Cornwall County Council* (Decn. No.146), the Registered Homes Tribunal
concluded that a house and a lodge "being within the same curtilage, and providing
respectively and exclusively the accommodation and board for the residents, cannot be
regarded as anything other than one establishment." This finding was upheld by the
Court of Appeal (*Harrison v Cornwall County Council* (1991) 90 L.G.R. 81 at 97). In
Swindells v Cheshire County Council, CO/0611/92, *The Times*, February 18, 1993. DC, a

bungalow was situated in the grounds of a house and shared the same services, call bell, nursing staff and pathway. The court found that the house and bungalow were one establishment and not two.

Offence: If an establishment is sold as a going concern, the registration does not run with it and the new owner will have to seek registration on his or her own account. A registration authority that believes that an unregistered establishment might be operating could use its power of inspection under s.31.

SUBS.(2)

3–010   *Separate agency:* A separate application for registration must be made in respect of each of the branches (s.12(4)). This is a very onerous requirement.

SUBS.(4)

3–011   *Regulations:* See the National Care Standards Commission (Registration) Regulations 2001 (SI 2001/3969), reg.8.

Applications for registration

3–012   **12.**—(1) A person seeking to be registered under this Part shall make an application to the registration authority.

(2) The application—

(a) must give the prescribed information about prescribed matters;

(b) must give any other information which the registration authority reasonably requires the applicant to give,

and must be accompanied by a fee of the prescribed amount.

(3) A person who applies for registration as the manager of an establishment or agency must be an individual.

(4) A person who carries on or manages, or wishes to carry on or manage, more than one establishment or agency must make a separate application in respect of each of them.

DEFINITIONS

3–013   agency: s.4(9).
establishment: s.4(8).
prescribed: s.121(1).
registration authority: s.5.
CHAI: s.121(13).
CSCI: s.121(13).

GENERAL NOTE

3–014   This section sets out the framework for applications for registration. The application must be either granted or refused (s.13).

The "responsible person" of the establishment or agency, as defined in reg.2(1) of the National Care Standards Commission (Registration) Regulations 2001 (SI 2001/3969), is required to be interviewed by the registration authority (*ibid.*, reg.5).

SUBS.(2)

3–015   *Prescribed information about prescribed matters:* See SI 2001/3969, above, regs 3, 4, 6, and 7.

Other information: In most cases, it will not be necessary for the authority to exercise this power because the information on the application form will be sufficient. However, there may be instances where the authority will require clarification of what is written on the form.

Subs.(3)

"The person carrying on an establishment or agency—essentially the owner—can be an **3–016** organisation or company, but we wanted to make clear that the role of manager, which is so important to the day-to-day running of the care service, is one that must be undertaken by a named person, although this [provision] does not preclude job-sharing arrangements" (*per* Lord Hunt of Kings Health, *Hansard*, HL, Vol.615, col.927).

Subs.(4)

In *Tiverton Group Homes v Devon County Council* (Decn. No.185), the Registered **3–017** Homes Tribunal, in confirming the appropriateness of a person managing three homes, said:

"Although the Tribunal has said in this particular case and on these very particular and special facts that the manager of two of these homes could manage a third, this is not to say that it advocates or even necessarily approves of a manager managing two or more homes. It must be reiterated that each case must be must be looked at on its merits. It might be totally inappropriate, for example, for the manager of a home for elderly, incontinent and/or otherwise heavily dependent residents, to be a manager of another home at the same time, particularly one some distance from the other. The present decision is in no way a 'precedent' for the conclusion that, as a matter of general application, managers may manage more than one home at a time."

The reasons why, in this case, the tribunal considered that the registration authority should move away from its "one home one manager" policy were:

(a) each home was very small;

(b) the homes were relatively close to each other;

(c) the residents were not in a high dependency category;

(d) most residents were mobile;

(e) the homes were well run by caring and dedicated people; and

(f) the appellants had enjoyed a long and constructive relationship with the registration authority.

Grant or refusal of registration

13.—(1) Subsections (2) to (4) apply where an application under section 12 has **3–018** been made with respect to an establishment or agency in accordance with the provisions of this Part.

(2) If the registration authority is satisfied that—

(a) the requirements of regulations under section 22; and

(b) the requirements of any other enactment which appears to the registration authority to be relevant, are being and will continue to be complied with (so far as applicable) in relation to the establishment or agency, it shall grant the application; otherwise it shall refuse it.

(3) The application may be granted either unconditionally or subject to such conditions as the registration authority thinks fit.

(4) On granting the application, the registration authority shall issue a certificate of registration to the applicant.

(5) The registration authority may at any time—

(a) vary or remove any condition for the time being in force in relation to a person's registration; or

(b) impose an additional condition.

DEFINITIONS

3–019   agency: s.4(9).
establishment: s.4(8).
registration authority: s.5.
regulation: s.121(1).

GENERAL NOTE

3–020   This section places a duty on the registration authority to register an establishment or agency if it is satisfied that the applicant has demonstrated that all relevant requirements are being and will continue to be complied with. The onus of satisfying the registration authority that an application should be granted, for example by provision of prescribed information (s.12(2)), falls on the applicant. If it grants the application, the registration authority must notify the applicant of its decision (s.19) and issue a certificate of registration (subs.(4)). Registration can be granted unconditionally or subject to conditions (subs.(3)). Conditions of registration can subsequently be varied, removed or added (subs.(5)). The provisions contained in ss.17 and 18 will be activated if the registration authority proposes to refuse the application or to vary, remove or impose an additional condition of registration.

If registration is granted, the registration authority will make an appropriate entry on the register that is kept pursuant to reg.8 of the National Care Standards Commission (Registration) Regulations 2001 (SI 2001/3969), and a certificate of registration will be issued (subs.(4)) A failure to display the certificate in a conspicuous place constitutes an offence under s.28.

SUBS.(2)

3–021   The registration authority cannot deny registration on the ground that the national minimum standards are not being or are not going to be complied with. The standards must be taken into account in any decision that the authority makes about non-compliance with a requirement (s.23).

Other enactments: In *The London Cosmetic Laser Centre Ltd v Commission for Healthcare Audit and Inspection* [2004] 278 EA, para.13, the Care Standards Tribunal unsurprisingly held that this phrase does not refer to other sections of the 2000 Act.

And will continue to be: The Minister of State gave the following example of the application of this provision:

"an applicant may want to set up a home in a leased building and the Commission may discover that the lease had only a couple of years left to run, or a year or 18 months. It would be justified in that case to reject the application, because older people entering a care home are, sadly, likely to live there for the rest of their lives, and it would not be right if they were forced to move after a relatively short time. In such circumstances the

Commission should have the power to refuse a registration, instead of having to go through the process of withdrawing it a short time later" (Standing Committee G, col.249).

Conditions: A breach of a condition of registration constitutes an offence under s.24. **3–022** Conditions may be generic or specific. Generic conditions could include conditions on care homes specifying the number and category of residents that may be accommodated. In some cases a specific condition may be required to take account of the circumstances in a particular home, centre, agency, private hospital or clinic. The Explanatory Notes (para.69) give the following example: "there might be a condition that a particular door be locked to prevent confused residents from wandering directly on to a busy road". The provisions contained in ss.17 and 18 will apply if the applicant does not agree with the imposition of a condition.

In *Avon County Council v Lang* CO/617/89 [1990] C.O.D. 365, Rose J. said in a case involving the interpretation of the 1984 Act that as the contents of a certificate of registration are capable of forming the basis of a criminal offence the conditions attached to a certificate must be in a simple and concise form and free from uncertainty or ambiguity. It was therefore not permissible for a registration authority to state in a registration certificate that the number of service users permitted by the registration might vary on the happening of a specified contingency, for example, a condition which says words to the effect of "eleven now but ten when Mrs T leaves" would be "wholly unsatisfactory". His Lordship also held that a registration authority (and a tribunal on appeal) is entitled to take into account the particular circumstances of potential as well as actual service users. It is submitted that these findings are equally applicable to this Act. Rose J.'s finding regarding the nature of the conditions to be imposed was not followed in *Grove Lodge Care Home v CSCI* [2003] 246 N.C. where the Care Standards Tribunal varied a condition of registration to the effect that the number of persons for whom accommodation is to be provided was to be reduced by one in the event of a particular person ceasing to be a resident.

Thinks fit: There are no mandatory conditions of registration.

3–023

Certificate of registration: The registration authority does not have the power to issue a temporary certificate of registration. A certificate of registration once issued does not remain in force for any particular period, but remains in force until such time, if ever, as it is varied or discharged or added to in pursuance of the powers contained in this Act (*Avon County Council v Lang,* above.

Cancellation of registration

14.—(1) The registration authority may at any time cancel the registration of a **3–024** person in respect of an establishment or agency—

(a) on the ground that that person has been convicted of a relevant offence;

(b) on the ground that any other person has been convicted of such an offence in relation to the establishment or agency;

(c) on the ground that the establishment or agency is being, or has at any time been, carried on otherwise than in accordance with the relevant requirements;

(d) on any ground specified by regulations.

(2) For the purposes of this section the following are relevant offences—

(a) an offence under this Part or regulations made under it;

(b) an offence under the Registered Homes Act 1984 or regulations made under it;

(c) an offence under the 1989 Act or regulations made under it;

(d) in relation to a voluntary adoption agency, an offence under regulations under section 9(2) of the Adoption Act 1976 or section 1(3) of the Adoption (Intercountry Aspects) Act 1999.

(3) In this section "relevant requirements" means—

(a) any requirements or conditions imposed by or under this Part; and

(b) the requirements of any other enactment which appear to the registration authority to be relevant.

DEFINITIONS

3–025   registration authority: s.5.
establishment: s.4(8).
agency: s.4(9).
the 1989 Act: s.12(13).

GENERAL NOTE

3–026   This section provides the registration authority with the power to cancel the registration of a person in respect of an establishment or agency if a relevant offence has been committed or if a condition of registration or other relevant regulatory requirement or ground specified in the regulations has been breached. Section 261E of the National Assistance Act 1948 (c.29), which prohibited a local authority from contacting residential care from a person who had been convicted of a regulatory offence, is repealed (Sch.6). Notice of the proposal to cancel has to be given to the registered person (s.17) who has a right to make representations (s.18). An urgent procedure for cancelling registration is provided for in s.20. The certificate of registration must be returned to the registration authority on the registration being cancelled. A failure do so is an offence (National Care Standards Commission (Registration) Regulations 2001, regs 10,11).

The importance of registration authorities adopting a responsible attitude toward cancellations was emphasised by Scott Baker J. in *The Secretary of State for Health v Prospect Care Services Ltd and Hyland* [2001] EWHC 164 (Admin) at para.72:

"This case contains a cautionary tale. The Inspectorate and Mr Hyland got across at each other when they should have been working together toward a common goal. Neither is exempt from blame. Each side seems to have been blind to the position and needs of the other. The Secretary of State, through the Inspectorate, holds a powerful weapon—a trump card—in being able to cancel the registration of a voluntary home. Where, as here, that weapon is used prematurely or inappropriately the consequences can be devastating. The very act of cancellation whether justified or not can (and it appears to have happened here) bring an organisation to its knees. A successful appeal may not undo the damage if in the result the home is closed down anyway. The power to cancel registration is therefore, it seems to me, matched by a great responsibility to see that it is not exercised unjustifiably."

The tribunal emphasised the need for a registration authority to adopt a proportionate approach to the question of cancellation in *Joyce v NCSC* [2003] 0190 N where an appeal against cancellation on the ground of a failure to appoint an individual to manage a care home was allowed in a situation where "the lack of a registered manager has not significantly or materially affected service users" and where "closure would have disproportionate effect upon the public health agencies, social care agencies, the users currently at the home, potential future users, owners and staff" (paras 85, 86).

A registered person is not entitled to use judicial review proceedings to challenge he **3–027** registration authority's decision to cancel the registration until the appeals procedure before the Care Standards Tribunal has been exhausted. This was the case even where there were defects in the decision making process (*R. v Birmingham City Council Ex p. Ferrero* (1991) 89 L.G.R. 997).

The cancellation of registration does not provide the registration authority with the power to physically close the establishment or to remove service users without their consent. Mentally incapable service users could be removed if this was deemed to be in their best interests (*F v West Berkshire Health Authority (Mental Health Act Commission intervening)* [1989] 2 All E.R. 545, HL). As continued operation of the establishment would render the person carrying on the establishment liable to prosecution, that person would doubtless wish to co-operate with the registration authority in making alternative arrangements for the service users. The registration authority would have a right of access to the premises by virtue of its power of inspection under s.31.

Subs.(1)

May at any time: The registration authority has discretion: it is not bound to cancel the **3–028** registration if a ground set out in this subsection is satisfied. As an alternative to cancellation, the authority could consider varying a condition of registration or imposing a new condition under s.13(5).

Person: Or corporation (Interpretation Act 1978, s.5, Sch.1).

Relevant offence: See subs.(2).

Any other person: "I shall give an example to illustrate what the provision is intended to achieve. If a member of the care staff in an establishment or agency was convicted of an offence covered by the clause, and the manager or person running the establishment or agency, refused to dismiss them or remove them from the relevant area, that would give rise to serious concern about the way in which the establishment or agency was being run. It would therefore be a proper matter for the Commission to take into account. That is precisely what is allowed under subsection (1)(b)" (*per* the Minister of State, Standing Committee G, col.253). An offence by "any other person" is a ground for cancellation only if the conviction relates to the establishment or agency in question. Compare this with para.(a).

Or has at any time been: Registration can be cancelled in circumstances where the breach of the relevant requirement is no longer apparent.

Relevant requirement: See subs.(3). The beach of the requirement need not have been the subject of proceedings for an offence.

Regulations: See the National Care Standards Commission (Registration) Regulations 2001 (SI 2001/3969), reg.14.

Subs.(2)

Offence under this Part: See ss.24 to 29.   **3–029**

Applications by registered persons

15.—(1) A person registered under this Part may apply to the registration **3–030** authority—

(a) for the variation or removal of any condition for the time being in force in relation to the registration; or

(b) for the cancellation of the registration.

(2) But a person may not make an application under subsection (1)(b)—

(a) if the registration authority has given him notice under section 17(4)(a) of a proposal to cancel the registration, unless the registration authority has decided not to take that step; or

(b) if the registration authority has given him notice under section 19(3) of its decision to cancel the registration and the time within which an appeal may be brought has not expired or, if an appeal has been brought, it has not been determined.

(3) An application under subsection (1) shall be made in such manner and state such particulars as may be prescribed and, if made under paragraph (a) of that subsection, shall be accompanied by a fee of such amount as may be prescribed.

(4) If the registration authority decides to grant an application under subsection (1)(a) it shall serve notice in writing of its decision on the applicant (stating, where applicable, the condition as varied) and issue a new certificate of registration.

(5) If different amounts are prescribed under subsection (3), the regulations may provide for the registration authority to determine which amount is payable in a particular case.

DEFINITIONS

3–031   registration authority: s.5.
CHAI: s.121(13).

GENERAL NOTE

3–032   This section enables the registered person to apply to the registration authority for a change in the conditions of registration or for the cancellation of registration. The registered person has no power to apply to the registration authority for the imposition of a new condition. A refusal by the authority to agree to a change in the conditions of registration triggers the procedure set out in ss.17 and 18. Subsection (2) prevents an application being made for the voluntary cancellation of registration if the registration authority has given notice of an intention to, or decided to cancel the registration.

Subs.(1)
Para.(a)

3–033   The registration authority must give the applicant notice of a proposal to refuse an application under para.(a) (s.17(5)). If the application is granted, a new certificate of registration will be issued (subs.(4)).

Apply ... for the variation or removal of any condition: See reg.12 of the National Care Standards Commission (Registration) Regulations 2001.

Para.(b)

3–034   There is no provision in this Act which allows for the automatic cancellation of registration on a change of circumstances or the surrender of registration by the registered person, even if the establishment or agency is no longer functioning. If a registered person wishes registration to be cancelled he or she must make an application under this provision (*Alternative Futures v National Care Standards Commission and Sefton MBC* [2002] EWHC 3032 (Admin), following *Kowlessur v Suffolk Health Authority* [2002] C/2000/ 2662, CA). *Per* Richards J.: "It seems to me unthinkable that registration could somehow be automatically cancelled or nullified simply by virtue of a change in the factual arrangements concerning a home without any intervention by the relevant authority and a judgement by that authority as to whether the changes were such as to take the homes outside the conditions of registration" (para.24). Subsequent to the decision in the *Alternative Futures* case the NCSC published a "Statement of Advice to Providers" (June 16, 2003) addressed to those providers who did "de-register" under 1984 Act and who may have concerns about the legitimacy of their current operations. The advice states: "Services which can demonstrate that they thought they were appropriately 'de-registered' under the 1984 Act and which can show that their services still clearly fall outside the scope of the current criteria requiring registration as a care home, should not have any grounds for concern arising from this and the Commission will not require them to go through the technicality of de-registering as a care home under the new Act, but will accept their current status."

The task of the registration authority on considering an application for de-registration is not to determine whether such action would be in the best interests of the service users: it is to determine whether the establishment or agency falls within the relevant definition contained in Part I.

An application under this provision should not be made after the registration authority has given notice under either s.17(4)(a) that it is proposing to cancel the registration or under s.19(3) that it has decided to cancel the registration. Such an application should also not be made if the business is being sold as a going concern. In these circumstances, the purchaser should apply to the registration authority at the earliest opportunity for registration. The seller of a care home or an independent hospital is required to notify the authority of his proposal to sell (Care Homes Regulations 2001 (SI 2001/3965), reg.39; Private and Voluntary Health Care (England) Regulations (SI 2001/3968), reg.30).

The NCSC issued guidance on this provision in so far as it relates to care homes: **3–035** "Registered Person's Application for Cancellation of Registration" (February 4, 2003). The guidance states at para.6 that the "key issues" for the NCSC when determining an application will be:

"(a) Will the registered person still be providing an establishment providing accommodation together with nursing or personal care and accommodation to the groups of people identified in s.3(1) of the Care Standards Act 2000?

(b) What arrangements will be made for the service users who hitherto have come to regard the service as their home?

(c) Will service users be safe and content during the period of transition until the 'effective date' of cancellation of registration takes effect?"

The burden of proof is on the registration authority which must satisfy itself that the requirements of registration are still being met (*Alternative Futures Ltd v NCSC* [2002] 101–111 N.C., para.26).

The dividing line between care homes and supported housing schemes is considered in the general note to s.3.

Apply ... for the cancellation of the registration: Following the procedure set out in reg.15 of the National Care Standards Commission (Registration) Regulations 2001.

Subs.(3)

Prescribed: See the Commission for Healthcare Audit and Inspection (Fees and **3–036** Frequency of Inspections) Regulations 2004 (SI 2004/661), reg.3 and the Commission for Social Care Inspection (Fees and Frequency of Inspections) Regulations 2004 (SI 2004/662), reg.3.

Regulations about registration

16.—(1) Regulations may make provision about the registration of persons **3–037** under this Part in respect of establishments or agencies, and in particular about—

(a) the making of applications for registration;

(b) the contents of certificates of registration.

(2) Regulations may provide that no application for registration under this Part may be made in respect of a fostering agency, or a voluntary adoption agency, which is an unincorporated body.

(3) Regulations may also require persons registered under this Part to pay to the registration authority an annual fee of such amount, and at such a time, as may be prescribed.

(4) A fee payable by virtue of this section may, without prejudice to any other method of recovery, be recovered summarily as a civil debt.

DEFINITIONS

3–038   agency: s.4(9).
establishment: s.4(8).
fostering agency: s.4.
prescribed: s.12(1).
voluntary adoption agency: s.4.
CHAI: s.121(13).
CSCI: s.121(13).

GENERAL NOTE

3–039   This section provides for regulation making powers with respect to registration.

SUBS.(1)

3–040   *Regulations:* See the National Care Standards Commission (Registration) Regulations 2001 (SI 2001/3969).

SUBS.(2)

3–041   This restates s.9(1) of the Adoption Act 1976 (c.36) in respect of voluntary adoption societies, and applies it to fostering agencies. Section 9(1) of the 1976 Act is repealed by Sch.6.

SUBS.(3)

3–042   *Fee:* "We have made it clear—for example in the White Paper 'Modernising Social Services'—that we want the Commission to fully recover the cost of regulation" (*per* the Minister of State, Standing Committee G, col.259). The amount of fee payable is set out in the Commission for Healthcare Audit and Inspection (Fees and Frequency of Inspections) Regulations 2004 (SI 2004/661), reg.5 and the Commission for Social Care Inspection (Fees and Frequency of Inspections) Regulations 2004 (SI 2004/662), reg.5.

Registration procedure

Notice of proposals

3–043   **17.**—(1) Subsections (2) and (3) apply where a person applies for registration in respect of an establishment or agency.

(2) If the registration authority proposes to grant the application subject to any conditions which have not been agreed in writing between it and the applicant, it shall give the applicant written notice of its proposal and of the conditions subject to which it proposes to grant his application.

(3) The registration authority shall give the applicant notice of a proposal to refuse the application.

(4) Except where it makes an application under section 20, the registration authority shall give any person registered in respect of an establishment or agency notice of a proposal—

(a) to cancel the registration (otherwise than in accordance with an application under section 15(1)(b));

(b) to vary or remove (otherwise than in accordance with an application under section 15(1)(a)) any condition for the time being in force in relation to the registration; or

(c) to impose any additional condition in relation to the registration.

(5) The registration authority shall give the applicant notice of a proposal to refuse an application under section 15(1)(a).

(6) A notice under this section shall give the registration authority's reasons for its proposal.

DEFINITIONS
    agency: s.4(9).   **3–044**
    establishment: s.4(8).
    registration authority: s.5.

GENERAL NOTE
    This section places a requirement on the registration authority to give notice to an appli- **3–045** cant or registered person of a decision that intends to take with respect to applications for registration, cancellation of registration or any change to a condition of registration. This requirement does not apply to applications that are made for urgent cancellation under s.20 (subs.(4)) or where the registration authority decides to grant an application for registration unconditionally, or subject to agreed conditions. A "notice of proposal" must set out the registration authority's reasons (subs.(6)). The person served with the notice has a right to make written representations to the registration authority (s.18).
    Reasons: The reasons should set out the relevant law and findings of fact. The Registered Homes Tribunal said that the registration authority should present "a clear, consistent and structured case, supported by reliable and creditable evidence" (*Fieldhouse v Devon County Council* (Decn. No.182)). In *Re Poyser and Mills Arbitration* [1964] 2 Q.B. 467, 478, Megaw J. said: "Parliament provided that reasons shall be given, and in my view that must be read as meaning that proper, adequate reasons must be given. The reasons that are set out must be reasons which will not only be intelligible, but which deal with the substantial points that have been raised."

Right to make representations

18.—(1) A notice under section 17 shall state that within 28 days of service of **3–046** the notice any person on whom it is served may make written representations to the registration authority concerning any matter which that person wishes to dispute.

(2) Where a notice has been served under section 17, the registration authority shall not determine any matter to which the notice relates until either—

(a) any person on whom the notice was served has made written representations to it concerning the matter;

(b) any such person has notified the registration authority in writing that he does not intend to make representations; or

(c) the period during which any such person could have made representations has elapsed.

DEFINITION
3–047   registration authority: s.5.

GENERAL NOTE
3–048   This section provides the person who has been the subject of a notice of proposal under s.17 with the right to make written representations to the registration authority within 28 days of the service of the notice. The registration authority cannot make a decision on its proposal until the 28-day period has expired unless it receives representations during that period or the person notifies the authority that he will not be making representations (subs.(2)). Although the right to make oral representations under the Registered Homes Act 1984 (c.23) is not replicated in this Act, the registration authority may wish to interview the person concerned before reaching a decision.

Although this section does not explicitly place an obligation on the authority to consider any representations before reaching its decision, this is clearly a requirement.

SUBS.(2)
3–049   *Within 28 days of service:* Excluding the date of service (*Dodds v Walker* [1981] 2 All E.R. 609, HL).

Notice of decisions

3–050   **19.**—(1) If the registration authority decides to grant an application for registration in respect of an establishment or agency unconditionally, or subject only to conditions which have been agreed in writing between it and the applicant, it shall give the applicant written notice of its decision.

(2) A notice under subsection (1) shall state the agreed conditions.

(3) If the registration authority decides to adopt a proposal under section 17, it shall serve notice in writing of its decision on any person on whom it was required to serve notice of the proposal.

(4) A notice under subsection (3) shall—

(a) explain the right of appeal conferred by section 21;

(b) in the case of a decision to adopt a proposal under section 17(2), state the conditions subject to which the application is granted; and

(c) in the case of a decision to adopt a proposal under section 17(4)(b) or (c), state the condition as varied, the condition which is removed or (as the case may be) the additional condition imposed.

(5) Subject to subsection (6), a decision of the registration authority to adopt a proposal under section 17(2) or (4) shall not take effect—

(a) if no appeal is brought, until the expiration of the period of 28 days referred to in section 21(2); and

(b) if an appeal is brought, until it is determined or abandoned.

(6) Where, in the case of a decision to adopt a proposal under section 17(2), the applicant notifies the registration authority in writing before the expiration of the

period mentioned in subsection (5)(a) that he does not intend to appeal, the decision shall take effect when the notice is served.

DEFINITIONS

agency: s.4(9).   **3–051**
establishment: s.4(8).
registration authority: s.5.

GENERAL NOTE

This section requires the registration authority to serve a written notice on the applicant if **3–052** it decides to grant an application unconditionally, or subject to agreed conditions (subs.(1)). If the representation stage set out in s.18 has been completed, the registration authority must serve a written notice of its decision on the person who received the notice of proposal (subs.(3)). This notice must explain the right of appeal conferred by s.21 and if the decision related to the granting or variation of conditions of registration, set out the conditions. An authority's decision to cancel registration, to grant registration subject to conditions which have not been agreed or to change a condition, will not take effect until either any appeal has been determined or the expiration of 28 days if no appeal is brought (subs.(5)). The authority's decision in the case of a decision to grant an application subject to conditions that have not been agreed, will take effect from the date when the notice was served if the applicant decides during the 28-day period not to pursue an appeal (subs.(6)).

Written notice: The notice should contain reference to the particular sections of this Act on which the registration authority can rely (*R. v Humberside County Council Ex p. Bogdal* (1992) 11 B.M.L.R. 46).

Urgent procedure for cancellation, etc.

20.—(1) If—   **3–053**

(a) the registration authority applies to a justice of the peace for an order—

    (i) cancelling the registration of a person in respect of an establishment or agency;

    (ii) varying or removing any condition for the time being in force by virtue of this Part; or

    (iii) imposing an additional condition; and

(b) it appears to the justice that, unless the order is made, there will be a serious risk to a person's life, health or well-being,

the justice may make the order, and the cancellation, variation, removal or imposition shall have effect from the time when the order is made.

(2) An application under subsection (1) may, if the justice thinks fit, be made without notice.

(3) As soon as practicable after the making of an application under this section, the registration authority shall notify the appropriate authorities of the making of the application.

(4) An order under subsection (1) shall be in writing.

(5) Where such an order is made, the registration authority shall, as soon as practicable after the making of the order, serve on the person registered in respect of the establishment of agency—

(a) a copy of the order; and

(b) notice of the right of appeal conferred by section 21.

(6) For the purposes of this section the appropriate authorities are—

(a) the local authority in whose area the establishment or agency is situated;

(b) the [Primary Care Trust or] Health Authority in whose area the establishment or agency is situated; and

(c) any statutory authority not falling within paragraph (a) or (b) whom the registration authority thinks it appropriate to notify.

(7) In this section "statutory authority" means a body established by or under an Act of Parliament.

AMENDMENT

3–054 The reference to Primary Care Trust in subs.(6)(b) was made by the NHS Reform and Health Care Professions Act 2002, s.2(5), Sch.2, Pt 2, para.70.

DEFINITIONS
agency: s.4(9).
establishment: s.4(8).
local authority: s.121(1).
registration authority: s.5.

GENERAL NOTE

3–055 This section provides a registration authority with the power to apply to a justice of the peace for the immediate cancellation of registration or change in the conditions of registration of an establishment or agency. The application can be made without notice, if the justice agrees (subs.(2)). The justice can only make an order if (1) there are grounds for cancelling the registration or for changing a condition of registration and (2) it appears to the justice that the absence of an order would result in a serious risk to a person's life, health or well-being (*Lyons v East Sussex CC*, 86 L.G.R. 369, CA). If an order is made, it has immediate effect (subs.(1)).

In *Lister v Bradford Metropolitan Council* (Decn. No.166), the Registered Homes Tribunal, made the following observations on the equivalent power contained in s.11 of the Registered Homes Act 1984:

"The powers of section 11 are Draconian and it is axiomatic that they should never ever be contemplated without the gravest and most serious thought. The tribunal is absolutely convinced that the respondent authorities, knowing of the dreadful upset to residents, to the problems of resettling them, to the inevitable problems which arise with relatives, to the enormous administrative difficulties involved, to the possibility of adverse comments in the press and to the time and expense which closure of this nature cause, would never ever proceed with such a step unless they felt it to be absolutely imperative. They are under a duty delegated to them by Parliament to protect and ensure the welfare of all people in their care, people who, because of age or disability, are particularly vulnerable. Therefore, if they believe, after taking into consideration all the serious consequences, that such a step is necessary to ensure that protection, they must take it. Even if they are subsequently found to have been wrong, this in no way should derogate from their duty to act."

There is no reason why, if the registration authority has material before it which it believes justifies an application under this section, but recognises that it may fail either in its application to the justice of the peace or on appeal against the justice to a tribunal under s.21, it should not simultaneously adopt the alternative route of indicating under s.17 that it proposes to cancel the registration. If the justice refuses the application or an appeal is allowed, the ordinary procedure can be followed (*Lyons v East Sussex CC*, above).

In *Jain and Jain v Nottingham Health Authority* (Decn. No.369) the Registered Homes **3–056** Tribunal said that it was "common ground before us that it follows from the approach taken by Phillips J. in *London Borough of Hillingdon v McLean* (1989) 88 L.G.R. 49 than an order should be made under [this section] only if it is the *only* way of avoiding a serious risk to the life, health or well-being of the patients".

Where a registration authority concludes on the evidence before it that an application under this section should be made, the court should not interfere with the statutory process on an application for judicial review unless there was bad faith, a true sense of *Wednesbury* perversity or substantive unfairness arising from a failure to disclose to the justice facts or documents which obviously infected the authority's case (*R. v Ealing, Hammersmith and Hounslow Health Authority Ex p. Wilson* (1996) 30 B.M.L.R. 92).

A registration authority which utilises the procedure set out in this section does not owe a duty of care to the owner of the establishment or agency so as to enable the owner to sue in the tort of negligence in the event of an allegation that the authority failed to fully and properly investigate the case (*Martine v South East Kent Health Authority* (1993) 20 B.M.L.R. 51, CA).

The procedure under this section is limited to situations where the establishment in question is registered under this Act. If an establishment is unregistered and urgent action is required to protect the residents, the registration authority could either apply to the High Court for an injunction to close the establishment, consider utilising the procedure under s.47 of the National Assistance Act 1948 or s.1 of the National Assistance (Amendment) Act 1951, or, if the residents appear to be mentally disordered, request an approved social worker to make an application to justice of the peace under s.135(1) of the Mental Health Act 1983.

The cancellation of registration does not provide the registration authority with the power to physically close the establishment or to remove service users without their consent. Mentally incapable service users could be removed if this was deemed to be in their best interests (*F v West Berkshire Health Authority (Mental Health Act Commission intervening)* [1989] 2 All E.R. 545, HL). As continued operation of the establishment would render the person carrying on the establishment liable to prosecution, that person would doubtless wish to co-operate with the registration authority in making alternative arrangements for the service users. The registration authority would have a right of access to the premises and the service users by virtue of its power of inspection under s.31.

THE HUMAN RIGHTS ACT 1998

An order made under this section involves the determination of the "civil rights and obli- **3–057** gations" of the proprietor for the purposes of Art.6(1) of the European Convention on Human Rights (*Konig v Federal Republic of Germany* (1978) 2 E.H.R.R. 170; *Bentham v Netherlands* (1986) 8 E.H.R.R. 1). A failure by the registration authority to take reasonable steps to inform either the proprietor or his or her legal representative of the pending hearing would violate the proprietors right to a fair hearing under that Article.

SUBS.(1)

Applies: The registration authority must notify relevant statutory authorities of the making **3–058** of the application (subs.(3)).

Appears to the justice: On the day on which the application is made. In *Harvey's Residential Care Home (Burnley) Ltd v Lancashire County Council* (Decn. No.129), the Registered Homes Tribunal said that an order should not be made under this section on the ground that certain anticipated events will occur in the future.

In *R. v Ealing, Hammersmith and Hounslow Health Authority Ex p. Wilson* (1996) above, at 99, Laws J. said that:

". . . behind any [application under the urgent procedure] there will always be a history of investigation and, as likely as not, disagreement, and I cannot think that the duty of disclosure systematically requires the authority . . . to expose to the magistrate the whole panoply of such a history in a case where . . . they conclude that there are compelling grounds for such urgent application."

Serious risk: In *Hillingdon LBC v McLean*, 88 L.G.R. 49, Phillips J. held that the risk to the residents of a home must be sufficiently serious to justify cancelling the registration, not merely serious in the abstract, for the court to make an order under this section. His Lordship said that the question for the justice is: "will there be a serious risk to the life, health or well-being of the residents if I do not make the order?" In practice, his Lordship did "not see how any tribunal could consider the question whether there would be a serious risk if the order were not made without comparing the degree of risk and the consequences of the order, whatever that order might be."

A person's: The person at risk could be a visitor, member of staff or service user.

Life, health or well-being: The words used are disjunctive and the registration authority would be justified in taking action under this section if any of these matters are thought to be seriously at risk.

Make the order: The registration authority must notify the person concerned of the right of appeal given by s.21 (subs.(5)).

Shall have effect from the time when the order is made: Any person who continued to run the establishment or agency after this time would be liable to be prosecuted under s.11.

Subs.(2)

3–059   A person against whom an order has been made under this section without notice has no right to make an application to the justice to set it aside (*Maritime v South Kent H.A.*, above).

If the justice thinks fit: It is submitted that the justices should only hear a without notice application where they are satisfied that either (a) it has proved to be impossible to locate the whereabouts of the registered person; (b) notifying the registered person would result in a delay which would significantly prejudice the welfare of the service users; or (c) notifying the registered person would significantly prejudice the welfare of the service users. Also see the note on "The Human Rights Act", above.

Subs.(3)

3–060   *Appropriate authorities:* See subs.(6). The reason for notification is to enable the local authority to consider the provision of alternative care pursuant to its obligations under s.47 of the National Health Service and Community Care Act 1990 (c.19) and for the Health Authority to consider whether to make provision for NHS Services.

Subs.(5)

3–061   *Right of appeal:* There is no provision for restoration of the registration prior pending an appeal to the tribunal.

THE NATIONAL CARE STANDARDS COMMISSION (REGISTRATION) REGULATIONS 2001

(SI 2001/3969)

Dated December 11, 2001, and made by the Secretary of State for Health under the Care Standards Act 2000 (c.14), ss.11(4), 12(2), (14)(1)(d), (15)(3), 16(1), 25(1) and 118(5) to (7).

GENERAL NOTE

These Regulations are made under the Care Standards Act 2000 and apply to England **3–062** only. They make provision in relation to the registration of establishments and agencies by the Commission for Healthcare Audit and Inspection and the Commission for Social Care Inspection.

ARRANGEMENT OF REGULATIONS   **3–063**

SCHEDULES

1. Information to be supplied on an application for registration as a person who carries on an establishment or agency
2. Documents to be supplied on an application for registration as a person who carries on an establishment or agency
3. Information and documents to be supplied on an application for registration as the manager of an establishment or agency
4. Information to be supplied on an application for registration in respect of a care home
5. Information to be supplied on an application for registration in respect of a children's home
6. Information to be supplied on an application for registration in respect of an independent hospital, independent clinic, or independent medical agency
7. Particulars to be recorded in the registers kept by the Commission

PART I

GENERAL

Citation, commencement and extent

3–064   **1.**—(1) These Regulations may be cited as the National Care Standards Commission (Registration) Regulations 2001 and shall come into force on 1st January 2002.

(2) These Regulations extend to England only.

Interpretation

3–065   **2.**—(1) In these Regulations, unless the context otherwise requires—

"the Act" means the Care Standards Act 2000;

"applicant" means a person seeking to be registered;

["Commission" means the Commission for Healthcare Audit and Inspection or the Commission for Social Care Inspection;]

["direct service provider" means a provider who supplies a domiciliary care worker who is employed by, and who acts for and under the control of, the provider;

"domiciliary care service user" means any person for whom a domiciliary care agency—

(a) supplies a domiciliary care worker who is employed by the agency (including domiciliary care workers supplied by a direct service provider); or

(b) provides services for the purpose of supplying him with a domiciliary care worker for employment by him;

"domiciliary care worker" means a person who—

(a) is employed by a domiciliary care agency to act for, and under the control of, another person;

(b) is introduced by a domiciliary care agency to a domiciliary care service user for employment by him; or

(c) is employed by a direct service provider,

in a position which is concerned with the provision of personal care in their own homes for persons who by reason of illness, infirmity or disability are unable to provide it for themselves without assistance;]

"half-way house" means a children's home in which children aged 16 or over may prepare, or be assisted in preparing, for independent living;

"holding company" has the meaning given to it by section 736 of the Companies Act 1985;

["nurse" mens a registered nurse, registered midwife or registered health visitor;

"nurses agency service user" means a person to whom a nurses agency—

(a) supplies a nurse who is employed by the agency; or
(b) provides services for the purpose of supplying him with a nurse for employment by him;]

"organisation" means a body corporate or any unincorporated association other than a partnership;

"placement plan" has the meaning given to it in regulation 12 (child's placement plan) of the Children's Homes Regulations 2001;

["Primary Care Trust" means a Primary Care Trust established under section 16A of the National Health Service Act 1977;]

"registered" means registered under Part II of the Act;

"registered manager" means a person who is registered as the manager of an establishment or agency;

"registered person" means a person who is the registered provider or registered manager in respect of an establishment or agency;

"registered provider" means a person who is registered as a person carrying on an establishment or agency;

"registration" means registration under Part II of the Act;

"relative", in relation to any person, means—

(a) the person's spouse;
(b) any parent, grandparent, child, grandchild, brother, sister, uncle, aunt, nephew or niece of his or his spouse;
(c) the spouse of any relative within sub-paragraph (b) of this definition,

and for the purpose of determining any such relationship a person's stepchild shall be treated as his child, and references to "spouse" in relation to any person include a former spouse and a person who is living with the person as husband and wife;

"representative" means, in relation to a service user, a person, other than the registered person or a person employed at or for the purposes of the establishment or agency, who with the service user's express or implied consent takes an interest in the service user's health and welfare;

"responsible individual" means an individual who is a director, manager, secretary or other officer of an organisation and is responsible for supervising the management of an establishment or agency;

"responsible person" means—

(a) where the applicant is an individual—

(i) the applicant; and

(ii) if the applicant carries on or intends to carry on the establishment or agency in partnership with others, each partner of his;

(b) where the applicant is a partnership, each member of the partnership;

(c) where the applicant is an organisation, the responsible individual;

"service user" means any person who is to be provided with accommodation or services in an establishment, or by an agency;

"statement of purpose" means—

(a) in relation to a care home, the written statement required to be compiled in relation to the care home in accordance with regulation 4(1) of the Care Homes Regulations 2001;

(b) in relation to a children's home, the written statement required to be compiled in relation to the children's home in accordance with regulation 4(1) of the Children's Homes Regulations 2001;

(c) in relation to an independent hospital, independent clinic, or independent medical agency, the written statement required to be compiled in relation to the independent hospital, independent clinic, or independent medical agency in accordance with regulation 5(1) of the Private and Voluntary Health Care (England) Regulations 2001;

[(ca) in relation to a residential family centre, the written statement required to be compiled in relation to the residential family centre in accordance with regulation 4(1) of the Residential Family Centres Regulations 2002;

(cb) in relation to a domiciliary care agency, the written statement required to be compiled in relation to the domiciliary care agency in accordance with regulation 4(1) of the Domiciliary Care Agencies Regulations 2002;

(cc) in relation to a fostering agency, the written statement required to be compiled in relation to the fostering agency in accordance with regulation 3(1) of the Fostering Services Regulations 2002;

(cd) in relation to a nurses agency, the written statement required to be compiled in relation to the nurses agency in accordance with regulation 4(1) of the Nurses Agencies Regulations 2002;

(ce) in relation to a voluntary adoption agency, the written statement required to be compiled in relation to the voluntary adoption agency in accordance with regulation 3(1) of the Voluntary Adoption Agencies and the Adoption Agencies (Miscellaneous Amendments) Regulations 2003;]

(d) in relation to an establishment or agency of any other description, a statement of the aims and objectives of the establishment or agency;

"subsidiary" has the meaning given to it by section 736 of the Companies Act 1985.

(2) In these Regulations, unless the context otherwise requires, references to an establishment or agency are to be construed as references—

(a) in the case of an applicant, to the establishment or agency in respect of which he is seeking to be registered;

(b) in the case of a registered person, to the establishment or agency in respect of which he is registered.

(3) In these Regulations, a reference—

(a) to a numbered regulation or Schedule is to the regulation in, or Schedule to, these Regulations bearing that number;

(b) in a regulation or Schedule to a numbered paragraph is to the paragraph in that regulation or Schedule bearing that number;

(c) in a paragraph to a lettered or numbered sub-paragraph is to the sub-paragraph in that paragraph bearing that letter or number.

[(4) In these Regulations—

(a) references to the supply of a nurse mean—

   (i) the supply of a nurse who is employed for the purposes of a nurses agency to act for and under the control of another person; and
   (ii) the introduction of a nurse by a nurses agency to a nurses agency service user for employment by him;

(b) references to the supply of a domiciliary care worker mean—

   (i) the supply of a domiciliary care worker who is employed by a domiciliary care agency to act for and under the control of another person;
   (ii) the introduction of a domiciliary care worker by a domiciliary care agency to a domiciliary care service user for employment by him; and
   (iii) the supply of a domiciliary care worker employed by a direct service provider to a domiciliary care service user;

(c) the terms "employed" and "employment" include employment under a contract of service or a contract for services, or otherwise than under a contract and whether or not for payment.]

AMENDMENT

The amendments to this regulation were made by SI 2003/369, reg.2(2), SI 2002/2469, **3–066** reg.11, Sch.8 and SI 2004/664, art.2, Sch.1, para.5.

PART II

APPLICATIONS FOR REGISTRATION

Information and documents to be provided by an applicant

3.—(1) An application for registration shall—   **3–067**

(a) be in writing on a form approved by the Commission;

(b) be sent or delivered to the Commission;

(c) be accompanied by a recent photograph of the responsible person, of whom the photograph shall be a true likeness;

(d) give the information that the applicant is required to provide in accordance with paragraphs (2) to (4).

(2) [Subject to paragraph (2A),] a person who is seeking to be registered as a person who carries on an establishment or agency shall provide to the Commission—

(a) full information in respect of the matters listed in Parts I and II of Schedule 1;

(b) the documents listed in [...] Schedule 2;

(c) [...]

[(2A) Where a person is seeking to be registered as the registered provider in respect of a care home and, if registered, would be an adult placement carer in respect of that care home, he shall not be required to provide to the Commission the information and documents listed in paragraph 4 of Schedule 1.]

(3) A person who is seeking to be registered as a manager in respect of an establishment or agency shall provide to the Commission—

(a) full information in respect of each of the matters listed in Part I of Schedule 3;

(b) the documents listed in [Part II] of that Schedule;

(c) [...]

(4) A person who is seeking to be registered in respect of an establishment or agency of a description specified in column (1) below shall provide to the Commission full information in respect of each of the matters listed in the Schedule specified in the corresponding entry in column (2) below.

(1)	*(2)*
Establishment or agency	*Schedule*
Care home	Schedule 4
Children's home	Schedule 5
Independent hospital, independent clinic, or independent medical agency	Schedule 6

(5) If the Commission so requests, the applicant shall provide full information to the Commission in respect of the matters listed in Part III of Schedule 1 in relation to any person specified for this purpose by the Commission who works, or is intended to work, at the establishment or for the purposes of the agency.

(6) The applicant shall provide to the Commission any other information or documents that it may reasonably require in relation to his application for registration.

AMENDMENTS

3–068   The amendments to this regulation were made by SI 2002/865, reg.8(2) and SI 2003/1845, reg.6.

DEFINITIONS
  Commission: reg.2(1).
  registration: reg.2(1).
  responsible person: reg.2(1).
  establishment: reg.2(1).
  agency: reg.2(1).
  registered: reg.2(1).

3–069

GENERAL NOTE
This regulation is concerned with the requirements placed on a person applying either to **3–070** carry on or to manage an establishment or agency. Modified requirements have been established in respect of a person who is seeking to be an adult placement carer: see para.(2A).

PARA.(2)
A person who makes a false statement in an application commits an offence under s.27 of **3–071** the Act.

Convictions

4. Where the Commission asks the responsible person for details of any crimi- **3–072** nal convictions which are spent within the meaning of section 1 of the Rehabilitation of Offenders Act 1974 and informs him at the time the question is asked that by virtue of the Rehabilitation of Offenders Act 1974 (Exceptions) Order 1975 spent convictions are to be disclosed, he shall supply in writing to the Commission details of any spent convictions that he has.

DEFINITIONS
  Commission: reg.2(1).
  responsible person: reg.2(1).   **3–073**

GENERAL NOTE
This regulation requires the applicant to divulge convictions that are spent within the **3–074** meaning of s.1 of the Rehabilitation of Offenders Act 1974.

Interview

5. The responsible person shall attend an interview for the purpose of enabling **3–075** the Commission to determine whether the applicant is fit to carry on or manage the establishment or agency in respect of which the applicant seeks to be registered.

DEFINITIONS
  responsible person: reg.2(1)   **3–076**
  Commission: reg.2(1).
  applicant: reg.2(1).
  establishment: reg.2(1).
  agency: reg.2(1).
  registered: reg.2(1).

GENERAL NOTE
As the interview could form the basis of a decision not to register the applicant, a minute **3–077** of the interview should be made by the authority and provided to the applicant.

Notice of changes

3–078   **6.** The applicant shall give notice in writing to the Commission of any change specified below which occurs after the application for registration is made and before it is determined—

   (a) any change of the name or address of the applicant or any responsible person;

   (b) where the applicant is a partnership, any change of membership of the partnership;

   (c) where the applicant is an organisation, any change of director, manager, secretary or other person responsible for the management of the organisation.

DEFINITIONS

3–079   applicant: reg.2(1).
Commission: reg.2(1).
registration: reg.2(1).
responsible person: reg.2(1).
organisation: reg.2(1).

GENERAL NOTE

3–080   This regulation requires the applicant to notify the registration authority of certain specified changes that have taken place after the application for registration has been made and before it is determined. It would be advisable for any change of substance that has occurred during this period to be notified to the registration authority.

Information as to staff engaged after application made

3–081   **7.**—(1) Where an applicant applies for registration as a person who carries on an establishment or agency, and before the application is determined, engages a person to work at the establishment or for the purposes of the agency, he shall, in respect of each person so engaged—

   (a) obtain the information specified in paragraphs 16 and 17 of Schedule 1 and, except where paragraph (2) applies, the documents specified in paragraph 10 of Schedule 2, in relation to the position in which the person is to work;

   (b) provide to the Commission, if it so requests, any of the information or documents which he is required to obtain under paragraph (a).

(2) This paragraph applies where any certificate or information on any matters referred to in paragraph 10 of Schedule 2 is not available to an individual because any provision of the Police Act 1997 has not been brought into force.

DEFINITIONS

3–082   applicant: reg.2(1).
registration: reg.2(1).
establishment: reg.2(1).
agency: reg.2(1).
registered: reg.2(1).
Commission: reg.2(1).

GENERAL NOTE
If an applicant for registration engages staff before the application is determined, this **3–083** regulation requires the applicant to obtain specified information about the staff and to obtain criminal record certificates in respect of the staff and to provide such information or documents to the registration authority on request.

PART III

CERTIFICATES OF REGISTRATION

Registers

8.—(1) The Commission shall keep a register in respect of each description of **3–084** establishment or agency specified in section 4(8)(a) or (9)(a) of the Act [...].

(2) Each register shall contain, in relation to each establishment or agency in respect of which a person's application for registration has been granted—

(a) the particulars specified in Part I of Schedule 7; and

(b) the particulars specified in respect of the register in Part II of that Schedule.

[(2A) For the purposes of paragraph 3 of Schedule 7, the reference to the address of an agency shall mean, in the case of a voluntary adoption agency, the address of the principal office and any branch of the agency.]

[(3) Subsections (1) and (2) of section 36 of the Act (provision of copies of registers) shall not apply to any part of the register relating to children's homes which consists of the restricted part of the address of any children's home.

(4) For the purposes of paragraph (3), the restricted part of the address of a children's home is the whole of the address except the name of the children's home.]

AMENDMENTS
The amendments to these regulations were made by SI 2002/865, reg.9(2) and SI 2003/ **3–085** 369, reg.2(3).

DEFINITIONS
Commission: reg.2(1). **3–086**
establishment: reg.2(1).
agency: reg.2(1).

Contents of certificate

9. Where the Commission is required to issue a certificate of registration it shall **3–087** ensure that the certificate contains the following particulars—

(a) the name, address and telephone number of the Commission;

(b) the name and address of the person who has been registered as the person who carries on the establishment or agency;

(c) where the person is an organisation, the name of the responsible individual;

(d) the name of the person registered as the manager of the establishment or agency;

(e) the description of the establishment or agency by reference to the description of establishment or agency specified in section 4(8)(a) or (9)(a) of the Act;

(f) where the registration is subject to any condition, details of the condition including any requirement in the condition as to—

    (i) the facilities or services that are to be provided;

    (ii) the number of service users for whom accommodation or services may be provided;

    (iii) the description of persons to whom facilities or services are to be provided;

    (iv) any period of time within which the condition is to be fulfilled;

    (v) the number and description of persons to be working at any specified place and time;

(g) the date of registration;

(h) a statement that if an establishment or agency is not carried on in accordance with the relevant requirements and conditions the registration is liable to be cancelled by the Commission;

(i) a statement that the certificate relates only to the person to whom it is issued by the Commission and is not capable of being transferred to another person.

[(j) in the case of a voluntary adoption agency, the address of the principal office and any branch of the agency.]

AMENDMENT

3–088   The amendment to this regulation was made by SI 2003/369, reg.2(4).

DEFINITIONS

3–089   Commission: reg.2(1).
registration: reg.2(1).
registered: reg.2(1).
establishment: reg.2(1).
agency: reg.2(1).
responsible individual: reg.2(1).
services user: reg.2(1).

GENERAL NOTE.

3–090   A failure to display the certificate of registration in a conspicuous place in the establishment or agency constitutes an offence under s.28 of the Act.

PARA.(B)

3–091   It is difficult to identify a rationale for the private address of an individual provider being identified on the certificate.

Return of certificate

3–092   **10.** If the registration of a person in respect of an establishment or agency is cancelled, he shall, not later than the day on which the decision or order cancelling the registration takes effect, return the certificate of registration to the Commission by—

(a) delivering it to the Commission; or

(b) sending it to the Commission by registered post or by recorded delivery.

DEFINITIONS
establishment: reg.2(1).   **3–093**
agency: reg.2(1).
registration: reg.2(1).
Commission: reg.2(1).

GENERAL NOTE
A failure to return the certificate is an offence under reg.11.   **3–094**

Offence

11.—(1) A failure to comply with regulation 10 shall be an offence.   **3–095**
(2) The Commission shall not bring proceedings against a person in respect of
any failure to comply with that regulation unless—

[(a) the Commission has served a notice on the persons specifying—

    (i) details of the person's failure to comply with that regulation, and
    (ii) the period, not exceeding one month, within which the person may
        make representations to the Commission about the notice, and]

(b) the period specified in the notice, beginning with the date of the notice, has
    expired; [...]

(3) Where the Commission considers that the person has failed to comply with
regulation 10, it may serve a notice on the person specifying—

(a) in what respect in its opinion the person has failed or is failing to comply
    with the requirements of that regulation;

(b) what action, in the opinion of the Commission, the person should take so as
    to comply with that regulation; and

(c) the period, not exceeding three months, within which the person should take
    action.

AMENDMENTS
The amendments to this regulation were made by SI 2002/865, reg.9(3).   **3–096**

DEFINITION
Commission: reg.2(1).   **3–097**

PART IV

CONDITIONS AND REPORTS

Application for variation or removal of a condition

12.—(1) In this regulation—   **3–098**

"application" means an application by the registered person under section
    15(1)(a) of the Act for the variation or removal of a condition in relation
    to his registration;
"proposed effective date" means the date requested by the registered person
    as the date on which the variation or removal applied for is to take effect.
(2) An application shall be—

(a) made in writing on a form approved by the Commission;

(b) sent or delivered to the Commission not less than six weeks before the proposed effective date or such shorter period (if any) before that date as may be agreed with the Commission;

(c) accompanied by the information specified in paragraph (3);

(d) accompanied by a fee of such amount as may be prescribed in relation to the variation or removal applied for by any regulation made under section 15(3) of the Act.

(3) The following information is specified—

(a) the proposed effective date;

(b) the registered person's reasons for making the application;

(c) details of changes that the registered person proposes to make in relation to the establishment or agency as a consequence of the variation or removal applied for, including details of—

    (i) proposed structural changes to the premises that are used as an establishment or for the purposes of an agency;

    (ii) additional staff, facilities or equipment, or changes in management that are required to ensure that the proposed changes are carried into effect.

(4) The registered person shall provide the Commission with any other information or any documents that it may reasonably require in relation to his application.

DEFINITIONS

3–099   registered person: reg.2(1).
registration: reg.2(1).
Commission: reg.2(1).
establishment: reg.2(1).
agency: reg.2(1).

Report as to financial viability

3–100   **13.** If it appears to the registered person that the establishment or agency is likely to cease to be financially viable at any time within the next following six months, the registered person shall give a report to the Commission of the relevant circumstances.

DEFINITIONS

3–101   registered person: reg.2(1).
establishment: reg.2(1).
agency: reg.2(1).
Commission: reg.2(1).

PART V

CANCELLATION OF REGISTRATION

Cancellation of registration

14. The following grounds are specified for the purposes of section 14(1)(d) of **3–102**
the Act as grounds on which the Commission may cancel the registration of a person in respect of an establishment or agency—

  (a) he has failed to pay at the time prescribed under subsection (3) of section 16
of the Act the annual fee payable by him by virtue of that subsection;

  (b) he has in relation to any application by him—

      (i) for registration; or
      (ii) for the variation or removal of a condition in relation to his registration,

made a statement which is false or misleading in a material respect or provided false information;

  (c) the establishment or agency has ceased to be financially viable, or is likely
to cease to be so within the next six months.

DEFINITIONS
  Commission: reg.2(1).   **3–103**
  registration: reg.2(1).
  establishment: reg.2(1).
  agency: reg.2(1).

Application for cancellation of registration

  15.—(1) In this regulation—   **3–104**

"application for cancellation" means an application by the registered person
under section 15(1)(b) of the Act for the cancellation of his registration;
"notice of application for cancellation" means a notice by the registered person stating that he has made, or intends to make, an application for
cancellation;
"proposed effective date" means the date requested by the registered person
as the date on which the cancellation applied for is to take effect.

(2) An application for cancellation shall be—

  (a) made in writing on a form approved by the Commission;

  (b) sent or delivered to the Commission not less than three months before the
proposed effective date or such shorter period (if any) before that date as
may be agreed with the Commission;

  (c) accompanied by the information specified in paragraph (4).

(3) If the registered person makes an application for cancellation he shall not
more than seven days thereafter give notice of application for cancellation to
each of the persons specified in paragraph (4)(d), other than a person to whom
he has given such notice within three months before he made the application
for cancellation.

(4) The following information is specified—

(a) the proposed effective date;

(b) a statement as to the arrangements (if any) that have been made by the registered person to ensure that on and after—

(i) the date of application for cancellation; and
(ii) the proposed effective date,

service users will continue to be provided with similar accommodation (if any) and services as those provided to them in the establishment or by the agency at the date on which the application for cancellation is made;

(c) the registered person's reasons for making the application for cancellation;

(d) particulars of any notice of application for cancellation that has been given to any of the following persons—

(i) service users;
(ii) persons who appear to the registered person to be representatives of service users;
(iii) the local authority and [Primary Care Trust] in whose areas the establishment or the premises used by the agency are situated;

(e) where the registered person has not given notice of application for cancellation to—

(i) each service user;
(ii) in respect of each service user, a person who appears to the registered person to be a representative of that service user; and
(iii) each of the bodies specified in sub-paragraph (4)(d)(iii),

a statement as to whether there were any circumstances which prevented the registered person from giving, or made it impracticable for him to give, notice of application for cancellation to any of the persons or bodies referred to in heads (i) to (iii) of this sub-paragraph before the date on which he applied for cancellation;

(f) where the registered person has applied for cancellation less than three months before the proposed effective date, a report as to whether the establishment or agency has ceased, or is likely to cease within the next following twelve months, to be financially viable.

(5) The registered person shall provide the Commission with any other information or any documents that it may reasonably require in relation to his application for cancellation.

AMENDMENT

3–105   The amendment to para.(d)(iii) was made by the National Health Service Reform and Health Care Professions Act 2002 (Supplementary, Consequential, etc. Provisions) Regulations 2002 (SI 2002/2469), reg.10, Sch.7.

DEFINITIONS

3–106   registered person: reg.2(1).
registration: reg.2(1).

Commission: reg.2(1).
service user: reg.2(1).
establishment: reg.2(1).
agency: reg.2(1).
representative: reg.2(1).
Primary Care Trust: reg.2(1).

Regulation 3(2)(a) and (5)   **SCHEDULE 1**

INFORMATION TO BE SUPPLIED ON AN APPLICATION FOR REGISTRATION AS A PERSON WHO CARRIED ON AN ESTABLISHMENT OR AGENCY

PART I

Information about the applicant

1. Where the applicant is an individual—   **3–107**

(a) if he intends to carry on the establishment or agency in partnership with others, the information specified in the following sub-paragraphs of this paragraph in relation to each partner of the firm;

(b) the responsible person's full name, date of birth, address and telephone number;

(c) details of his professional or technical qualifications, and experience of carrying on an establishment or agency, so far as such qualifications and experience are relevant to providing services for persons to whom services are to be provided at the establishment or by the agency;

(d) details of his employment history, including the name and address of his present employer and of any previous employers;

(e) details of any business he carries on or has carried on;

(f) the name and addresses of two referees—

    (i) who are not relatives of the responsible person;
    (ii) each of whom is able to provide a reference as to the responsible person's competence to carry on an establishment or agency of the same description as the establishment or agency; and
    (iii) one of whom has employed the responsible person for a period of at least 3 months,

but the requirement for the name and address of a referee who has employed the responsible person for a period of at least 3 months shall not apply where it is impracticable to obtain a reference from a person who fulfils that requirement;

(g) [. . .]

2. Where the applicant is a partnership—

(a) the name and address of the partnership;

(b) in relation to each member of the partnership, the information specified in paragraph [1(b) to (f)].

3. Where the applicant is an organisation—

(a) the name of the organisation and the address of the registered office or principal office of the organisation;

(b) the full name, date of birth, address and telephone number of the responsible individual;

(c) details of the professional or technical qualifications of the responsible individual and his experience of carrying on an establishment or agency of the same description as the establishment or agency, so far as such qualifications and experience are relevant to providing services for persons for whom services are to be provided at the establishment or by the agency;

(d) if the organisation is a subsidiary of a holding company, the name and address of the registered or principal office of the holding company and of any other subsidiary of that holding company.

4. [In all cases (unless otherwise provided in these Regulations]—

(a) a reference from a bank expressing an opinion as to the applicant's financial standing;

(b) a statement as to whether the responsible person has been adjudged bankrupt, or sequestration of his estate has been ordered, or he has made a composition or arrangement with, or granted a trust deed for, his creditors;

(c) a statement as to the applicant's ability to ensure the financial viability of the establishment or agency for the purpose of achieving the aims and objectives of the establishment or agency set out in its statement of purpose;

(d) a business plan in respect of the establishment or agency;

(e) details as to cash-flow in respect of the establishment or agency.

PART II

Information about the establishment or agency

3–108   **5.** The name, address, telephone number, facsimile number, and electronic mail address (if any) of the establishment or agency.

6. The description of establishment or agency specified in section 4(8)(a) or (9)(a) of the Act in respect of which the applicant seeks to be registered.

7. The statement of purpose of the establishment or agency.

8. A statement as to the accommodation, facilities and services which are to be provided by the establishment or agency including the extent and, where appropriate, location of such accommodation, facilities and services.

9. The date on which the establishment or agency was established or is proposed to be established.

10. Details of the scale of charges payable by the service users.

11. In respect of the premises to be used by an establishment—

(a) a description of the premises, including a statement as to whether the premises are purpose-built or have been converted for use as an establishment;

(b) a description of the area in which the premises are located.

12. In respect of the premises to be used by an establishment or for the purposes of an agency, a statement as to whether at the date the application is made the premises are capable of being used for the purpose of—

(a) achieving the aims and objectives set out in the statement of purpose of the establishment or agency; and

(b) providing facilities and services in accordance with the statement referred to in paragraph 8,

without the need for planning permission, building works, or conversion of the premises and, if the premises are not capable of such use at the date the application is made, details of the permission, works or conversion needed.

13. A statement as to the security arrangements, including arrangements for the purposes of—

(a) safeguarding access to information held by the establishment or agency; and

(b) restricting access from adjacent premises or, when the premises form part of a building, from other parts of the building.

14. The name and address of any other establishment or agency of a description specified in section 4(8)(a) or (9)(a) of the Act in which the applicant has or has had a business or financial interest, or at which he is or has been employed, and details of such interest or employment.

15. Whether any other business is or will be carried on in the same premises as those of the establishment or agency and, if so, details of such business.

Information about staff

16. In respect of any person, other than the applicant, who works at, or is intended to work at the establishment or for the agency— **3–109**

(a) the person's name, sex and date of birth;

(b) the person's duties and responsibilities in relation to his work.

PART III

Further information about staff

17. In respect of any person, other than the applicant, who works at, or is intended to work at the establishment or for the purposes of the agency— **3–110**

(a) whether the person is, or is intended to be, resident in the premises used as the establishment or for the purposes of the agency;

(b) if he is a relative of any person who has made an application in respect of the establishment or agency, his relationship to such person;

(c) whether the person works or is intended to work, on a full-time basis or on a part-time basis and, if on a part-time basis, the number of hours per week for which it is intended that the person will work;

(d) the date on which the person commenced, or is intended to commence, working at the establishment or for the purposes of the agency;

(e) information as to the person's qualifications, experience and skills in so far as is relevant to the work that the person is to perform;

(f) a statement by [the] applicant that he is satisfied as to the authenticity of the qualifications, and has verified the experience and skills that are referred in subparagraph (e);

(g) a statement as to—

(i) the suitability of the person's qualifications for the work that the person is to perform;

(ii) whether the person has the skills necessary for such work;

(iii) the person's fitness to work, and have regular contact, with service users;

(h) a statement by the person as to the state of his physical and mental health;

(i) a statement by the applicant that the person is physically and mentally fit for the purposes of the work which he is to perform;

(j) a statement by the applicant as to whether he is satisfied as to the person's identity, the means by which he so satisfied himself and whether he has obtained a copy of the person's birth certificate;

(k) confirmation by the applicant that he has a recent photograph of the person;

(l) a statement by the applicant that he has obtained two references relating to the person and that he is satisfied as to the authenticity of those references;

(m) details of any criminal offences of which the person has been convicted, including details of any convictions which are spent within the meaning of section 1 of the Rehabilitation of Offenders Act 1974 and which may be disclosed by virtue of the Rehabilitation of Offenders Act 1974 (Exceptions) Order 1975, and, in relation to each such offence, a statement by the person—

(i) as to whether in his view the offence is relevant to his suitability to care for, train, supervise or be in sole charge of any person and, if so,

(ii) as to why he considers that he is suitable to perform the work in which he is to be employed;

(n) details of any criminal offences in respect of which he has been cautioned by a constable and which, at the time the caution was given, he admitted.

AMENDMENTS

3–111   The amendments to this Schedule were made by SI 2002/865, reg.9(4) and SI 2003/1845, reg.6.

DEFINITIONS

3–112   applicant: reg.2(1).
establishment: reg.2(1).
agency: reg.2(1).
employment: reg.2(4).
relative: reg.2(1).
responsible person: reg.2(1).
organisation: reg.2(1).
responsible individual: reg.2(1).
subsidiary: reg.2(1).
holding company: reg.2(1).
statement of purpose: reg.2(1).
service user: reg.2(1).
employed: reg.2(4).

Regulation 3(2)(b)   **SCHEDULE 2**

DOCUMENTS INFORMATION TO BE SUPPLIED ON AN APPLICATION FOR REGISTRATION AS A PERSON
WHO CARRIED ON AN ESTABLISHMENT OR AGENCY

Documents concerning applicant

3–113   **1.** The responsible person's birth certificate.
2. Certificates or other suitable evidence relating to the responsible person's professional or technical qualifications, so far as such qualifications are relevant to providing services for persons for whom services are to be provided at the establishment or by the agency.

3.—(1) Subject to sub-paragraph (2), a report by a general medical practitioner as to whether the responsible person is physically and mentally fit to carry on an establishment or agency of the same description as the establishment or agency.

(2) Where the responsible person is unable to obtain the report referred to in sub-paragraph (1), a statement by the responsible person as to the state of his physical and mental health.

4. The following documents in relation to the responsible person—

(a) a criminal record certificate—

   (i) which has been issued under section 113 of the Police Act 1997; and
   (ii) the application for which was countersigned by the Commission,

   including, where applicable, the matters specified in [section 113(3A)(a) and (b) of that Act and the following provisions once they are in force, namely section 113(3C)(a) and (b) of that Act;]

(b) an enhanced criminal record certificate—

   (i) which has been issued under section 115 of that Act; and
   (ii) the application for which was countersigned by the Commission,

   including, where applicable, the matters specified in [section 115(6A)(a) and (b) of that Act and the following provisions once they are in force, namely section 115(6B)(a) and (b) of that Act.]

5. Where the applicant is a corporate body, a copy of each of its last two annual reports.

6. Where the organisation is a subsidiary of a holding company, the name and address of the registered or principal office and the last two annual reports (if any) of the holding company and of any other subsidiary of that holding company.

7. The last annual accounts (if any) of the establishment or agency.

8. Except where the applicant is a local authority[, NHS trust or NHS foundation trust], a reference from a bank expressing an opinion as to the applicant's financial standing.

9. A certificate of insurance for the applicant in respect of liability which may be incurred by him in relation to the establishment or agency in respect of death, injury, public liability, damage or other loss.

Criminal record certificates in respect of staff
10.—(1) [. . .], a statement] confirming that—   **3–114**

(a) the documents specified in sub-paragraph (2) have been issued—

   (i) in the case of any applicant, to every person, other than the applicant, who works, or is intended to work, for the purposes of the establishment or agency; and
   (ii) where the applicant is an organisation, to the responsible individual; and

(b) the applicant will make the documents so issued available for inspection by the Commission if the Commission so requires.

[(2) The following documents are specified—

(a) where the position falls within section 115(3) or (4) of the Police Act 1997 (registration under Part II of the Care Standards Act 2000), an enhanced criminal record certificate issued under section 115 of that Act; or

(b) in any other case, a criminal record certificate issued under section 113 of that Act, including, where applicable, the matters specified in sections 113(3A) and 115(6A) of that Act and the following provisions once they are in force, namely section 113(3C)(a) and (b) and section 115(6B)(a) and (b) of that Act.]

(3)–(5) *[Repealed by SI 2003/2323, reg.4]*

AMENDMENTS

3–115   The amendments to this Schedule were made by SI 2002/865, reg.8(3), SI 2003/369, reg.2(5), SI 2003/2323, reg.4 and SI 2004/696, art.3(5), Sch.5.

DEFINITIONS

3–116   responsible person: reg.2(1).
organisation: reg.2(1).
subsidiary: reg.2(1).
holding company: reg.2(1).
applicant: reg.2(1).
responsible individual: reg.2(1).
supply of a domiciliary care worker: reg.2(4).
supply of a nurse: reg.2(4).
Commission: reg.2(1).

Regulation 3(3)   **SCHEDULE 3**

INFORMATION AND DOCUMENTS TO BE SUPPLIED ON AN APPLICATION FOR REGISTRATION AS A PERSON
WHO CARRIED ON AN ESTABLISHMENT OR AGENCY

PART I

Information

3–117   1. The applicant's full name, date of birth, address and telephone number.

2. Details of the applicant's professional or technical qualifications, and experience of managing an establishment or agency, so far as such qualifications and experience are relevant to providing services for persons for whom services are to be provided at the establishment or by the agency.

3. Details of the applicant's professional training relevant to carrying on or managing an establishment or agency.

4. Details of the applicant's employment history, including the name and address of his present employer and of any previous employers.

5. Details of any business the applicant carries on or manages or has carried on or managed.

6. The name and addresses of two referees—

(a) who are not relatives of the applicant;

(b) each of whom is able to provide a reference as to the applicant's competence to carry on an establishment or agency of the same description as the establishment or agency; and

(c) one of whom has employed the applicant for a period of at least 3 months,

but the requirement for the name and address of a referee who has employed the applicant for a period of at least 3 months shall not apply where it is impracticable to obtain a reference from a person who fulfils that requirement.

7. The name, address, telephone number, facsimile number, and electronic mail address (if any) of the establishment or agency.

8. [...]

PART II

Documents

9. The applicant's birth certificate.

3–118

10. Certificates or other suitable evidence relating to the applicant's professional or technical qualifications, so far as such qualifications are relevant to providing services for persons for whom services are to be provided at the establishment or by the agency.

11. [...]

[**11A.**]—(1) Subject to sub-paragraph (2), a report by a general medical practitioner as to whether the applicant is physically and mentally fit to carry on an establishment or agency of the same description as the establishment or agency.

(2) Where the applicant is unable to obtain the report referred to in sub-paragraph (1), a statement by the applicant as to the state of his physical and mental health.

12. A criminal record certificate—

(a) which has been issued to the applicant under section 113 of the Police Act 1997; and

(b) the application for which was countersigned by the Commission,

including, where applicable, the matters specified in [section 113(3A)(a) and (b) of that Act and the following provisions once they are in force, namely section 113(3C)(a) and (b) of that Act.]

13. An enhanced criminal record certificate—

(a) which has been issued to the applicant under section 115 of that Act; and

(b) the application for which was countersigned by the Commission,

including, where applicable, the matters specified in [section 115(6A)(a) and (b) of that Act and the following provisions once they are in force, namely section 115(6B)(a) and (b) of that Act.]

<small>AMENDMENTS</small>

The amendments to this Schedule were made by SI 2002/865, reg.8(4).

3–119

<small>DEFINITIONS</small>

applicant: reg.2(1).

3–120

employment: reg.2(4).

employer: reg.2(4): reg.2(1).

relative: reg.2(1).

Commission: reg.2(1).

Regulation 3(4)   **SCHEDULE 4**

<small>INFORMATION TO BE SUPPLIED ON AN APPLICATION FOR REGISTRATION IN RESPECT OF A CARE HOME</small>

1. In this Schedule "service user" means any person in the care home who is in need of nursing or personal care by reason of disability, infirmity, past or present illness, past or present mental disorder or past or present dependence on alcohol or drugs.

3–121

2. Details of the accommodation available for—

(a) service users; and

(b) persons working at the care home.

3. Whether it is proposed to provide nursing at the care home.

4. Whether it is proposed to provide at the care home accommodation, nursing or personal care to service users who are children.

5. The maximum number of service users for whom the care home is proposed to be used, and the number of such users by reference to—

(a) their sex;

(b) the categories listed in paragraph 6(c) of Schedule 7;

(c) service users who are children.

Regulation 3(4)   **SCHEDULE 5**

INFORMATION TO BE SUPPLIED ON AN APPLICATION FOR REGISTRATION IN RESPECT OF A CHILDREN'S
HOME

3–122   **1.** The following details about the children who are intended to be accommodated at the children's home—

(a) their age range;

(b) their sex;

(c) the maximum number of such children;

(d) whether the children to be accommodated are selected by reference to other criteria than age or sex, and if so those criteria.

2. The organisational structure of the children's home.
3. The facilities and services to be provided within the children's home for the children accommodated.
4. The arrangements for protecting and promoting the health of any children accommodated.
5. The fire precautions and emergency procedures.
6. The arrangements to allow children to follow religious observance.
7. The arrangements for contact between a child and his parents, relatives and friends.
8. Details as to the use of restraint and discipline, the circumstances in which they will be used, and who is permitted to authorise such use.
9. The procedure for dealing with any unauthorised absence of a child from the children's home.
10. The arrangements for allowing children in the children's home to raise issues, and the procedure for dealing with complaints.
11. The arrangements for the education of any child accommodated.
12. The arrangements for dealing with reviews of the placement plans of any children accommodated.

Regulation 3(4)   **SCHEDULE 6**

INFORMATION TO BE SUPPLIED ON AN APPLICATION FOR REGISTRATION IN RESPECT OF AN
INDEPENDENT HOSPITAL, INDEPENDENT CLINIC, OR INDEPENDENT MEDICAL AGENCY

3–123   **1.** The nature of the services to be provided including, in particular, details of any listed services.
2. The equipment and facilities to be provided.
3. The number of patient beds to be provided in an independent hospital or independent clinic.
4. The anticipated number of patients to be treated annually.
5. The arrangements made for the supply of blood and blood products.
6. The arrangements made for the provision of pathology and radiology services.

7. The number of registered medical practitioners who are to be involved in the treatment of patients.

8. Details of any services which are to be provided to children.

DEFINITION

relative: reg.2(1).   **3–124**

Regulation 8   **SCHEDULE 7**

PARTICULARS TO BE RECORDED IN THE REGISTERS KEPT BY THE COMMISSION

PART I

1. The full name, address and date of birth of each person registered in respect of the **3–125** establishment or agency.

2. Where the registered person is an organisation—

(a) the address of the registered office or principal office of the organisation;

(b) the full names, dates of birth and addresses of any individual who is a director, manager, secretary or other officer of an organisation and is responsible for supervising the management of the establishment or agency.

3. The full name, address and telephone number of the establishment or agency.

4. The date of registration and of the issue of the certificate of registration and, where applicable, the date of any cancellation of registration.

5. The details of any conditions imposed on registration, any additional conditions imposed and any variation of any condition.

PART II

Care homes register

6. In the case of the register relating to care homes—   **3–126**

(a) which (if any) of the following categories of care home are applicable, each category to be indicated by reference to the following code—

care home only	PC
care home with nursing	N
care home providing adult placement	AP
care home not providing medicines or medical treatment	NM

(b) the number of service users of each sex;

(c) which (if any) of the following categories in respect of service users are applicable, each category to be indicated by reference to the following code—

old age, not falling within any other category	OP
service users who are over 65 years of age but do not fall within the category of old age	E
dementia	DE
mental disorder, excluding learning disability or dementia	MD
learning disability	LD

physical disability	PD
past or present drug dependence	D
past or present alcohol dependence	A
terminally ill	TI
sensory impairment	SI

Children's homes register

3–127   7. In the case of the register relating to children's homes—

(a) which (if any) of the following categories of children's home are applicable, each category to be indicated by reference to the following code—

children's home (excluding any of the following categories in this sub-paragraph)	CH
schools (not nursing)	SCH
secure unit	SU
half-way house for child aged 16 or over	HH

(b) the number of service users of each sex;

(c) which (if any) of the following categories in respect of service users are applicable, each category to be indicated by reference to the following code—

children (with none of the following conditions)	X
children with emotional or behavioural difficulties	EBD
children with physical disabilities	PD
children with learning disabilities	LD
children with mental disorders, excluding learning disability	MD
children with present drug dependence	D
children with present alcohol dependence	A
sensory impairment	SI

Registers relating to independent hospitals, independent hospitals in which treatment or nursing (or both) are provided for persons liable to be detained under the Mental Health Act 1983, independent clinics and independent medical agencies

3–128   8.—(a) In the case of the register relating to—
(i) independent hospitals, the code IH;
(ii) independent clinics, the code IC;
(iii) independent medical agencies, the code IMA.

(b) In the case of each of the registers relating respectively to independent hospitals, independent hospitals in which treatment or nursing (or both) are provided for persons liable to be detained under the Mental Health Act 1983, independent clinics and independent medical agencies, which (if any) of the following categories in respect of service users are applicable, each category to be indicated by reference to the following code—

acute hospitals (with overnight beds)	AH
acute hospitals (day surgery only)	AH(DS)
mental health treatment establishments, not including those where people are liable to be detained	MH
mental health establishments taking people liable to be detained	MD(D)
hospices for adults	H(A)
hospices for children	H(C)
maternity hospitals/clinics	MAT
abortion clinics	TOP
prescribed techniques or prescribed technology: establishments using Class 3B or Class 4 lasers	PT(L)
prescribed techniques or prescribed technology: establishments using intense light sources	PT(IL)
prescribed techniques or prescribed technology: establishments providing dialysis	PT(DL)
prescribed techniques or prescribed technology: establishments using endoscopy	PT(E)
prescribed techniques or prescribed technology: establishments providing in vitro fertilisation	PT(IVF)
prescribed techniques or prescribed technology: establishments providing hyperbaric oxygen treatment	PT(HBO)
private doctors: walk-in medical centres	PD(M)
private doctors (other)	PD
private doctors: independent medical agencies	PD(IMA)

Registers relating to residential family centres, domiciliary care agencies, nurses agencies and fostering agencies

9. In the case of the register relating to—   **3–129**

(a) residential family centres, the code RFC;

(b) domiciliary care agencies, the code DCA;

(c) nurses agencies, the code NA;

(d) fostering agencies, the code IFA.

[Voluntary adoption agencies register

10.—(1) In the case of the register relating to voluntary adoption agencies, which of the **3–130** following categories of voluntary agency is applicable, each category to be indicated by reference to the following code—

domestic adoption services only	DA
intercountry adoption services only	ICA
domestic and intercountry adoption services	DICA

(2) For the purposes of sub-paragraph (1)—
"domestic adoption services" means services in relation to adoptions other than inter-country adoptions;
"domestic and intercountry adoption services" means domestic adoption services and intercountry adoption services;
"intercountry adoption" means—

(a) the adoption of a child habitually resident in the British Islands by prospective adopters habitually resident outside the British Islands; or

(b) the adoption of a child habitually resident outside the British Islands;
"intercountry adoption services" means services in relation to intercountry adoptions.]

AMENDMENT
3–131   Paragraph 10 was added by SI 2003/369, reg.2(6).

DEFINITIONS
3–132   relative: reg.2(1).
establishment: reg.2(1).
agency: reg.2(1).
organisation: reg.2(1).
service user: reg.2(1).
half-way house: reg.2(1).

GENERAL NOTE
PARA.6
3–133   The position of the NCSC regarding the OP category for care homes was set out in para.2 of the decision of the Care Standards Tribunal in *Fairburn v NCSC* [2002] 0076 N.C.:

"The OP category allows the accommodation of and provision of care services to service users whose sole or primary need for accommodation and care is because of illness, disorder, disability, infirmity or dependency which results from their being elderly (this would include treatment for or convalescence from physical or mental conditions resulting from ageing). Service users may also be properly accommodated when suffering from degrees of these various physical or mental conditions which do not result from the service users being elderly but only if these are secondary reasons for their needing accommodation and care. Service users may also be properly accommodated if subsequent to their entry to the home, they are assessed as being terminally ill and the home has the facilities, staffing and services to meet their needs."

THE COMMISSION FOR HEALTHCARE AUDIT AND INSPECTION (FEES AND FREQUENCY OF INSPECTIONS) REGULATIONS 2004

(SI 2004/661)

Dated March 10, 2004 and made by the Secretary of State for Health under the Care Standards Act (c.14), ss.12(2), 15(3), 16(3), 31(7) and 118(5) to 7.

GENERAL NOTE
3–134   These Regulations partly replace, with amendments, the National Care Standards Commission (Fees and Frequency of Inspections) Regulations 2003 and prescribe the fees that are to be paid to the Commission for Healthcare Audit and Inspection by certain

establishments and agencies, namely independent hospitals, independent clinics and independent medical agencies.

The fees are payable—

(a) on an application for registration in respect of an establishment or agency (reg.3); and

(b) on an application for the variation or removal of any condition for the time being in force in relation to the registration (reg.4).

In addition, reg.5 prescribes the annual fee that is to be paid in respect of these establishments and agencies under s.16(3) of the Act.

Regulation 6 prescribes the frequency of inspections of premises used for the purposes of these establishments and agencies.

ARRANGEMENT OF REGULATIONS   **3–135**

PART I

GENERAL

PART II

FEES

PART III

FREQUENCY OF INSPECTIONS

PART I

GENERAL

Citation, commencement and application

1.—(1) These Regulations may be cited as the Commission for Healthcare **3–136** Audit and Inspection (Fees and Frequency of Inspections) Regulations 2004 and shall come into force on 1st April 2004.

(2) These Regulations apply in relation to England only.

Interpretation

2. In these Regulations—   **3–137**

"the Act" means the Care Standards Act 2000;

"the 1984 Act" means the Registered Homes Act 1984;

"acute hospital" means a hospital of the type referred to in section 2(3)(a)(i) of the Act (not being a hospice) which has approved places;

"agency" means an independent medical agency;

"approved place" means a bed provided for the use of a service user at night;

"certificate" means a certificate of registration;

"establishment" means an independent hospital or independent clinic;

"existing provider" means a person who immediately before 1st April 2002—

(a) was registered under Part 1 of the 1984 Act in respect of a residential care home; or

(b) was registered under Part 2 of the 1984 Act in respect of a nursing home or mental nursing home;

"hospice" means an establishment the whole or main purpose of which is to provide palliative care;

"listed services" has the same meaning as in section 2(7) of the Act, as modified by regulation 3(4) of the Private and Voluntary Health Care (England) Regulations 2001, but in these Regulations excludes treatment using prescribed techniques or prescribed technology;

"mental health hospital" means a hospital of the type referred to in section 2(3)(b) of the Act;

"new provider" means a person who carries on an independent hospital, independent clinic or independent medical agency and did so for the first time on or after 1st April 2002;

"prescribed techniques or prescribed technology" means the techniques or technology set out in regulation 3(1)(a) to (f) of the Private and Voluntary Health Care (England) Regulations 2001;

"previously exempt provider" means a provider who immediately before 1st April 2002 carried on an establishment other than a residential care home, nursing home or mental nursing home in respect of which a person was required to be registered under Part 1 or 2 of the 1984 Act;

"registered manager" means a person who is registered under Part 2 of the Act as the manager of the establishment or agency;

"registered person" means any person who is the registered provider or registered manager in respect of an establishment or agency;

"registered provider" in relation to an establishment or agency means a person who is registered under Part 2 of the Act as the person carrying on the establishment or agency;

"service user" means any person who is to be provided with accommodation or services in an establishment, or by an agency, but excludes registered persons or persons employed or intended to be employed in an establishment or by an agency, and their relatives;

"small establishment" means an establishment which has less than four approved places.

PART II

FEES

Registration fees

3—138 **3.**—(1) For the purposes of section 12(2) of the Act, and subject to paragraph (2), the fee to accompany an application by a person seeking to be registered under Part 2 of the Act as a person who carries on an establishment or agency shall be £1,584.

(2) Where the establishment is a small establishment the fee shall be £432.

(3) For the purposes of section 12(2) of the Act, the fee to accompany an application by a person seeking to be registered under Part 2 of the Act as a person who manages an establishment or agency other than a small establishment shall be £432.

Variation fees

4.—(1) For the purposes of section 15(3) of the Act, the fee to accompany an **3–139** application by the registered provider under section 15(1)(a) of the Act ("the variation fee") shall, subject to paragraphs (2) and (3), be £792.

(2) Where the establishment is a small establishment the fee shall be £432.

(3) In a case where the variation of a condition is a minor variation, the variation fee shall be £72.

(4) For the purposes of paragraph (3), a "minor variation" is a variation which, in the opinion of the CHAI, if the application for the variation of the condition were granted, would involve no material alteration in the register kept by the CHAI in accordance with regulations made under section 11(4) of the Act.

Annual fees

5.—(1) Subject to paragraphs (2) and (3), the registered provider, in respect of **3–140** an establishment or agency specified in column (1) of the Table below, shall pay an annual fee and—

  (a) the amount of the annual fee shall be—

      (i) in a case where no amount is specified in column (3) or (4), the amount specified in column (2);

     (ii) in any other case, the sum of the amount specified in column (2) and the amounts specified in column (3), and (if applicable) column (4), multiplied by the number of approved places specified in respect of each column; and

  (b) shall be payable for the year beginning 1st April 2004 and subsequent years in accordance with column (5).

Column (1)	Column (2)	Column (3)	Column (4)	Column (5)
Establishment or agency	*Flat rate payable in all cases*	*Rate payable for each approved place from the 4th to the 29th place inclusive*	*Rate payable for the 30th and each subsequent approved place*	*Annual fee due on*
(a) Hospice	£216	£72	£72	(a) in the case of an existing provider, on the anniversary of the date on which the annual fee was payable under the 1984 Act; (b) in the case of a previously exempt provider, on 1st April 2004 and thereafter on the anniversary of that date; and (c) in the case of a new provider— (i) if the certificate was issued before 1st April 2004 each year on the anniversary of the date of issue; (ii) otherwise, on the date on which the certificate is issued, and thereafter on the anniversary of that date.

(b) Acute hospital or mental health hospital	£3,600	£144	£72	(a) in the case of an existing provider, on the anniversary of the date on which the annual fee was payable under the 1984 Act; (b) in the case of a previously exempt provider, on 1st April 2004 and thereafter on the anniversary of that date; and (c) in the case of a new provider— (i) if the certificate was issued before 1st April 2004 each year on the anniversary of the date of issue; (ii) otherwise, on the date on which the certificate is issued, and thereafter on the anniversary of that date.
(c) Hospital using prescribed techniques or prescribed technology	£1,080	£144	£72	(a) in the case of an existing provider, on the anniversary of the date on which the annual fee was payable under the 1984 Act; (b) in the case of a previously exempt provider, on 1st April 2004 and thereafter on the anniversary of that date; and (c) in the case of a new provider— (i) if the certificate was issued before 1st April 2004 each year on the anniversary of the date of issue; (ii) otherwise, on the date on which the certificate is issued, and thereafter on the anniversary of that date.

(d) Hospital providing listed services	£1,440	£144	£72	(a) in the case of an existing provider, on the anniversary of the date on which the annual fee was payable under the 1984 Act; (b) in the case of a previously exempt provider, on 1st April 2004 and thereafter on the anniversary of that date; and (c) in the case of a new provider— (i) if the certificate was issued before 1st April 2004 each year on the anniversary of the date of issue; (ii) otherwise, on the date on which the certificate is issued, and thereafter on the anniversary of that date.
(e) Independent clinic or independent medical agency	£1,440			(a) in the case of a previously exempt provider, on 1st April 2004 and thereafter on the anniversary of that date; and (b) in the case of a new provider— (i) if the certificate was issued before 1st April 2004 each year on the anniversary of the date of issue; (ii) otherwise, on the date on which the certificate is issued, and thereafter on the anniversary of that date.

(2) In the case of an establishment which is a small establishment, the annual fee shall be the flat rate specified in column (2).

(3) Where an independent hospital falls into more than one of the categories listed in paragraph (a), (b), (c) or (d) of column (1) of the Table above, the category that applies to it for the purposes of this regulation shall be the category

with the highest flat rate fee payable as set out in column (2) in relation to paragraphs (a), (b), (c) or (d).

PART III
FREQUENCY OF INSPECTIONS

Frequency of inspections

6.—(1) Subject to paragraphs (2) and (3), the CHAI shall arrange for premises **3–141** which are used as an establishment, or for the purposes of an agency, to be inspected a minimum of once in every 12 month period.

(2) In the case of an establishment or agency, carried on by a person other than an existing provider in respect of which a person is registered for the first time in a 12 month period, no inspection shall be required in that period.

(3) Any inspection referred to in paragraph (1) may be unannounced.

(4) In this regulation "12 month period" means a period commencing on 1st April in any year and ending on 31st March in the following year.

THE COMMISSION FOR SOCIAL CARE INSPECTION (FEES AND FREQUENCY OF INSPECTIONS) REGULATIONS 2004

(SI 2004/662)

Dated March 10, 2004 and made by the Secretary of State for Health under the Care Standards Act 2000 (c.14), ss.12(2), 15(3), 16(3), 31(7), 45(4), 51(1) and 118(5) to (7) and the Children Act 1989 (c.41), s.87D(2).

GENERAL NOTE

These Regulations partly replace, with amendments, the National Care Standards **3–142** Commission (Fees and Frequency of Inspections) Regulations 2003 and prescribe the fees that are to be paid to the Commission for Social Care Inspection by establishments and agencies (other than voluntary adoption agencies, independent hospitals, independent clinics and independent medical agencies).

The fees are payable—

(a) on an application for registration in respect of an establishment or agency (reg.3); and

(b) on an application for the variation or removal of any condition for the time being in force in relation to the registration (reg.4).

In addition, reg.5 prescribes the annual fee that is to be paid in respect of certain establishments and agencies under s.16(3) of the Act, the annual fee that is to be paid by a local authority fostering service under s.51(1) of the Act and the annual fee that is to be paid by boarding schools, residential special schools and residential colleges under s.87D of the Children Act 1989.

Regulation 6 prescribes the frequency of inspections of premises used for the purposes of certain establishments and agencies and of premises used for the purposes of a local authority fostering service.

The 2003 Regulations are revoked by reg.7.

PART I

GENERAL

REG.
1. Citation, commencement and application
2. Interpretation

PART II

FEES

3. Registration fees
4. Variation fees
5. Annual fees

PART III

FREQUENCY OF INSPECTIONS

6. Frequency of inspections
7. Revocation

PART I

GENERAL

Citation, commencement and application

3–144   **1.**—(1) These Regulations may be cited as the Commission for Social Care Inspection (Fees and Frequency of Inspections) Regulations 2004 and shall come into force on 1st April 2004.

(2) These Regulations apply in relation to England only.

Interpretation

3–145   **2.**—(1) In these Regulations—

"the Act" means the Care Standards Act 2000;

"the 1957 Act" means the Nurses Agencies Act 1957;

"the 1984 Act" means the Registered Homes Act 1984;

"the 1989 Act" means the Children Act 1989;

"adult placement home" means a care home in respect of which the registered provider is an adult placement carer within the meaning of regulation 45 of the Care Homes Regulations 2001;

"approved place" means—

(a) in relation to an establishment, boarding school, residential college or residential special school, a bed provided for the use of a service user at night; or

(b) in relation to a residential family centre, overnight accommodation which is appropriate to a single family;

"boarding school" means a school (not being a residential special school or a school which is a children's home or a care home) providing

accommodation for any child, and "school" has the meaning given to it
in section 105(1) of the 1989 Act;
"certificate" means a certificate of registration;
"existing provider" means—

(a) a person who immediately before 1st April 2002—

 (i) was registered under Part 1 of the 1984 Act in respect of a residential
care home;
 (ii) was registered under Part 2 of the 1984 Act in respect of a nursing
home or mental nursing home;
 (iii) carried on a home that was registered in a register kept for the purposes
of section 60 of the 1989 Act;
 (iv) carried on a home that was registered under Part 8 of the 1989 Act; or

(b) a nurses agency provider;

"local authority fostering service" means the discharge by a local authority of
relevant fostering functions within the meaning of section 43(3)(b) of
the Act;
"new provider" means a person who—

(a) carries on a residential family centre, nurses agency or domiciliary care
agency, and first carried on that establishment or agency after 1st April
2003; or
(b) carries on any other description of establishment or agency, and first
carried on that establishment or agency after 1st April 2002;

"nurses agency provider" means a person—

(a) who, immediately before 1st April 2003, carried on an agency for the
supply of nurses within the meaning of the 1957 Act; and
(b) was the holder of—

 (i) a valid licence which had been granted to him by a local authority
under section 2 of that Act and which authorised him to carry on that
agency from premises specified in the licence; or
 (ii) a licence which would have ceased to be valid on 31st December 2002
by virtue of section 2(6) of the 1957 Act, but which continued to be
treated as valid by virtue of article 4 of the Care Standards Act 2000
(Commencement and Transitional Provisions) (Amendment No.2)
(England) Order 2002 ("the relevant order");

"previously exempt provider" means a provider—

(a) who, immediately before 1st April 2002, carried on an establishment
other than—

(i) a residential care home, nursing home or mental nursing home in respect of which a person was required to be registered under Part 1 or 2 of the 1984 Act;

(ii) a home that was required to be registered in a register kept for the purposes of section 60 of the 1989 Act or under Part 8 of that Act; or

(b) who, immediately before 1st April 2003, carried on an agency other than an agency for the supply of nurses within the meaning of the 1957 Act which the person was authorised to carry on from those premises under a licence granted to him under section 2 of that Act;

"registered manager" in relation to an establishment or agency means a person who is registered under Part 2 of the Act as the manager of the establishment or agency;

"registered person" means any person who is the registered provider or registered manager in respect of an establishment or agency;

"registered provider" in relation to an establishment or agency means a person who is registered under Part 2 of the Act as the person carrying on the establishment or agency;

"residential college" means a college as defined in section 87(10) of the 1989 Act which provides accommodation for any child;

"residential special school" means—

(a) a special school in accordance with sections 337 and 347(1) of the Education Act 1996; or

(b) an independent school not falling within (a) which has as its sole or main purpose the provision of places, with the consent of the Secretary of State, for pupils with special educational needs or who are in public care,
and which provides accommodation for any child;

"service user" means—

(a) any person who is to be provided with accommodation or services in an establishment, or by an agency, but excludes registered persons or persons employed or intended to be employed in an establishment or by an agency, and their relatives; or

(b) a child accommodated in a boarding school, residential college or residential special school;

"small agency" means a domiciliary care agency or nurses agency where no more than two members of staff, including registered persons but excluding someone employed solely as a receptionist, are employed at any one time;

"small establishment" means an establishment, other than an adult placement home, which has less than four approved places.

(2) In these Regulations—

(a) "agency" does not include a voluntary adoption agency or an independent medical agency; and

(b) "establishment" does not include an independent hospital or an independent clinic.

PART II

FEES

Registration fees

3.—(1) For the purposes of section 12(2) of the Act, and, subject to paragraph **3–146** (2), the fee to accompany—

(a) an application by a person seeking to be registered under Part 2 of the Act as a person who carries on an establishment or agency, other than an establishment or agency referred to in sub-paragraph (b), shall be £1,584; and

(b) an application by a person seeking to be registered under Part 2 of the Act as a person who carries on a residential family centre, nurses agency or domiciliary care agency, shall be £1,320.

(2) Where the establishment is a small establishment or an adult placement home or the agency is a small agency the fee shall be—

(a) in the case of an application referred to in paragraph (1)(a), £432; and

(b) in the case of an application referred to in paragraph (1)(b), £360.

(3) For the purposes of section 12(2) of the Act, the fee to accompany an application by a person seeking to be registered under Part 2 of the Act as a person who manages an establishment or agency other than a small establishment or an adult placement home or a small agency—

(a) in respect of an establishment or agency other than an establishment or agency referred to in sub-paragraph (b), shall be £432;

(b) in respect of a residential family centre, nurses agency or domiciliary care agency, shall be £360.

Variation fees

4.—(1) For the purposes of section 15(3) of the Act, the fee to accompany an **3–147** application by the registered provider under section 15(1)(a) of the Act ("the variation fee") shall, subject to paragraphs (2) and (3), be—

(a) in respect of an establishment or agency other than an establishment or agency referred to in sub-paragraph (b), £792;

(b) in respect of a residential family centre, nurses agency or domiciliary care agency, £660.

(2) Where the establishment is a small establishment or an adult placement home or the agency is a small agency the fee shall be—

(a) in the case of an application referred to in paragraph (1)(a), £432;

(b) in the case of an application referred to in paragraph (1)(b), £360.

(3) In a case where the variation of a condition is a minor variation, the variation fee shall be—

(a) in the case of an application referred to in paragraph (1)(a), £72; and

(b) in the case of an application referred to in paragraph (1)(b), £60.

(4) For the purposes of paragraph (3) a "minor variation" is a variation which, in the opinion of the CSCI, if the application for the variation of the condition were granted, would involve no material alteration in the register kept by the CSCI in accordance with regulations made under section 11(4) of the Act.

Annual fees

3–148   **5.**—(1) Subject to paragraphs (2) to (4), the registered provider, in respect of an establishment or agency, a relevant person in respect of a boarding school, residential college or residential special school or a local authority in respect of a local authority fostering service, specified in column (1) of the Table below shall pay an annual fee and—

(a) the amount of the annual fee shall be—

    (i) in a case where no amount is specified in column (3) or (4), the amount specified in column (2);

    (ii) in any other case, the sum of the amount specified in column (2) and the amounts specified in column (3), and (if applicable) column (4), multiplied by the number of approved places specified in respect of each column; and

(b) shall be payable for the year beginning 1st April 2004 and subsequent years in accordance with column (5).

Column (1)	Column (2)	Column (3)	Column (4)	Column (5)
Establishment, agency, school or college, local authority fostering service	*Flat rate payable in all cases*	*Rate payable for each approved place from the 4th to the 29th place inclusive*	*Rate payable for the 30th and each subsequent approved place*	*Annual fee due on*

(a) Care home	£216	£72	£72	(a) in the case of an existing provider, the anniversary of the date on which the annual fee was payable under the 1984 Act or the 1989 Act;
				
				(b) in the case of a previously exempt provider, on 1st April 2004 and thereafter on the anniversary of that date; and
				(c) in the case of a new provider—
				  (i) if the certificate was issued before 1st April 2004 each year on the anniversary of the date of issue;
				  (ii) otherwise, on the date on which the certificate is issued, and thereafter on the anniversary of that date.

(b) Children's home	£720	£72	£72	(a) in the case of an existing provider, on the anniversary of the date on which the annual fee was payable under the 1984 Act or the 1989 Act; (b) in the case of an existing provider, where an annual fee was not previously payable under the 1989 Act, on 1st April in each year; (c) in the case of a previously exempt provider, on 1st April 2004 and thereafter on the anniversary of that date; and (d) in the case of a new provider— (i) if the certificate was issued before 1st April 2004 each year on the anniversary of the date of issue; (ii) otherwise, on the date on which the certificate is issued, and thereafter on the anniversary of that date.

(c) Fostering agency	£1,440			(a) if the certificate was issued— (i) before 1st April 2003, on 1st April 2004 and thereafter on the anniversary of that date; or (ii) on or after 1st April 2003 and before 1st April 2004, each year on the anniversary of the date of issue; or (b) otherwise on the date on which the certificate is issued and thereafter on the anniversary of that date.
(d) Residential family centre	£480	£60	£60	(a) in the case of an existing provider, on the anniversary of the date on which the annual fee was payable under the 1984 Act or the 1989 Act; (b) in the case of a previously exempt provider, on 1st April 2004 and thereafter on the anniversary of that date; and (c) in the case of a new provider, on the date on which the certificate is issued, and thereafter on the anniversary of that date.

(e) Domicili- ary care agency	£900			(a) if the certificate was issued— (i) before 1st April 2003, on 1st April 2004 and thereafter on the anniversary of that date; or (ii) on or after 1st April 2003 and before 1st April 2004, each year on the anniver- sary of the date of issue; or (b) otherwise, on the date on which the cer- tificate is issued and thereafter on the anni- versary of that date.
(f) Nurses agency	£600			(a) in the case of an existing provider— (i) where the licence under the 1957 Act was granted to the provider by the local authority between 1st January 2002 and 31st March 2002, on the anniversary first occurring after 1st April 2004 of the date on which the certificate was issued, and there- after on the anniversary of that date; (ii) where the licence under the 1957 Act was granted to the provider by the local authority on or after 1st April 2002 but before 1st April 2003, on the anniversary first occurring on or after 1st April 2004 of the date on which the licence was granted, and thereafter on the anniversary of that date;

(iii) whose licence under the 1957 Act continued to be treated as valid after 31st December 2002 by virtue of article 4(1)(a) of the relevant order, on the anniversary first occurring on or after 1st April 2004 of the date on which the fee payable in relation to the making of an application for a licence under the 1957 Act was last paid, and thereafter on the anniversary of that date;

(iv) whose licence under the 1957 Act continued to be treated as valid after 31st December 2002 by virtue of article 4(1)(b) of the relevant order—

   (aa) where the licence was granted to the provider by the local authority on or after 1st January 2001 but before 1st April 2001, on the anniversary first occurring on or after 1st April 2004 of the date on which the certificate was issued, and thereafter on the anniversary of that date;

				(bb) where the licence was granted to the provider by the local authority on or after 1st April 2001 but before 1st January 2002, on the anniversary first occurring on or after 1st April 2004 of the date on which the fee payable in relation to the making of an application for a licence under the 1957 Act was last paid, and thereafter on the anniversary of that date; and (b) in the case of a new provider, on the date on which the certificate is issued, and thereafter on the anniversary of that date.
(g) Boarding school and residential college	£360	£21.60	£10.80	(a) in the case of a school or college which was providing accommodation for any child on 1st January 2002, on 1st September in each year; (b) in the case of a school or college established after 1st January 2002 and before 1st April 2004, on the anniversary of the date on which it was established; (c) otherwise, on the date of the establishment of the school or college, and thereafter on the anniversary of that date.

(h) Residential special school	£576	£57.60	£28.80	(a) in the case of a school which was providing accommodation for any child on 1st January 2002, on 1st September in each year; (b) in the case of a school established after 1st January 2002 and before 1st April 2004, on the anniversary of the date on which it was established; (c) otherwise, on the date of the establishment of the school, and thereafter on the anniversary of that date.
(i) Local authority fostering service	£1,440			in the case of a local authority which was discharging relevant fostering functions on 1st January 2002, on 1st April in each year, and in all other cases, on the first occasion on which such functions are first discharged, and thereafter on the anniversary of that date.

(2) In the case of a care home which is an adult placement home, or a care home which is a small establishment, the annual fee shall be £144.

(3) In the case of an establishment which is a small establishment, other than a care home which is a small establishment, the annual fee shall be the flat rate specified in column (2).

(4) In the case of an agency which is a small agency, the annual fee payable shall be 50 per cent. of the flat rate specified in column (2).

PART III

FREQUENCY OF INSPECTIONS

Frequency of inspections

6.—(1) Subject to paragraphs (2) to (5), the CSCI shall arrange for premises **3–149** which are used as an establishment, or for the purposes of an agency, to be inspected—

(a) in the case of a care home or children's home, a minimum of twice in every 12 month period; and

(b) in any other case, a minimum of once in every 12 month period.

(2) Subject to paragraph (4), the CSCI shall arrange for premises which are used for the purposes of a local authority fostering service to be inspected once in every 12 month period.

(3) In the case of an establishment or agency, carried on by a person other than an existing provider, which is a care home or a children's home and in respect of which a person is registered for the first time—

(a) between 1st April and 30th September in a 12 month period, only one inspection is to be carried out in that period;

(b) between 1st October and 31st March in a 12 month period, no inspection shall be required in that period.

(4) In the case of an establishment or agency, carried on by a person other than an existing provider or a home mentioned in paragraph (3), in respect of which a person is registered for the first time in a 12 month period, no inspection shall be required in that period.

(5) Any inspection referred to in paragraphs (1) or (2) may be unannounced.

(6) In this regulation "12 month period" means a period commencing on 1st April in any year and ending on 31st March in the following year.

Revocation

3–150   **7.** The National Care Standards Commission (Fees and Frequency of Inspections) Regulations 2003 are hereby revoked.

PART 4

REGULATIONS AND NATIONAL MINIMUM STANDARDS

Throughout its short life, the National Care Standards Commission failed to fully appreci- **4–001** ate the crucial distinction between regulations made by Parliament under the authority of s.22 and the national minimum standards issued by the Government under s.23. Regulations and standards were seen as having an equivalent legal status. For example, the advice published by the Commission in 2003 on the implementation of the standards that had been issued for domiciliary care states that registered providers "will be required to meet the requirements of the regulations and national standards." Providers are legally obliged to comply with the regulations. No such obligations arise with respect to the standards, although adverse regulatory consequences could flow from a failure to comply with them. The regulator does that have the power to transform standards, which it must take account of (s.23(4)), into requirements placed on providers. To do so would subvert the intention of Parliament.

In *Fatile (Ebenezer House) v NCSC* [2004] 237 N.C., counsel for the registration authority submitted that the "National Minimum Standards . . . should only be departed from in exceptional circumstances" (para.21). A more extreme position was adopted by the registration authority and accepted by the Care Standards Tribunal in *Woodlands Court Residential Home v National Care Standards Commission* [2003] 209 N.C. where the tribunal accepted the submission of the authority that where there was a new home or an extension to an existing home the standards "would have to be complied with" (para.4). The obligation placed on the registration authority is to take the standards into account when taking certain decisions. This Act neither states nor implies that only exceptional circumstances can justify a departure from the standards or that the standards must be complied with in certain circumstances. It is submitted that a departure from the standards is permissible if the registration authority, having taken all relevant circumstances into account, concludes that this would be reasonable course of action for the applicant or the registered person to take. It is unfortunate that in the *Fatile* case the tribunal, having misquoted s.23, said that the standards are not "an absolute condition of registration" (para.25). The tribunal appears to have acted on the assumption that a refusal of registration can be justified on the ground that the relevant national minimum standard has not been satisfied. This is not the case as the registration authority can only refuse an application for registration if it is satisfied that the requirements of the regulations (or other enactment) have not been satisfied (s.13(2)). The tribunal failed to identify which regulation was being breached by the applicant.

Confusion about the legal status of the standards is not confined to England. The Care Standards Inspectorate for Wales has given guidance to its staff on the circumstances whereby a breach of the standards can be prosecuted (Guidance to CSIW Staff on Applying the National Minimum Standards (Physical Standards) to Existing Care Homes for Older People and Younger Adults, para.13). Prosecution is not an option that can be considered as a breach of the standards does not constitute an offence.

Regulation of establishments and agencies

4–002   **22.**—(1) Regulations may impose in relation to establishments and agencies any requirements which the appropriate Minister thinks fit for the purposes of this Part and may in particular make any provision such as is mentioned in subsection (2), (7) or (8).

(2) Regulations may—

(a) make provision as to the persons who are fit to carry on or manage an establishment or agency;

(b) make provision as to the persons who are fit to work at an establishment or for the purposes of an agency;

(c) make provision as to the fitness of premises to be used as an establishment or for the purposes of an agency;

(d) make provision for securing the welfare of persons accommodated in an establishment or provided with services by an establishment, an independent medical agency or a domiciliary care agency;

(e) make provision for securing the welfare of children placed, under section 23(2)(a) of the 1989 Act, by a fostering agency;

(f) make provision as to the management and control of the operations of an establishment or agency;

(g) make provision as to the numbers of persons, or persons of any particular type, working at an establishment or for the purposes of an agency;

(h) make provision as to the management and training of such persons;

(i) impose requirements as to the financial position of an establishment or agency;

(j) make provision requiring the person carrying on an establishment or agency to appoint a manager in prescribed circumstances.

(3) Regulations under subsection (2)(a) may, in particular, make provision for prohibiting persons from managing an establishment or agency unless they are registered in, or in a particular part of, one of the registers maintained under section 56(1).

(4) Regulations under subsection (2)(b) may, in particular, make provision for prohibiting persons from working in such positions as may be prescribed at an establishment, or for the purposes of an agency, unless they are registered in, or in a particular part of, one of the registers maintained under section 56(1).

(5) Regulations under paragraph (d) of subsection (2) may, in particular, make provision—

(a) as to the promotion and protection of the health of persons such as are mentioned in that paragraph;

(b) as to the control and restraint of adults accommodated in, or provided with services by, an establishment;

(c) as to the control, restraint and discipline of children accommodated in, or provided with services by, an establishment.

(6) Regulations under paragraph (e) of subsection (2) may, in particular, make provision—

(a) as to the promotion and protection of the health of children such as are mentioned in that paragraph;

(b) as to the control, restraint and discipline of such children.

(7) Regulations may make provision as to the conduct of establishments and agencies, and such regulations may in particular—

(a) make provision as to the facilities and services to be provided in establishments and by agencies;

(b) make provision as to the keeping of accounts;

(c) make provision as to the keeping of documents and records;

(d) make provision as to the notification of events occurring in establishments or in premises used for the purposes of agencies;

(e) make provision as to the giving of notice by the person carrying on an establishment or agency of periods during which he or (if he does not manage it himself) the manager proposes to be absent from the establishment or agency, and specify the information to be supplied in such a notice;

(f) provide for the making of adequate arrangements for the running of an establishment or agency during a period when the manager is absent from it;

(g) make provision as to the giving of notice by a person registered in respect of an establishment or agency of any intended change in the identity of the manager or the person carrying it on;

(h) make provision as to the giving of notice by a person registered in respect of an establishment or agency which is carried on by a body corporate of changes in the ownership of the body or the identity of its officers;

(i) make provision requiring the payment of a fee of such amount as may be prescribed in respect of any notification required to be made by virtue of paragraph (h);

(j) make provision requiring arrangements to be made by the person who carries on, or manages, an establishment or agency for dealing with complaints made by or on behalf of those seeking, or receiving, any of the services provided in the establishment or by the agency and requiring that person to take steps for publicising the arrangements;

(k) make provision requiring arrangements to be made by the person who carries on, or manages, an independent hospital, independent clinic or independent medical agency for securing that any medical or psychiatric treatment, or listed services, provided in or for the purposes of the establishment or (as the case may be) for the purposes of the agency are of appropriate quality and meet appropriate standards;

(l) make provision requiring arrangements to be made by the person who carries on, or manages, a care home for securing that any nursing provided by the home is of appropriate quality and meets appropraite standards.

(8) Regulations may make provision—

(a) [. . .];

(b) imposing other requirements (in addition to those imposed by section 25 of the 1989 Act (use of accommodation for restricting liberty)) as to the placing of a child in accommodation provided for the purpose mentioned in paragraph (a), including a requirement to obtain the permission of any local authority who are looking after the child;

(c) as to the facilities which are to be provided for giving religious instruction to children in children's homes.

(9) Before making regulations under this section, except regulations which amend other regulations made under this section and do not, in the opinion of the appropriate Minister, effect any substantial change in the provision made by those regulations, the appropriate Minister shall consult any persons he considers appropriate.

(10) References in this section to agencies do not include references to voluntary adoption agencies.

(11) In subsection (7)(k), "listed services" has the same meaning as in section 2.

AMENDMENT

The word omitted in subs.(8) were repealed by s.196, Sch.9, Pt 2 of the Health and Social Care (Community Health and Standards) Act 2003.

DEFINITIONS

4–004 agency: s.4(9).
appropriate minister: s.122(1).
care home: s.3.
child: s.121(1).
domiciliary care agency: s.4.
establishment: s.4(8).
fostering agency: s.4.
independent clinic: s.2.
independent hospital: s.2.
independent medical agency: s.2.
prescribed: s.121(1).
regulations: s.121(1).
voluntary adoption agency: s.4.

GENERAL NOTE

4–005 This section provides for wide ranging regulation-making powers. Different services have different sets of regulations. The following regulations have been made: the Care Homes Regulations 2001 (SI 2001/3865), the Children's Homes Regulations 2001 (SI 2001/3967), the Private and Voluntary Health Care (England) Regulations 2001 (SI 2001/3968), the Nurses Agencies Regulations 2003 (SI 2002/3212), the Residential Family Centres Regulations 2002 (SI 2002/3213), the Domiciliary Care Agencies

Regulations 2002 (SI 2002/3214) and the Fostering Services Regulations 2002 (SI 2002/57). The following regulations have been made in respect of adoption services: the Voluntary Adoption Agencies and Adoption Agencies (Miscellaneous Amendments) Regulations 2003 (SI 2003/367) and the Local Authority Adoption Service (England) Regulations 2003 (SI 2003/370). The registration authorities will, in enforcing the regulations, take into account the standards issued under s.23.

The following guidance on the implementation of the regulations was issued by the Department of Health in a letter dated January 29, 2002, from the Minister of State, Department of Health to the Chair of the NCSC:

"The regulations must be applied to all registered services. Services that are newly registered after 1 April 2002 must comply with the regulations when they are registered. Currently registered services must also comply with the regulations. However, we do not expect the Commission to assess whether regulations are complied with for currently registered services until the first programmed inspection takes place. If any regulations are not complied with on inspection the commission should agree actions and a time scale with the provider for compliance to be achieved. This should be reviewed at the end of the period through a follow up visit. If compliance is not achieved at the end of this period then the Commission will need to prosecute (if a breach of the relevant regulation is an offence) or consider other enforcement action. The exception to this approach would be where concerns have been raised about the provider with the Commission prior to the first inspection or where it is considered that vulnerable service users are at risk if the Commission does not act at a faster pace. The Commission should take swift action regarding dangerous or unsafe practice."

The Care Standards Tribunal has jurisdiction to determine any challenge to the vires of a provision of regulations made by the Secretary of State as being beyond the scope of this section "whenever it is necessary to do so in determining whether a decision under appeal was erroneous in point of law" (*Chief Adjudications Officer v Foster* [1993] 1 All E.R. 705, HL, *per* Lord Bridge at 712).

PARA.(2)(D)

This provision was inserted at the Committee stage because the Government was concerned that the Bill as originally drafted did "not give us all the powers we need to make regulations to protect children and promote their welfare in establishments and agencies covered by the Commission. That is, in particular, the case in relation to children in hospices and private healthcare establishments" (*per* Lord Hunt of Kings Heath, *Hansard*, HL, Vol.608, col.804). **4–006**

SUBS.(7)(C)

Documents and records: The Minister of State identified the type of document that would be covered by this provision: "A care home, for example, will be required to keep a gas certificate to show that all gas appliances are safe and have been serviced annually. If the home has lifts, it will need to keep certificates to show that those, too, have been serviced regularly. All establishments will of course need a certificate of insurance showing their public liability cover" (Standing Committee G, col.297). **4–007**

SUBS.(7)(J)

The Government will use this power to require all establishments and agencies to have proper procedure for dealing with complaints. Any person who is dissatisfied with the outcome of the internal procedure will be able to take his complaint to the Commission (*per* Lord Hunt of Kings Heath, *Hansard*, HL, Vol. 611, col.1211). **4–008**

4–009   Provision for the regulation of voluntary adoption agencies is contained in s.9 of the Adoption Act 1976, which is amended by para.5(6) of Sch.4 to this Act.

National minimum standards

4–010   **23.**—(1) The appropriate Minister may prepare and publish statements of national minimum standards applicable to establishments or agencies.

(2) The appropriate Minister shall keep the standards set out in the statements under review and may publish amended statements whenever he considers it appropriate to do so.

(3) Before issuing a statement, or any amended statement which in the opinion of the appropriate Minister effects a substantial change in the standards, the appropriate Minister shall consult any persons he considers appropriate.

(4) The standards shall be taken into account—

(a)   in the making of any decision by the registration authority under this Part;

(b)   in any proceedings for the making of an order under section 20;

(c)   in any proceedings on an appeal against such a decision or order; and

(d)   in any proceedings for an offence under regulations under this Part [or proceedings against a voluntary adoption agency for an offence under s.9(4) of the Adoption Act 1976 or [against a voluntary adoption agency or adoption support agency for an offence under] s.9 of the Adoption and Children Act 2002].

AMENDMENTS

4–011   The words in square brackets in subs.(4)(d) were inserted by the Adoption and Children Act 2002, s.139, Sch.3, para.110 and the Health and Social Care (Community Health and Standards) Act 2003, s.147, Sch.9, Pt 2, para.21.

DEFINITIONS

4–012   agency: s.4(9).
establishment: s.4(8).
registration authority: s.5.
the appropriate Minister: s.121(1).

GENERAL NOTE

4–013   This section provides, to the appropriate Minister, the power to publish statements of national minimum standards applicable to establishments or agencies. The role of the standards is to set out Parliament's expectations of those providing social and healthcare services. The standards must be taken into account in the situations identified in subs.(4). They therefore do not have a free-standing effect. The Minister is required to keep the standards under review and, before issuing a statement or amendment to it, to consult any person he considers appropriate. Among the issues that the standards address are: privacy and dignity; service user's choice and control over their own lives; how cultural and social, spiritual and educational needs are met; health and well-being; the quality of the physical environment; and protection from harm and abuse.

4–014   The following guidance on the implementation of the standards was issued by the Department of Health in a letter dated January 29, 2002, from the Minister of State, Department of Health to the Chair of the NCSC:

"Compliance with the national minimum standards is not enforceable, but compliance with the regulations is enforceable subject to the NMS being taken into account. There is no legal requirement to comply with the standards as such.

The national minimum standards should be used to fulfil two main functions:

- To amplify the legal framework (the CSA and the regulations)
- To provide a tool for the Commission and providers to jointly improve the quality of services (CSA Section 7(2)).

The national minimum standards must be used by the Commission as the basis for inspection and registration and applied in full. Services that are newly registered after 1 April 2002 must comply with the national minimum standards in order to be registered.

The Commission should not generally assess whether services comply with the standards until the first programmed inspection (or registration in the case of services new to regulation). If any of the national minimum standards are not complied with we would expect the Commission to agree an action plan and time scale with the provider to achieve compliance. This should be reviewed at the end of the period through a follow-up visit. If there is still non-compliance the Commission should consider enforcement action at this point. However, unless there is significant risk to vulnerable people, the Commission should endeavour to pursue a strategy of working with the provider over time to meet the standards. The Department wishes to see the Commission using its regulatory powers as a means of raising standards. At the same time the Commission should take swift action regarding dangerous and unsafe practice. Provided non-compliance with national minimum standards does not present such dangers appropriate time should be allowed for providers to put in place actions required to comply.

The Commission must consider very carefully in any case whether enforcement action is appropriate, focussing particularly on allowing providers sufficient time to make improvements. In relation to the environmental national minimum standards for care homes, the Commission should consider carefully certain factors such as whether the accommodation overall is satisfactory and service users views, before coming to any final decision.

The Commission should take particular care in applying the following standards for care homes for older people in order to avoid good quality care homes being removed from registration by their application:

Standard 21.3 Assisted Baths—the ratio should be interpreted flexibly with disabled showers being considered as an assisted bath. The Commission should not require a care home to have a second assisted bath facility for nine residents and should consider the overall quality of care and architectural constraints before deciding how many service users there should be before a second assisted bath is required. If there is any doubt about what constitutes an assisted bath the Commission should consult an occupational therapist.

Standard 22.2 Passenger Lifts—When considering whether a passenger lift is required the Commission should take account of any guidance from the Health and Safety Executive and Fire Service. The Commission should also consider the needs of the residents, and provided that these can be met in an alternative way a passenger lift may not be required. This should be agreed with the care home following the first inspection and set out clearly in writing. Stair lifts will continue to be acceptable in appropriate circumstances and they could be one of the alternative options to a passenger lifts provided this meets the needs of service users.

Standard 22.5 Doorways—when applying this standard the Commission should take account of the definition of wheelchair users in the standards, this refers to a person for whom the main source of independent mobility is a wheelchair. It should not be applied in respect of service users who are pushed in a wheelchair by staff. The standard does not require that all doorways should be at least 800mm in width. However, the Commission will need to be satisfied that wheelchair users are not discriminated against as a result of not having independent clear access to any rooms.

Standard 23.3 and 23.4 Room Sizes—the Commission should not apply this standard until 2007. The Commission is reminded that whilst it is required to take account of the NMS it should consider individual circumstances when deciding whether it is appropriate to apply them or not. The Commission is entitled to take account of special circumstances in particular cases, which may lead to the conclusion that it is not appropriate for some aspect of the NMS to be applied with full rigour in those particular cases. In deciding whether special circumstances apply the Commission should consider in particular whether the needs of service users are best served by the accommodation without alteration to meet the standards. For example if it were harmful for a resident to be moved, it would be open to the Commission to decide that a room which falls below the standards nevertheless suits the persons' needs.

Standard 23.11 Shared Rooms—the Commission should not apply this standard until 2007. As with standards 23.3 and 23.4 above, the Commission is entitled to take account of special circumstances in particular cases which may lead to the conclusion that that it is not appropriate for some aspect of the NMS to be applied with full rigous in those particular cases. In deciding whether special circumstances apply the Commission should consider in particular whether the needs of service users are best served by accommodation in shared rooms. For example in a particular home there may be a high proportion of rooms occupied by couples who chose to share rooms."

4–015   In *How do we care?* (March 2004), the NCSC undertook research to assess how services were performing against the national minimum standards. Preliminary analysis of interim data for the second year of the NCSC's operation showed that at least:

- 48% of care homes for older people met each standard (up from 26% in year 1);

- 46% of care homes for younger adults met each standard (up from 17% in year 1);

- 41% of children's homes met each standard (up from 22% in year 1).

SUBS.(1)

4–016   The following statements of national minimum standards have been published:

- Care Homes for Older People

- Independent Health Care

- Care Homes for Children

- Fostering services

- Adult Placements

- Boarding Schools

- Residential Special Schools

- Accommodation of students under eighteen by Further Education Colleges

- Domiciliary Care

- Nurses Agencies

- Adoption Services

- Residential Family Centres

● Care Homes for Adults (18–65)

The standards can be accessed via the websites of the CSCI (*www.csci.org.uk*) and the CHAI (*www.chai.org.uk*).

Subs.(4)

Taken into account: Along with other relevant matters. No legal duty is placed on registered persons to comply with the national minimum standards. Compliance with the standards is therefore not directly enforceable. The standards should be considered and applied by the registration authority in the situations set out in this provision. They should not be read as if they were binding on the decision-maker because the regulator would be entitled to depart from them if it was considered that there was a good reason so to do. However, it is submitted that the decision-maker should not take a substantially different course from that identified in the standards: see *R. v Islington LBC Ex p. Rixon* (1998) 1 C.C.L.R. 119. The standards should be applied in a flexible and sensitive manner with the aim of achieving the overall objective of ensuring that the best interests of the service user are secured.

The guidance issued by the Department of Health on the implementation of standards, which is set out above, states that newly registered services "must comply" with the standards in order to be registered. The registration authority should not adopt this approach as to do so would fetter its discretion with regard to its decision on registration. This aspect of the guidance attempts to convert the statutory requirement to take the standards into account into a requirement that the registration authority insists that the applicant for registration slavishly complies with the standards. Such an approach is clearly inconsistent with the requirement for the standards to be "taken into account". A decision of the registration authority not to register which is made solely on the ground that not every standard had been complied with could be challenged on an application for judicial review as being unlawful.

A condition of registration granted under s.13(3) to the effect that the registered person comply with the standards that apply to the registered establishment or agency could be challenged on the ground that the registration authority is seeking to subvert the statutory intention by converting standards into conditions and thereby making a failure to comply with a standard a criminal offence under s.24.

4–017

Para.(d)

The amendment to this provision has only been brought into force in so far as it relates to the Adoption Act (SI 2003/366, art.2(4)(c)).

THE CARE HOMES REGULATIONS 2001

(SI 2001/3965)

Dated December 11, 2001, and made by the Secretary of State for Health under the Care Standards Act 2000 (c.14), ss.3(3), 22(1), (2)(a) to (d) and (f) to (j), (5), (7)(a) to (h), (j) and (l), 25(1), 34(1), 35 and 118(5) to (7).

GENERAL NOTE

These Regulations apply to England only.

Regulation 43 provides for offences. A breach of the regulations specified in reg.43 may found an offence on the part of the registered person. However, no prosecution may be brought unless the Commission has first given the registered person a notice which sets out in what respect it is alleged he is not complying with a regulation, and what action the Commission considers it is necessary for him to take in order to comply. The notice must specify a time period for compliance, not exceeding three months.

4–018

PART I

G<small>ENERAL</small>

PART II

R<small>EGISTERED</small> P<small>ERSONS</small>

PART III

C<small>ONDUCT OF</small> C<small>ARE</small> H<small>OMES</small>

PART IV

P<small>REMISES</small>

PART V

M<small>ANAGEMENT</small>

PART VI

CHILDREN

PART VII

MISCELLANEOUS

SCHEDULES

PART I

GENERAL

Citation, commencement and extent

1.—(1) These Regulations may be cited as the Care Homes Regulations 2001 **4–020** and shall come into force on 1st April 2002.

(2) These Regulations extend to England only.

Interpretation

2.—(1) In these Regulations—   **4–021**

"the Act" means the Care Standards Act 2000;

["Commission" means the Commission for Social Care Inspection;]

"environmental health authority" means the authority responsible for environmental health for the area in which the care home is situated;

"fire authority", in relation to a care home, means the authority discharging in the area in which the care home is situated the function of fire authority under the Fire Services Act 1947;

"general practitioner" means a registered medical practitioner who—

(a) provides general medical services under Part II of the National Health Service Act 1977;

(b) performs personal medical services in connection with a pilot scheme under the National Health Service (Primary Care) Act 1997; or

(c) provides services which correspond to services provided under Part II of the National Health Service Act 1977, otherwise than in pursuance of that Act;

"health care professional" means a person who is registered as a member of any profession to which section 60(2) of the Health Act 1999 applies or who is clinical psychologist, child psychotherapist or speech therapist;

"inspection report" means a report prepared in relation to the care home under section 32(5) of the Act;

"organisation" means a body corporate or any unincorporated association other than a partnership;

"registered manager", in relation to a care home, means a person who is registered under Part II of the Act as the manager of the care home;

"registered person", in relation to a care home, means any person who is the registered provider or registered manager in respect of the care home;

"registered provider", in relation to a care home, means a person who is registered under Part II of the Act as a person carrying on the care home;

"relative", in relation to any person, means—

(a) the person's spouse;

(b) any parent, grandparent, child, grandchild, brother, sister, uncle, aunt, nephew or niece of his or his spouse;

(c) the spouse of any relative within sub-paragraph (b) of this definition,

and for the purpose of determining any such relationship a person's step-child shall be treated as his child, and references to "spouse" in relation to any person include a former spouse and a person who is living with the person as husband and wife;

"representative" means, in relation to a service user, a person, other than the registered person or a person employed at the care home, who with the service user's express or implied consent takes an interest in the service user's health and welfare;

"responsible individual" shall be construed in accordance with regulation 7(2)(c)(i);

"service user" means any person accommodated in the care home who is in need of nursing or personal care by reason of disability, infirmity, past or present illness, past or present mental disorder or past or present dependence on alcohol or drugs;

"service user's guide" means the written guide produced in accordance with regulation 5(1);

"service user's plan" means the written plan prepared in accordance with regulation 15(1);

"staff" means persons employed by the registered person to work at the care home but does not include a volunteer or a person employed under a contract for services;

"statement of purpose" means the written statement compiled in accordance with regulation 4(1).

(2) In these Regulations, unless the context otherwise requires, a reference—

(a) to a numbered regulation or Schedule is to the regulation in, or Schedule to, these Regulations bearing that number;

(b) in a regulation or Schedule to a numbered paragraph is to the paragraph in that regulation or Schedule bearing that number;

(c) in a paragraph to a lettered or numbered sub-paragraph is to the sub-paragraph in that paragraph bearing that letter or number.

(3) In these Regulations, references to employing a person include employing a person whether or not for payment and whether under a contract of service or a contract for services and allowing a person to work as a volunteer; and references to an employee or to a person being employed shall be construed accordingly.

Amendment

The reference to the "Commission" was inserted by SI 2004/664, art.3, Sch.2. **4–022**

General Note

This regulation is applied by reg.28 where a child is accommodated in the care home. **4–023**

Excepted establishments

3.—(1) For the purposes of the Act, an establishment is excepted from being a **4–024** care home if—

(a) it is a health service hospital at which nursing is provided;

(b) it provides accommodation, together with nursing, and is vested—

(i) in the Secretary of State for the purposes of his functions under the National Health Service Act 1977; or
(ii) in an NHS trust; [or
(iii) in an NHS foundation trust;]

(c) it is a university;

(d) it is an institution within the further education sector as defined by section 91(3) of the Further and Higher Education Act 1992; [...]

(e) it is a [school; or]

[(f) it does not provide accommodation except—

    (i) for a period or periods which do not exceed 28 days in aggregate during any period of 12 months; and

    (ii) for not more than 3 persons at any one time who fall within section 3(2) of the Act;

(g) it provides accommodation solely for a person (or persons) who—

    (i) was placed with a local authority foster parent ("the carer" under the Children Act 1989;

    (ii) remained in that placement for a period of not less than 5 years immediately prior to his 18th birthday; and

    (iii) continues to live with the carer after his 18th birthday.]

(2) For the purposes of paragraph (1), "university" includes—

(a) any university college;

(b) any college, or institution in the nature of a college, of a university.

(3) The exception in paragraph (1)(d) does not apply if—

(a) the establishment provides accommodation together with nursing or personal care to any person; and

(b) the number of such persons is more than one tenth of the number of students to whom it provides both education and accommodation.

AMENDMENT

4–025 The amendments to para.(1) were made by SI 2003/1845, reg.2 and SI 2004/696, art.3(1), Sch.1, para.40.

GENERAL NOTE

PARA.(1)(F)

4–026 This exempts from registration carers who provide respite care or holiday breaks for service users.

PARA.(1)(G)

4–027 This exempts from registration carers who have cared for someone for at least five years before their eighteenth birthday and who are considered therefore to be part of the carer's family.

Statement of purpose

4–028 **4.**—(1) The registered person shall compile in relation to the care home a written statement (in these Regulations referred to as "the statement of purpose") which shall consist of—

(a) a statement of the aims and objectives of the care home;

(b) a statement as to the facilities and services which are to be provided by the registered person for service users; and

(c) a statement as to the matters listed in Schedule 1.

(2) The registered person shall supply a copy of the statement of purpose to the Commission and shall make a copy of it available on request for inspection by every service user and any representative of a service user.

(3) Nothing in regulation 16(1) or 23(1) shall require or authorise the registered person to contravene, or not to comply with—

(a) any other provision of these Regulations; or

(b) the conditions for the time being in force in relation to the registration of the registered person under Part II of the Act.

DEFINITIONS
    registered person: reg.2(1).   **4–029**
    service user: reg.2(1).
    representative: reg.2(1).
    Commission: reg.2(1).

GENERAL NOTE
    The registration authority will judge the operation of the home against the statement of **4–030** purpose. The statement must be kept under review and, where appropriate, revised (reg.6). A summary of the statement must be included in the service users guide (reg.5(1)(a)). Guidance on the statement of purpose is contained in Appendix 3 to *Choice, Power, Performance: The Need for Information on Care Services in England* which was published by the NCSC in March 2004. A contravention or failure to comply with this regulation is an offence (reg.43(1)).

    This regulation is applied by reg.29 where a child is accommodated in the care home.

PARA.*(1)(B)*
    Facilities: The facilities to be provided in a care home are set out in reg.16.   **4–031**

Service user's guide

    5.—(1) The registered person shall produce a written guide to the care home (in **4–032** these Regulations referred to as "the service user's guide") which shall include—

(a) a summary of the statement of purpose;

(b) the terms and conditions in respect of accommodation to be provided for service users, including as to the amount and method of payment of fees;

(c) a standard form of contract for the provision of services and facilities by the registered provider to service users;

(d) the most recent inspection report;

(e) a summary of the complaints procedure established under regulation 22;

(f) the address and telephone number of the Commission.

(2) The registered person shall supply a copy of the service user's guide to the Commission and each service user.

[(2A) If a person other than a service user or the Commission requests a copy of the service user's guide, the registered person shall either—

(a) make the service user's guide available for inspection by that person at the care home; or

(b) supply a copy to that person.]

(3) Where a local authority has made arrangements for the provision of accommodation, nursing or personal care to the service user at the care home, the registered person shall supply to the service user a copy of the agreement specifying the arrangements made.

AMENDMENT
4–033   Paragraph (2A) was inserted by SI 2003/1703, reg.2(2).

DEFINITIONS
4–034   registered person: reg.2(1).
service user: reg.2(1).
inspection report: reg.2(1).
Commission: reg.2(1).

GENERAL NOTE
4–035   The service user's guide must be kept under review and, where appropriate, revised (reg.6).
It would appear that the duty under paras (2) and (3) to supply the service user with a copy of the guide and, where applicable, a copy of the agreement will apply even though the service user lacks to mental capacity to understand the documents. It is suggested that in this situation a copy of the documents should be also be supplied to the service user's representative or, if the service user does not have a representative, the relative of the patient who takes the closest interest in the service user's welfare. If such a person makes a request for a copy of the guide, it must be supplied to that person (para.(2A)).

[Information about fees
4–036   **5A.**—(1) This regulation shall apply where nursing is provided by the care home.
(2) The registered person shall provide to each service user, by not later than the day on which he becomes a service user, a statement specifying—

(a) the fees payable by or in respect of the service user for the provision to the service user of any of the following services—

(i) accommodation, including the provision of food;
(ii) nursing; and
(iii) personal care,

and, except where a single fee is payable for those services, the services to which each fee relates;

(b) the method of payment of the fees and the person or persons by whom the fees are payable.

(3) The registered person shall notify the service user at least one month in advance of—

(a) any increase in the fees referred to in paragraph (2)(a) and payable by or in respect of the service user;

(b) any variation in the matters referred to in paragraph (2)(b).

(4) The registered person shall inform the service user—

(a) if it is practicable to do so, by not later than 28 days after the day on which he becomes a service user; or

(b) in any other case, as soon as it becomes practicable to do so,

as to whether a nursing contribution is to be paid in respect of nursing to be provided at the care home to the service user.

(5) Where a nursing contribution is paid in respect of nursing provided at the care home to the service user, the registered person shall provide to the service user a statement specifying—

(a) the date of payment and the amount of the nursing contribution; and

(b) either—

(i) the date (if any) on which the registered person is to pay the amount of the nursing contribution to the service user or deduct that amount from the fees referred to in paragraph (2)(a); or

(ii) if the nursing contribution is not to be so paid or deducted, whether and if so how it is taken into account for the purpose of calculating those fees.

(6) In this regulation, "nursing contribution" means a payment by a Primary Care Trust to the registered person in respect of nursing to be provided to a service user at the care home, but does not include a payment where—

(a) the Primary Care Trust has made arrangements with the care home for the provision of accommodation to the service user; and

(b) the payment relates to any period for which under those arrangements accommodation is provided at the care home to the service user.]

AMENDMENT
This regulation was inserted by SI 2003/1703, reg.2(3).   **4–037**

DEFINITIONS
registered person: reg.2(1).   **4–038**
service user: reg.2(1).

GENERAL NOTE
This regulation was made as a result of the introduction of NHS-funded nursing care in **4–039** care homes. It is aimed at achieving transparency by ensuring that service users and others

are clear about those parts of fees that they are expected to pay themselves and those parts that are funded from other sources.

A contravention or failure to comply with this regulation is an offence (reg.43(1)).

PARA.(1)

4–040　This regulation does not apply to service users in care homes with nursing who are only in receipt of personal care.

Review of statement of purpose and service user's guide

4–041　**6.** The registered person shall—

(a) keep under review and, where appropriate, revise the statement of purpose and the service user's guide; and

(b) notify the Commission and service users of any such revision within 28 days.

DEFINITIONS

4–042　registered person: reg.2(1).
statement of purpose: reg.2(1).
service user's guide: reg.2(1).
service user: reg.2(1).
Commission: reg.2(1).

GENERAL NOTE

4–043　A contravention or failure to comply with this regulation is an offence (reg.43(1)).

PART II

REGISTERED PERSONS

Fitness of registered provider

4–044　**7.**—(1) A person shall not carry on a care home unless he is fit to do so.

(2) A person is not fit to carry on a care home unless the person—

(a) is an individual who carries on the care home—

(i) otherwise than in partnership with others, and he satisfies the requirements set out in paragraph (3);
(ii) in partnership with others, and he and each of his partners satisfies the requirements set out in paragraph (3);

(b) is a partnership, and each of the partners satisfies the requirements set out in paragraph (3);

(c) is an organisation and—

(i) the organisation has given notice to the Commission of the name, address and position in the organisation of an individual (in these Regulations referred to as "the responsible individual") who is a director, manager, secretary or other officer of the organisation and is responsible for supervising the management of the care home; and
(ii) that individual satisfies the requirements set out in paragraph (3).

(3) The requirements are that—

110

(a) he is of integrity and good character; and

(b) he is physically and mentally fit to carry on the care home; and

(c) full and satisfactory information is available in relation to him in respect of the following matters—

(i) the matters specified in paragraphs 1 to 5 and 7 of Schedule 2;
(ii) [...];
(iii) [...].

(4) [...].
(5) A person shall not carry on a care home if—

(a) he has been adjudged bankrupt or sequestration of his estate has been awarded and (in either case) he has not been discharged and the bankruptcy order has not been annulled or rescinded; or

(b) he has made a composition or arrangement with his creditors and has not been discharged in respect of it.

AMENDMENTS
The amendments to this regulation were made by SI 2002/865, reg.2(2).   **4–045**

DEFINITIONS
Commission: reg.2(1).   **4–046**
organisation: reg.2(1).

GENERAL NOTE
In *R. (on the application of National Care Standards Commission) v Jones* [2004] **4–047**
EWHC 918 (Admin), Sullivan J. held that:

(i) this regulation and reg.9 do not merely provide a statutory definition of "fitness" for the purposes of the 2000 Act; they do so in mandatory terms;

(ii) the registration authority and the Care Standards Tribunal should consider the issue of fitness by giving intelligible answers to the questions posed by para.(3), *i.e.* is the applicant/appellant a person of integrity and good character, etc.;

(iii) in requiring an applicant for registration to be of integrity and good character, the regulation should not be construed as requiring perfection. His Lordship said at para.30: "Even if in the past an applicant for registration has been dishonest, or has been convicted of a criminal offence, or has been found guilty of professional misconduct, he or she may still, as at the time of the application for registration and/or by the time of an appeal to the tribunal, be fairly described as a person of integrity and good character."

His Lordship doubted, *obiter*, whether the situation that obtained under the 1984 Act, where the burden of proof in fitness cases at the tribunal was placed on the registration authority, is replicated in the 2000 Act. His Lordship said at para.35:

"It seems to me that it is at least arguable that under the new statutory regime the burden lies upon an appellant to satisfy the tribunal to the civil standard that he or she is a fit person to manage a care home as defined by reg.9 and Part II of the Act. It appears to be common ground that this is the position at first instance when an application is made to the Commission. The applicant for registration must satisfy the Commission that he or she is a fit person. Why that burden should shift to the Commission on appeal is by no means clear to me. Insofar as it is correct to speak of a 'burden of proof' when deciding such judgmental issues, one would expect the onus to be upon the appellant to persuade the tribunal that the Commission's decision was wrong."

In *Azzopardi v London Borough of Havering* (Decn. No.76) the Registered Homes Tribunal offered the following general comments on the meaning of fitness:

"It is probably much easier to recognise the qualities of fitness than to attempt to define it. However, the words 'trust', 'integrity', 'uprightness', 'honourable', and 'truthful' spring to mind. A fit person is one who can be trusted, in whom one has confidence, who acts according to high principles. It follows that a person will be unfit if he or she is untrustworthy or dishonest. The 1984 Act requires that a proprietor of a care home be such a fit person, since the elderly people in their care are often frail and vulnerable and the person in control of them is in a powerful position to exploit that frailty. It is imperative that residents' well-being can be assured and that they must be protected from harm. It is a high standard that the law requires..."

Fitness, "in the sense used in the [1984] Act, must imply more than competence at a job" (*Coormish v Cheshire County Council* (Decn. No.101)). If a person has been convicted of a criminal offence, enquiries should be made "into the broad circumstances of and surrounding the offences as well as the past history of [the applicant]" (*Love v Wiltshire County Council* (Decn. No.88)). A "conviction has to be considered in the context of whether to allow the applicant to run the ... home would be likely to affect adversely the interests of the residents" (*Phillips v Peterborough Health Authority* (Decn. No.6)), although it is not necessary to establish a connection between the crime and the possible adverse effect it might have on the care and well-being of the residents (Decn. No.76, above). If the circumstances of the crime involve a breach of trust, it is likely that the applicant will be deemed to be unfit even if the service users have not been adversely affected by the conviction (*Murphy v NCSC* [2003] 199. N.C.). In *Murphy* the Care Standards Tribunal said that decisions of the Registered Homes Tribunal concerning the issue and standard of fitness "continue to provide guidance" (para.38).

4–048 In *R. v Humberside County Council Ex p. Bogdal* (1992) 11 B.M.L.R. 46 at 56, Brooke J. said that a person could be fit to be involved in a home in a small way but not fit to "carry on" the home. In a decision under the 1984 Act, the Court of Appeal held that the question of fitness is not to be assessed in some abstract way independently of the application to which the question of fitness relates or the registration to which the cancellation relates. It is therefore the case that the tribunal should apply their minds to the test of the fitness of the applicant in relation to the establishment that they are investigating and they are under no further obligation to consider the characteristics of the applicant in relation to his other activities, such as his conduct at his other establishments (*Crammer v Harrogate Health Authority*, QBCOF 94/0071/D, March 3, 1995). At first instance, Pill J. said that the applicant "could be fit to run one home and unfit to run another" (CO/ 2479/90, May 19, 1993).

There is nothing illogical in the tribunal saying that one breach of the rules would not of itself justify a finding of unfitness, but then going on to consider the attitude of the applicant appearing before it to the breach. There might be considerable differences between an applicant who promptly acknowledged his or her error, recorded it in the proper manner and thus showed his or her determination that it would never happen again, and an applicant who shrugged off the error, failed to report it and then sought to minimise it, thus appearing to be unaware of its significance (*Ruggee v The Registered Homes Tribunal and Bradford Health Authority*, CO/3925, December 1, 1998).

In *Fieldhouse v Devon County Council* (Decn. No.182), the Registered Homes Tribunal said that because of the potential serious consequences for all concerned following a finding of unfitness, the tribunal would expect the registration authority "to present a clear, consistent and structured case, supported by reliable and creditable evidence."

The responsible individual must undertake training to ensure that he or she possesses the necessary skills for carrying on the care home (reg.10(2)).

This regulation is applied by reg.30(1) where a child is accommodated in the care home.

PARA.(1)

Shall not: This provision is mandatory—unfitness must be found if any one of the criteria set out in para.(3) is not met.

PARA.(2)

Responsible individual: This individual, who must receive appropriate training (reg.10), **4–049** does not have to be approved by the registration authority. He or she can be responsible for more than one care home. The care home must be visited by responsible individual at least once a month (reg.26).

PARA.(3)

The criteria of fitness contained in this provision are largely based on decisions of the **4–050** Registered Homes Tribunal under the 1984 Act.

Integrity and good character: The registration authority is entitled to expect "very high standards of integrity and honesty from a home owner and/or manager" (*Murphy v NCSC*, above, para.46). Also see *R. (on the application of National Care Standards Commission) v Jones*, above.

Appointment of manager

8.—(1) The registered provider shall appoint an individual to manage the care **4–051** home where—

(a) there is no registered manager in respect of the care home; and

(b) the registered provider—

    (i) is an organisation or partnership;

    (ii) is not a fit person to manage a care home; or

    (iii) is not, or does not intend to be, in full-time day to day charge of the care home.

(2) Where the registered provider appoints a person to manage the care home he shall forthwith give notice to the Commission of—

(a) the name of the person so appointed; and

(b) the date on which the appointment is to take effect.

DEFINITIONS

    registered provider: reg.2(1). **4–052**
    registered manager: reg.2(1).
    Commission: reg.2(1).

GENERAL NOTE

This regulation identifies the situations that require the appointment of a manager for a **4–053** care home. A person cannot be appointed unless he or she is fit to manage the home (reg.9). A person can be appointed to manage more than one home: see s.12(4) of the Act.

In *Joyce v NCSC* [203] 0190 N., the tribunal held that the "individual" referred to in para.(1) must be a registered manager and that the requirement of that paragraph will endure throughout the time that there is no registered manager in respect of the care home, whether or not an unregistered manager or person to manage the home has been appointed. The tribunal further found that the "person" referred to in para.(2) also refers to a registered manager. It is therefore the case that para.(2) cannot be breached if a manager within the terms of para.(1) has not been appointed. The registration authority is required to notify the registration authority if a person ceases to manage a care home (reg.39). A failure to notify constitutes an offence and a breach of s.14(1)(c).

In *Joyce* the tribunal, having noted that this regulation does not provide flexibility in the requirement for employment as a registered manager, said at para.88:

"This is severe and may not reflect everyday reality, staff leave for a variety of reasons, sometimes without warning. NCSC appears to have responded by development of informal policy, an 'extra statutory concession'. It may be that future amendments to legislation may formalise and clarify procedures and steps that need to be taken."

The concession takes the form of a three-month period of grace for recruitment of a manager and three-month target for processing registration. The tribunal concluded that "a six month period, the extreme of the two steps required, is the maximum reasonable time it should take for a manager to be appointed and registered" (para.90).

Fitness of registered manager

4–054   **9.**—(1) A person shall not manage a care home unless he is fit to do so.
(2) A person is not fit to manage a care home unless—

(a) he is of integrity and good character;

(b) having regard to the size of the care home, the statement of purpose, and the number and needs of the service users—

   (i) he has the qualifications, skills and experience necessary for managing the care home; and
   (ii) he is physically and mentally fit to manage the care home; and

(c) full and satisfactory information is available in relation to him in respect of the following matters—

   (i) the matters specified in paragraphs 1 to 5 and 7 of Schedule 2;
   (ii) [...];
   (iii) [...].

(3) [...].

AMENDMENTS
4–055   The amendments to this regulation were made by SI 2002/865, reg.2(3).

GENERAL NOTE
4–056   This regulation is applied by reg.30(2) where a child is accommodated in the care home.
In *J v NCSC* [2003] 0168 N.C., the NCSC had refused to grant the appellant registration as a manager. The interview stage of the fitness assessment conduced by the NCSC was described as follows: "The interviewers have a proforma with tick-boxes. The interviewee does not see the proforma, the interviewers tick boxes to indicate appropriate responses given by the interviewee in answer to specific questions." The NCSC confirmed that the

appellant would have been refused registration on the basis of his performance at that interview alone. The tribunal expressed its reservations about the fit person interview and the use of the proforma: "The standard proforma suffers from many of the disadvantages of what is fashionably called the 'one size fits all' approach. Its most obvious danger is any candidate with an average or better memory and a copy of the form could readily 'mug up' the appropriate answers and thus achieve a high mark while having little or no real knowledge of the care of the vulnerable". Having concluded that the interviewers had to an extent before the interview formed a view about the appellant's fitness and that the consequent prejudice was reflected in some of the answers on the proforma, the tribunal found the fit person interview to have serious inherent defects. The tribunal also found that "the appellant whose background was largely 'hands on' with a minimum of theoretical input was at a disadvantage in a theoretical discussion" and that the appellant "is undoubtedly one of those who are better at handling a situation than at putting that situation into its theoretical context". The manager's appeal against the decision of the NCSC was allowed.

The tribunal allowed an appeal by a manager against the refusal of the NCSC to grant him registration in *Wilkinson v NCSC* [2003] 231 E.A. In this case the decision to refuse refusal was founded on the manager's response to a question on the application form concerning past disciplinary action. The manager had stated that subsequent to his dismissal by a previous employer his case had been taken to a tribunal where he had won damages, whereas in fact the case had been settled through ACAS with a payment of £4,000 being made to the manager by his employer. The tribunal found that the answer that the manager had given had not compromised his integrity and undermined the trust of the registration authority to such an extent that the standard required by this regulation was not satisfied.

Also see the note on reg.7.

PARA.(1)

This provision is mandatory—unfitness must be found if any one of the criteria set out in para.(2) is not met.

Registered person: general requirements

10.—(1) The registered provider and the registered manager shall, having **4–057** regard to the size of the care home, the statement of purpose, and the number and needs of the service users, carry on or manage the care home (as the case may be) with sufficient care, competence and skill.

(2) If the registered provider is—

(a) an individual, he shall undertake;

(b) an organisation, it shall ensure that the responsible individual undertakes;

(c) a partnership, it shall ensure that one of the partners undertakes,

from time to time such training as is appropriate to ensure that he has the experience and skills necessary for carrying on the care home.

(3) The registered manager shall undertake from time to time such training as is appropriate to ensure that he has the experience and skills necessary for managing the care home.

DEFINITIONS

    registered provider: reg.2(1).   **4–058**
    registered manager: reg.2(1).
    statement of purpose: reg.2(1).
    responsible individual: reg.2(1).
    organisation: reg.2(1).

4–059   This regulation is applied by reg.30(3) where a child is accommodated in the care home.

Notification of offences
4–060   **11.** Where the registered person or the responsible individual is convicted of any criminal offence, whether in England and Wales or elsewhere, he shall forthwith give notice in writing to the Commission of—

(a) the date and place of the conviction;

(b) the offence of which he was convicted; and

(c) the penalty imposed on him in respect of the offence.

DEFINITIONS
4–061   registered person: reg.2(1).
responsible individual: reg.2(1).
Commission: reg.2(1).

GENERAL NOTE
4–062   A contravention or failure to comply with this regulation is an offence (reg.43(1)).
Criminal offence: This could be unrelated to the operation of a care home.

PART III

CONDUCT OF CARE HOME

Health and welfare of service users
4–063   **12.**—(1) The registered person shall ensure that the care home is conducted so as—

(a) to promote and make proper provision for the health and welfare of service users;

(b) to make proper provision for the care and, where appropriate, treatment, education and supervision of service users.

(2) The registered person shall so far as practicable enable service users to make decisions with respect to the care they are to receive and their health and welfare.
(3) The registered person shall, for the purpose of providing care to service users, and making proper provision for their health and welfare, so far as practicable ascertain and take into account their wishes and feelings.
(4) The registered person shall make suitable arrangements to ensure that the care home is conducted—

(a) in a manner which respects the privacy and dignity of service users;

(b) with due regard to the sex, religious persuasion, racial origin, and cultural and linguistic background and any disability of service users.

(5) The registered provider and registered manager (if any) shall, in relation to the conduct of the care home—

(a) maintain good personal and professional relationships with each other and with service users and staff; and

(b) encourage and assist staff to maintain good personal and professional relationships with service users.

DEFINITIONS

registered person: reg.2(1).   **4–064**
service user: reg.2(1).
registered manager: reg.2(1).
staff: reg.2(1).

GENERAL NOTE

A contravention or failure to comply with paras (1) to (4) of this regulation is an offence   **4–065**
(reg.43(1)).
This regulation is applied by reg.32 where a child is accommodated in the care home.

PARA.(1)

Welfare: In *Domah v Hertfordshire CC (Decn. No.147)*, a case under the 1984 Act, the   **4–066**
Registered Homes Tribunal said: "Good care practice does not require a home to be run
like an over hearty holiday camp, but it does require that residents be treated as individuals
and helped to follow their individual interests".

Supervision: In *O'Neil v Sefton MBC (Decn. No.195)*, a case under the 1984 Act, the
Registered Homes Tribunal said that it regarded the use of electronic listening devices in
a care home as "being a very serious breach of the right to privacy of staff and residents".

Further requirements as to health and welfare

13.—(1) The registered person shall make arrangements for service users—   **4–067**

(a) to be registered with a general practitioner of their choice; and

(b) to receive where necessary, treatment, advice and other services from any health care professional.

(2) The registered person shall make arrangements for the recording, handling, safekeeping, safe administration and disposal of medicines received into the care home.

(3) The registered person shall make suitable arrangements to prevent infection, toxic conditions and the spread of infection at the care home.

(4) The registered person shall ensure that—

(a) all parts of the home to which service users have access are so far as reasonably practicable free from hazards to their safety;

(b) any activities in which service users participate are so far as reasonably practicable free from avoidable risks; and

(c) unnecessary risks to the health or safety of service users are identified and so far as possible eliminated,

and shall make suitable arrangements for the training of staff in first aid.

(5) The registered person shall make suitable arrangements to provide a safe system for moving and handling service users.

(6) The registered person shall make arrangements, by training staff or by other measures, to prevent service users being harmed or suffering abuse or being placed at risk of harm or abuse.

(7) The registered person shall ensure that no service user is subject to physical restraint unless restraint of the kind employed is the only practicable means of securing the welfare of that or any other service user and there are exceptional circumstances.

(8) On any occasion on which a service user is subject to physical restraint, the registered person shall record the circumstances, including the nature of the restraint.

DEFINITIONS

4–068   registered person: reg.2(1).
service user: reg.2(1).
general practitioner: reg.2(1).
health care professional: reg.2(1).
staff: reg.2(1).

GENERAL NOTE

4–069   This regulation is modified by reg.47(2)(5) in relation to an adult placement carer providing a short-term break for a service user.

4–070   In November 2002, the National Care Standards Commission, the Local Government Association and the Health and Safety Executive issued a Memorandum of Understanding that sets out how they will work together to regulate and enforce health and safety legislation in establishments and agencies regulated under the 2000 Act.

A contravention or failure to comply with paras (1) to (4) and (6) to (8) of this regulation is an offence (reg.43(1)).

PARA.(2)

4–071   The Royal Pharmaceutical Society of Great Britain has published "The Administration and Control of Medicines in Care Homes and Children's Services" (June 2003) which is "designed to assist owners and managers of care homes to safely handle medicines; and to meet the medication standards that now form an integral part of the process to regulate private care" (para.1).

In *The Management of Medication in Care Services* (March 2004), the NCSC examined the performance of care homes for older people and younger adults and children's homes in relation to the national minimum standards on medication. The report found that compliance with the standards varied widely.

PARA.(6)

4–072   The NCSC, the Association of Directors of Social Services and the Association of Chief Police Officers have agreed an "Adult Protection Protocol" (December, 2003) which sets out the processes and procedures to be followed by the three parties when protecting vulnerable adults from abuse. Also see the House of Commons Select Committee on Health, 2nd Report Session 2003–4 on Elder Abuse, paras 50–69.

PARA.(7)

4–073   It is submitted that if the use of restraint is the only practicable means of responding to the situation, it should be used irrespective of whether exceptional circumstances can be identified.

Assessment of service users

14.—(1) The registered person shall not provide accommodation to a service **4–074** user at the care home unless, so far as it shall have been practicable to do so—

(a) needs of the service user have been assessed by a suitably qualified or suitably trained person;

(b) the registered person has obtained a copy of the assessment;

(c) there has been appropriate consultation regarding the assessment with the service user or a representative of the service user;

(d) the registered person has confirmed in writing to the service user that having regard to the assessment the care home is suitable for the purpose of meeting the service user's needs in respect of his health and welfare.

(2) The registered person shall ensure that the assessment of the service user's needs is—

(a) kept under review; and

(b) revised at any time when it is necessary to do so having regard to any change of circumstances.

DEFINITIONS
registered person: reg.2(1).   **4–075**
service user: reg.2(1).
representative: reg.2(1).

GENERAL NOTE
Under s.47 of the National Health Service and Community Care Act 1990, a local auth- **4–076** ority has a duty to assess any person who may be in need of community care services and to decide whether the assessed needs call for the provision of such services. The arrangements that local authorities make to provide residential accommodation for vulnerable persons under Part III of the National Assistance Act 1948 are community care services for the purposes of s.47. The assessment under s.47 will satisfy the requirements under sub-paras (a) and (c) of para.(1). If the local authority makes arrangements for accommodation pursuant to Part III, the authority shall, subject to certain conditions, ensure that the person concerned is accommodated at the place of his or her choice (National Assistance Act 1948 (Choice of Accommodation) Directions 1992).
A contravention or failure to comply with this regulation is an offence (reg.43(1)).

PARA.(2)
The review and revision of the assessment should, in practice, be part of the process that **4–077** leads to the review and revision of the service user's plan under reg.15.

Service user's plan

15.—(1) Unless it is impracticable to carry out such consultation, the registered **4–078** person shall, after consultation with the service user, or a representative of his, prepare a written plan ("the service user's plan") as to how the service user's needs in respect of his health and welfare are to be met.
(2) The registered person shall—

(a) make the service user's plan available to the service user;

(b) keep the service user's plan under review;

(c) where appropriate and, unless it is impracticable to carry out such consultation, after consultation with the service user or a representative of his, revise the service user's plan; and

(d) notify the service user of any such revision.

DEFINITIONS

4–079 registered person: reg.2(1).
service user: reg.2(1).
representative: reg.2(1).

GENERAL NOTE

4–080 A contravention or failure to comply with this regulation is an offence (reg.43(1)).

Facilities and services

4–081 **16.**—(1) Subject to regulation 4(3), the registered person shall provide facilities and services to service users in accordance with the statement required by regulation 4(1)(b) in respect of the care home.

(2) The registered person shall having regard to the size of the care home and the number and needs of service users—

(a) provide, so far as is necessary for the purpose of managing the care home—

(i) appropriate telephone facilities;
(ii) appropriate facilities for communication by facsimile transmission;

(b) provide telephone facilities which are suitable for the needs of service users, and make arrangements to enable service users to use such facilities in private;

(c) provide in rooms occupied by service users adequate furniture, bedding and other furnishings, including curtains and floor coverings, and equipment suitable to the needs of service users and screens where necessary;

(d) permit service users, so far as it is practicable to do so, to bring their own furniture and furnishings into the rooms they occupy;

(e) arrange for the regular laundering of linen and clothing;

(f) so far as it is practicable to do so, provide adequate facilities for service users to wash, dry and iron their own clothes if they so wish and, for that purpose, to make arrangements for their clothes to be sorted and kept separately;

(g) provide sufficient and suitable kitchen equipment, crockery, cutlery and utensils, and adequate facilities for the preparation and storage of food;

(h) provide adequate facilities for service users to prepare their own food and ensure that such facilities are safe for use by service users;

(i) provide, in adequate quantities, suitable, wholesome and nutritious food which is varied and properly prepared and available at such time as may reasonably be required by service users;

(j) after consultation with the environmental health authority, make suitable arrangements for maintaining satisfactory standards of hygiene in the care home;

(k) keep the care home free from offensive odours and make suitable arrangements for the disposal of general and clinical waste;

(l) provide a place where the money and valuables of service users may be deposited for safe keeping, and make arrangements for service users to acknowledge in writing the return to them of any money or valuables so deposited;

(m) consult service users about their social interests, and make arrangements to enable them to engage in local, social and community activities and to visit, or maintain contact or communicate with, their families and friends;

(n) consult service users about the programme of activities arranged by or on behalf of the care home, and provide facilities for recreation including, having regard to the needs of service users, activities in relation to recreation, fitness and training.

(3) The registered person shall ensure that so far as practicable service users have the opportunity to attend religious services of their choice.

(4) In this regulation "food" includes drink.

DEFINITIONS

registered person: reg.2(1). **4–082**
service user: reg.2(1).
environmental health authority: reg.2(1).

GENERAL NOTE

A contravention or failure to comply with paras (1), (2)(a) to (j) and (l) to (n) and (3) of **4–083** this regulation is an offence (reg.43(1)).

PARA.(2)(G)

This paragraph does not apply in relation to an adult placement carer providing a short- **4–084** term break for a service user (reg.47(3)(5)).
Storage of food: Care homes are subject to the provisions of the Food Safety Act 1990.

PARA.(2)(H)

Having regard to the registered persons duty under reg.12, service users should not be **4–085** provided with facilities to provide their own food if they have been assessed as not having the required mental and/or physical agility to engage in such activity.

Records
17.—(1) The registered person shall— **4–086**

(a) maintain in respect of each service user a record which includes the information, documents and other records specified in Schedule 3 relating to the service user;

(b) ensure that the record referred to in sub-paragraph (a) is kept securely in the care home.

(2) The registered person shall maintain in the care home the records specified in Schedule 4.

(3) The registered person shall ensure that the records referred to in paragraphs (1) and (2)—

    (a) are kept up to date; and

    (b) are at all times available for inspection in the care home by any person authorised by the Commission to enter and inspect the care home.

(4) The records referred to in paragraphs (1) and (2) shall be retained for not less than three years from the date of the last entry.

DEFINITIONS

4–087   registered person: reg.2(1).
service user: reg.2(1).
record: reg.2(1).
Commission: reg.2(1).

GENERAL NOTE

4–088   A contravention or failure to comply with this regulation is an offence (reg.43(1)). A prosecution for a failure to comply with this regulation can be brought even though the person concerned is no longer the registered person of the home (reg.43(4)).

In *Farooq and Farooq v Croydon LBC (Decn. No.219)*, a case under the 1984 Act, the tribunal said that "records are not simply a description of what is happening. Good, accurate and reliable records are essential to, and indicative of, the whole process of care in a well run home. Only with accurate meaningful records can the respondents know what is going on in the home, how the residents are progressing, whether there are matters which should be investigated, and so forth. Further, for continuity of care of residents, all the staff need to have clear records to which they can turn, so that, for example absences of staff or incidents with residents do not take anyone by surprise."

PARA.*(3)(B)*

4–089   *Enter and inspect:* A power to enter and inspect is provided for in s.31 of the Act.

Staffing

4–090   **18.**—(1) The registered person shall, having regard to the size of the care home, the statement of purpose and the number and needs of service users—

    (a) ensure that at all times suitably qualified, competent and experienced persons are working at the care home in such numbers as are appropriate for the health and welfare of service users;

    (b) ensure that the employment of any persons on a temporary basis at the care home will not prevent service users from receiving such continuity of care as is reasonable to meet their needs;

    (c) ensure that the persons employed by the registered person to work at the care home receive—

        (i) training appropriate to the work they are to perform; and

        (ii) suitable assistance, including time off, for the purpose of obtaining further qualifications appropriate to such work.

(2) The registered person shall ensure that persons working at the care home are appropriately supervised.

(3) Where the care home—

(a) provides nursing to service users; and

(b) provides, whether or not in connection with nursing, medicines or medical treatment to service users,

the registered person shall ensure that at all times a suitably qualified registered nurse is working at the care home.

(4) The registered person shall make arrangements for providing persons who work at the care home with appropriate information about any code of practice published under section 62 of the Act.

DEFINITIONS

    registered person: reg.2(1).   **4–091**
    statement of purpose: reg.2(1).
    service user: reg.2(1).
    employment: reg.2(2).

GENERAL NOTE

    "Guidance on staffing levels in care homes" was issued in March 27, 2002 in a letter **4–092** from the Minister to the Chairperson of the NCSC. This guidance sets out the approach that should be adopted by the Commission in respect of both existing homes and for new applications for registration. With regard to the former, the guidance states that there must be no regression from staffing levels that existed at March 31, 2002. With regard to the latter, the guidance states that the Commission should use the guidance produced by the "Residential Forum". The guidance, which applied to the first year of the Commission's life, was extended by a further letter from the Minister dated April 2, 2003 pending further statutory guidance being issued.

    A contravention or failure to comply with this regulation is an offence (reg.43(1)).

PARA.(3)

    For a suggested definition of nursing care, see the note on s.3(1).   **4–093**

Fitness of workers

    19.—(1) The registered person shall not employ a person to work at the care **4–094** home unless—

(a) the person is fit to work at the care home;

(b) subject to paragraph (6), he has obtained in respect of that person the information and documents specified in—

    (i) paragraphs [1 to 7] of Schedule 2;
    (ii) [...];
    (iii) [...]; and

(c) he is satisfied on reasonable grounds as to the authenticity of the references referred to in paragraph 5 of Schedule 2 in respect of that person.

    (2) This paragraph applies to a person who is employed by a person ("the employer") other than the registered person.

(3) This paragraph applies to a position in which a person may in the course of his duties have regular contact with service users at the care home or with any other person of a description specified in section 3(2) of the Act.

(4) The registered person shall not allow a person to whom paragraph (2) applies to work at the care home in a position to which paragraph (3) applies, unless—

(a) the person is fit to work at the care home;

(b) the employer has obtained in respect of that person the information and documents specified in—

(i) paragraphs [1 to 7] of Schedule 2;
(ii) [...];
(iii) [...]; and

(c) the employer is satisfied on reasonable grounds as to the authenticity of the references referred to in paragraph 5 of Schedule 2 in respect of that person, and has confirmed in writing to the registered person that he is so satisfied.

(5) For the purposes of paragraphs (1) and (4), a person is not fit to work at a care home unless—

(a) he is of integrity and good character;

(b) he has qualifications suitable to the work that he is to perform, and the skills and experience necessary for such work;

(c) he is physically and mentally fit for the purposes of the work which he is to perform at the care home; and

(d) full and satisfactory information is available in relation to him in respect of the following matters—

(i) each of the matters specified in paragraphs [1 to 7] of Schedule 2;
(ii) [...];
(iii) [...];

(6) Paragraphs (1)(b) and (5)(d), in so far as they relate to paragraph 7 of Schedule 2, shall not apply until [31st October 2004] in respect of a person who immediately before 1st April 2002 is employed to work at the care home.

(7) [...].

AMENDMENTS

4–095   The amendments to this regulation were made by SI 2002/865, reg.2(4) and SI 2003/534, reg.2.

DEFINITIONS

4–096   registered person: reg.2(1).
employ: reg.2(3).
service user: reg.2(1).

A contravention or failure to comply with this regulation is an offence (reg.43(1)).   **4–097**
This regulation is applied by reg.33 where a child is accommodated in the care home.

CRIMINAL RECORDS BUREAU CHECKS
See the note on Sch.2, para.7.   **4–098**

PARA.(5)
See the notes on reg.7.   **4–099**

Restrictions on acting for service user

20.—(1) Subject to paragraph (2), the registered person shall not pay money   **4–100**
belonging to any service user into a bank account unless—

(a) the account is in the name of the service user, or any of the service users, to which the money belongs; and

(b) the account is not used by the registered person in connection with the carrying on or management of the care home.

(2) Paragraph (1) does not apply to money which is paid to the registered person in respect of charges payable by a service user for accommodation or other services provided by the registered person at the care home.

(3) The registered person shall ensure so far as practicable that persons working at the care home do not act as the agent of a service user.

DEFINITIONS
registered person: reg.2(1).   **4–101**
service user: reg.2(1).

GENERAL NOTE
A contravention or failure to comply with this regulation is an offence (reg.43(1)).   **4–102**

PARA.(3)
Agent: A mentally capable person who receives social security benefits or a state pension   **4–103**
may nominate a person as their agent to collect the money for them. The nomination of an
agent is an informal arrangement between claimant and agent.

Staff views as to conduct of care home

21.—(1) This regulation applies to any matter relating to the conduct of the care   **4–104**
home so far as it may affect the health or welfare of service users.

(2) The registered person shall make arrangements to enable staff to inform the
registered person and the Commission of their views about any matter to which
this regulation applies.

DEFINITIONS
service user: reg.2(1).   **4–105**
registered person: reg.2(1).
staff: reg.2(1).
Commission: reg.2(1).

GENERAL NOTE
A contravention or failure to comply with this regulation is an offence (reg.43(1)).   **4–106**

The Public Interest Disclosure Act 1998, which is part of employment legislation, applies to people at work who raise genuine concerns about crime, breach of a legal obligation, miscarriage of justice, danger to health and safety or the environment and the cover up of any of these. It applies whether or not the information is confidential. An internal disclosure within the organisation or with the person responsible for the malpractice will be protected if the "whistleblower" has an honest and reasonable suspicion that the malpractice has occurred, is occurring or is likely to occur. Disclosure to a prescribed regulator, such as the CSCI or the CHAI, will be protected where the whistleblower meets the test for internal disclosure and, additionally, honestly and reasonably believes that the information and any allegation in it are substantially true. Wider disclosure such as those to the police, the media and MPs are protected if, in addition to the tests for regulatory disclosures, they are reasonable in all the circumstances and they are not made for personal gain. However, there are various preconditions to be satisfied if the whistleblower is to win protection for a wider disclosure. Where a whistleblower is victimised in breach of the Act he or she can bring a claim to an employment tribunal for compensation. Dismissals in breach of the Act are automatically unfair.

Although the Act does not require organisations to set up whistleblowing procedures, the existence of the Act will encourage this. Key aspects of such procedures, as endorsed by the Committee on Standards on Public Life (Second Report, Cm. 3270–1) are:

- a clear statement that malpractice is taken seriously in the organisation;
- respect for confidentiality of staffing raising concerns, if they wish;
- the opportunity to raise concerns outside the line management structure;
- penalties for making false allegations maliciously; and
- an indication of the proper way in which concerns may be raised outside the organisation if necessary.

Complaints

4–107 **22.**—(1) The registered person shall establish a procedure ("the complaints procedure") for considering complaints made to the registered person by a service user or person acting on the service user's behalf.

(2) The complaints procedure shall be appropriate to the needs of service users.

(3) The registered person shall ensure that any complaint made under the complaints procedure is fully investigated.

(4) The registered person shall, within 28 days after the date on which the complaint is made, or such shorter period as may be reasonable in the circumstances, inform the person who made the complaint of the action (if any) that is to be taken.

(5) The registered person shall supply a written copy of the complaints procedure to every service user and to any person acting on behalf of a service user if that person so requests.

(6) Where a written copy of the complaints procedure is to be supplied in accordance with paragraph (5) to a person who is blind or whose vision is impaired, the registered person shall so far as it is practicable to do so supply, in addition to the written copy, a copy of the complaints procedure in a form which is suitable for that person.

(7) The copy of the complaints procedure to be supplied in accordance with paragraphs (5) and (6) shall include—

(a) the name, address and telephone number of the Commission; and

(b) the procedure (if any) that has been notified by the Commission to the registered person for the making of complaints to the Commission relating to the care home.

(8) The registered person shall supply to the Commission at its request a statement containing a summary of the complaints made during the preceding twelve months and the action that was taken in response.

DEFINITIONS

registered person: reg.2(1).   **4–108**
service user: reg.2(1).
Commission: reg.2(1).

GENERAL NOTE

A contravention or failure to comply with this regulation is an offence (reg.43(1)).   **4–109**

PART IV

PREMISES

Fitness of premises

23.—(1) Subject to regulation 4(3), the registered person shall not use premises **4–110** for the purposes of a care home unless—

(a) the premises are suitable for the purpose of achieving the aims and objectives set out in the statement of purpose; and

(b) the location of the premises is appropriate to the needs of service users.

(2) The registered person shall having regard to the number and needs of the service users ensure that—

(a) the physical design and layout of the premises to be used as the care home meet the needs of the service users;

(b) the premises to be used as the care home are of sound construction and kept in a good state of repair externally and internally;

(c) equipment provided at the care home for use by service users or persons who work at the care home [is] maintained in good working order;

(d) all parts of the care home are kept clean and reasonably decorated;

(e) adequate private and communal accommodation is provided for service users;

(f) the size and layout of rooms occupied or used by service users are suitable for their needs;

(g) there is adequate sitting, recreational and dining space provided separately from the service user's private accommodation;

(h) the communal space provided for service users is suitable for the provision of social, cultural and religious activities appropriate to the circumstances of service users;

(i) suitable facilities are provided for service users to meet visitors in communal accommodation, and in private accommodation which is separate from the service users' own private rooms;

(j) there are provided at appropriate places in the premises sufficient numbers of lavatories, and of wash-basins, baths and showers fitted with a hot and cold water supply;

(k) any necessary sluicing facilities are provided;

(l) suitable provision is made for storage for the purposes of the care home;

(m) suitable storage facilities are provided for the use of service users;

(n) suitable adaptations are made, and such support, equipment and facilities, including passenger lifts, as may be required are provided, for service users who are old, infirm or physically disabled;

(o) external grounds which are suitable for, and safe for use by, service users are provided and appropriately maintained;

(p) ventilation, heating and lighting suitable for service users is provided in all parts of the care home which are used by service users.

(3) The registered person shall provide for staff—

(a) suitable facilities and accommodation, other than sleeping accommodation, including—

  (i) facilities for the purpose of changing;
  (ii) storage facilities;

(b) sleeping accommodation where the provision of such accommodation is needed by staff in connection with their work at the care home.

(4) The registered person shall after consultation with the fire authority—

(a) take adequate precautions against the risk of fire, including the provision of suitable fire equipment;

(b) provide adequate means of escape;

(c) make adequate arrangements—

  (i) for detecting, containing and extinguishing fires;
  (ii) for giving warnings of fires;
  (iii) for the evacuation, in the event of fire, of all persons in the care home and safe placement of service users;
  (iv) for the maintenance of all fire equipment; and
  (v) for reviewing fire precautions, and testing fire equipment, at suitable intervals;

(d) make arrangements for persons working at the care home to receive suitable training in fire prevention; and

(e) to ensure, by means of fire drills and practices at suitable intervals, that the persons working at the care home and, so far as practicable, service users, are aware of the procedure to be followed in case of fire, including the procedure for saving life.

(5) The registered person shall undertake appropriate consultation with the authority responsible for environmental health for the area in which the care home is situated.

AMENDMENT
   The amendment to para.(2)(c) was made by SI 2002/865, reg.3(2).   **4–111**

DEFINITIONS   **4–112**
   registered person: reg.2(1).
   statement of purpose: reg.2(1).
   service user: reg.2(1).
   staff: reg.2(1).
   fire authority: reg.2(1).
   environmental health authority: reg.2(1).

GENERAL NOTE
   A contravention or failure to comply with this regulation is an offence (reg.43(1)).   **4–113**

PART V

MANAGEMENT

Review of quality of care
   24.—(1) The registered person shall establish and maintain a system for—   **4–114**

(a) reviewing at appropriate intervals; and

(b) improving,

the quality of care provided at the care home, including the quality of nursing where nursing is provided at the care home.
   (2) The registered person shall supply to the Commission a report in respect of any review conducted by him for the purposes of paragraph (1), and make a copy of the report available to service users.
   (3) The system referred to in paragraph (1) shall provide for consultation with service users and their representatives.

DEFINITIONS   **4–115**
   registered person: reg.2(1).
   Commission: reg.2(1).
   service user; reg.2(1).
   representative: reg.2(1).

GENERAL NOTE
   A contravention or failure to comply with this regulation is an offence (reg.43(1)).   **4–116**
   This regulation is applied by reg.35 where a child is accommodated in the care home.

Financial position

4–117   **25.**—(1) The registered provider shall carry on the care home in such manner as is likely to ensure that the care home will be financially viable for the purpose of achieving the aims and objectives set out in the statement of purpose.

(2) The registered person shall, if the Commission so requests, provide the Commission with such information and documents as it may require for the purpose of considering the financial viability of the care home, including—

(a) the annual accounts of the care home certified by an accountant;

(b) a reference from a bank expressing an opinion as to the registered provider's financial standing;

(c) information as to the financing and financial resources of the care home;

(d) where the registered provider is a company, information as to any of its associated companies;

(e) a certificate of insurance for the registered provider in respect of liability which may be incurred by him in relation to the care home in respect of death, injury, public liability, damage or other loss.

(3) The registered person shall—

(a) ensure that adequate accounts are maintained in respect of the care home and kept up to date;

(b) ensure that the accounts give details of the running costs of the care home, including rent, payments under a mortgage and expenditure on food, heating and salaries and wages of staff; and

(c) supply a copy of the accounts to the Commission at its request.

(4) In this regulation a company is an associated company of another if one of them has control of the other or both are under the control of the same person.

DEFINITIONS

4–118   registered provider: reg.2(1).
statement of purpose: reg.2(1).
registered person: reg.2(1).
company: para.(4).
Commission: reg.2(1).

GENERAL NOTE

4–119   Regulation 13 of the National Care Standards Commission (Registration) Regulations 2001 requires the registered person to notify the registration authority if the establishment or agency is likely to become financially unviable.

A contravention or failure to comply with this regulation is an offence (reg.43(1)).

Visits by registered provider

4–120   **26.**—(1) Where the registered provider is an individual, but not in day to day charge of the care home, he shall visit the care home in accordance with this regulation.

(2) Where the registered provider is an organisation or partnership, the care home shall be visited in accordance with this regulation by—

(a) the responsible individual or one of the partners, as the case may be;

(b) another of the directors or other persons responsible for the management of the organisation or partnership; or

(c) an employee of the organisation or the partnership who is not directly concerned with the conduct of the care home.

(3) Visits under paragraph (1) or (2) shall take place at least once a month and shall be unannounced.

(4) The person carrying out the visit shall—

(a) interview, with their consent and in private, such of the service users and their representatives and persons working at the care home as appears necessary in order to form an opinion of the standard of care provided in the care home;

(b) inspect the premises of the care home, its record of events and records of any complaints; and

(c) prepare a written report on the conduct of the care home.

(5) The registered provider shall supply a copy of the report required to be made under paragraph (4)(c) to—

(a) the Commission;

(b) the registered manager; and

(c) in the case of a visit under paragraph (2)—

(i) where the registered provider is an organisation, to each of the directors or other persons responsible for the management of the organisation; and

(ii) where the registered provider is a partnership, to each of the partners.

DEFINITIONS

registered provider: reg.2(1). **4–121**
responsible individual: reg.2(1).
service user: reg.2(1).
representative: reg.2(1).
registered manager: reg.2(1).
Commission: reg.2(1).

GENERAL NOTE

In June 2003, the National Care Standards Commission made available to providers a **4–122** format for reporting on the conduct of care homes in accordance with this regulation. Use of the format is not obligatory.

The requirement for a monthly report to be submitted to the registration authority and others (see paras (4)(c), (5)) appears is onerous burden that provides no obvious benefit.

A contravention or failure to comply with this regulation is an offence (reg.43(1)).

PART VI

CHILDREN

Application of this Part

4–123   **27.** The provisions of this Part shall apply where any child is accommodated in the care home.

Interpretation

4–124   **28.** In regulation 2, paragraph (1) shall have effect as if—

(a) at the end of the definition of "service user" there were added the words ", or any child who is accommodated in the care home";

(b) the following definitions were added at the appropriate places—

"placement plan" has the meaning given to it in regulation 12 (child's placement plan) of the Children's Homes Regulations 2001;

"placing authority" has the meaning given to it in regulation 2(1) (interpretation) of the Children's Homes Regulations 2001;".

Statement of purpose

4–125   **29.** In regulation 4, paragraph (1) shall have effect as if at the end of that paragraph there were added the following—
      " and

(d) the information specified in Schedule 5."

Registered person

4–126   **30.**—(1) In regulation 7, paragraph (3) shall have effect as if at the end of that paragraph there were added the following—
      " and

(d) his skills and experience are suitable for the purpose of his working with children."

(2) In regulation 9, paragraph (2) shall have effect as if at the end of that paragraph there were added the following—
      " and

(d) his skills and experience are suitable for the purpose of his working with children and either—
  (i) his qualifications are suitable for the purpose of his working with children; or
  (ii) another person has been appointed for the purpose of assisting him in the management of the care home, and the qualifications of the person so appointed are suitable for the purpose of his working with children."

(3) In regulation 10, paragraph (1) shall have effect as if for the words "and the number and needs of the service users," there were substituted the words "the number and needs of the service users and the need to safeguard and promote the welfare of children accommodated in the care home,".

Separate provision for children
   31.—(1) Subject to paragraph (2), the registered person shall ensure that—   **4–127**

(a) the provision to be made for the care, treatment and supervision of children accommodated in the care home; and

(b) the provision of facilities and services to them,

shall, so far as it is practicable to do so, be made separately from other service users.
   (2) Paragraph (1) shall not prevent the registered person from making provision jointly for children and other service users whose age does not significantly differ from those children.

DEFINITION
   registered person: reg.2(1).   **4–128**

GENERAL NOTE
PARA.(2)
   Age: This is a reference to a persons chronological age.   **4–129**

Welfare and protection of children
   32.—(1) Regulation 12 of these Regulations shall have effect as if, at the end of **4–130** sub-paragraph (a) of paragraph (1) of that regulation there were added the words ", including provision for safeguarding the welfare of children accommodated in the care home".
   (2) The provisions of regulations 12, 15 to 18, 23 and 30 of, and Schedule 5 to, the Children's Homes Regulations 2001 (child's placement plan; contact and access to communications; arrangements for the protection of children; behaviour management, discipline and restraint; education, employment and leisure activity; hazards and safety; notifiable events) shall apply to the registered person as if—

(a) any reference to the registered person were to the registered person as defined in these Regulations;

(b) any reference to the children's home or the home were to the care home.

   (3) Where the registered person notifies the Commission in accordance with regulation 30 of the Children's Homes Regulations 2001 of any of the following events, namely—

(a) serious illness or a serious accident sustained by a child accommodated at the care home;

(b) the outbreak of any infectious disease at the care home or involving children accommodated at the care home,

he will not be required to give separate notice of that event to the Commission under regulation 37 (notification of death, illness and other events) of these Regulations.

DEFINITIONS
4–131   registered person: reg.2(1).
Commission: reg.2(1).

Fitness of workers

4–132   **33.** Regulation 19 shall have effect as if—

(a) in sub-paragraph (b) of paragraph (1) and sub-paragraph (b) of paragraph (4), for head (i) in each of those sub-paragraphs there were substituted the following head—

"(i) paragraphs 1 to 6 of Schedule 2 and in Schedule 6;";

(b) in sub-paragraph (d) of paragraph (5), for head (i) there were substituted the following head—

"(i) each of the matters specified in paragraphs 1 to 6 of Schedule 2 and in Schedule 6;";

(c) at the end of paragraph (5) there were added the following—

" and

(d) his qualifications, skills and experience are suitable for the purpose of working with children."

Staff disciplinary procedure

4–133   **34.** The registered person shall operate a staff disciplinary procedure which, in particular—

(a) provides for the suspension of an employee of his where necessary in the interests of the safety or welfare of children accommodated in the care home; and

(b) provides that the failure on the part of an employee of his to report an incident of abuse, or suspected abuse of a child accommodated in the care home to an appropriate person is a ground on which disciplinary proceedings may be instituted.

DEFINITION
4–134   registered person: reg.2(1).

Review of quality of care

4–135   **35.** Regulation 24 shall have effect as if—

(a) the system referred to in paragraph (1) of regulation 24 included monitoring at appropriate intervals the matters set out in Schedule 7;

(b) in paragraph (2) of regulation 24, after the words "any review conducted by him" there were added the words ", or any matters monitored";

(c) in paragraph (3) of regulation 24, for the words "and their representatives" there were substituted the words ", their representatives, the parents of the children accommodated at the care home and, in relation to those children, the placing authorities".

Offences

36. Regulation 43 shall have effect as if for paragraph (1) there were substituted **4–136** the following paragraph—

"(1) A contravention or failure to comply with any of the following provisions shall be an offence—

(a) regulations 4, 5, [5A,] 11, 12(1) to (4), 13(1) to (4) and (6) to (8), 14, 15, 16(1), (2)(a) to (j) and (l) to (n) and (3), 17 to 26 and 37 to 40, to the extent that those regulations have effect subject to Part VI of these Regulations;

(b) regulations 31 and 34; and

(c) the provisions referred to in paragraph (2) of regulation 32, to the extent that they apply to the registered person by virtue of that paragraph."

AMENDMENT
The amendment to this regulation was made by SI 2003/1703, reg.2(4).   **4–137**

PART VII

MISCELLANEOUS

Notification of death, illness and other events

37.—(1) The registered person shall give notice to the Commission without **4–138** delay of the occurrence of—

(a) the death of any service user, including the circumstances of his death;

(b) the outbreak in the care home of any infectious disease which in the opinion of any registered medical practitioner attending persons in the care home is sufficiently serious to be so notified;

(c) any serious injury to a service user;

(d) serious illness of a service user at a care home at which nursing is not provided;

(e) any event in the care home which adversely affects the well-being or safety of any service user;

(f) any theft, burglary or accident in the care home;

(g) any allegation of misconduct by the registered person or any person who works at the care home.

(2) Any notification made in accordance with this regulation which is given orally shall be confirmed in writing.

DEFINITIONS
registered person: reg.2(1).   **4–139**
Commission: reg.2(1).
service user: reg.2(1).

GENERAL NOTE
The registered person is also placed under a legal obligation to inform bodies other than **4–140** the Commission in the event of certain occurrences. In particular, note should be made of

the reporting requirements contained in the Reporting of Injuries, Diseases and Dangerous Occurrences Regulations 1995 (SI 1995/3163). Information about these regulations can found at *www.riddor.gov.uk*.

The NCSC published a guidance note on the implementation of this regulation. Appendix 1 to this document sets out clarification of the type of events that the Commission considers fall within the ambit of the regulation. Some of the events identified by the Commission, especially in relation to para.(1)(e), clearly fall outside of the scope of this regulation, for example "admission to the home of persons subject to a guardianship order or other sections of the Mental Health Act"

A contravention or failure to comply with this regulation is an offence (reg.43(1)).

PARA.(1)(E).

4–141   *Adversely affects:* The potentiality of an event to adversely affect the well-being or safety of the service user is not covered by this provision.

Notice of absence

4–142   **38.**—(1) Where—

(a) the registered provider, if he is an individual; or

(b) the registered manager,

proposes to be absent from the care home for a continuous period of 28 days or more, the registered person shall give notice in writing to the Commission of the proposed absence.

(2) Except in the case of an emergency, the notice referred to in paragraph (1) above shall be given no later than one month before the proposed absence commences or within such shorter period as may be agreed with the Commission and the notice shall specify—

(a) the length or expected length of the absence;

(b) the reason for the absence;

(c) the arrangements which have been made for the running of the care home during that absence;

(d) the name, address and qualifications of the person who will be responsible for the care home during that absence; and

(e) in the case of the absence of the registered manager, the arrangements that have been, or are proposed to be, made for appointing another person to manage the care home during that absence, including the proposed date by which the appointment is to be made.

(3) Where the absence arises as a result of an emergency, the registered person shall give notice of the absence within one week of its occurrence specifying the matters mentioned in sub-paragraphs (a) to (e) of paragraph (2).

(4) Where—

(a) the registered provider, if he is an individual; or

(b) the registered manager,

has been absent from the care home for a continuous period of 28 days or more, and the Commission has not been given notice of the absence, the registered person shall without delay give notice in writing to the Commission of the absence, specifying the matters mentioned in sub-paragraphs (a) to (e) of paragraph (2).

(5) The registered person shall notify the Commission of the return to duty of the registered provider or (as the case may be) the registered manager not later than 7 days after the date of his return.

DEFINITIONS

registered person: reg.2(1).   **4–143**
registered manager: reg.2(1).
Commission: reg.2(1).

GENERAL NOTE

This regulation is modified by reg.47(4), (5) in relation to an adult placement carer pro- **4–144**
viding a short-term break for a service user.

A contravention or failure to comply with this regulation is an offence (reg.43(1)).

Notice of changes

39. The registered person shall give notice in writing to the Commission as soon **4–145**
as it is practicable to do so if any of the following events takes place or is proposed
to take place—

(a) a person other than the registered person carries on or manages the care home;

(b) a person ceases to carry on or manage the care home;

(c) where the registered person is an individual, he changes his name;

(d) where the registered provider is a partnership, there is any change in the membership of the partnership;

(e) where the registered provider is an organisation—

  (i) the name or address of the organisation is changed;
  (ii) there is any change of director, manager, secretary or other similar officer of the organisation;
  (iii) there is to be any change of responsible individual;

(f) where the registered provider is an individual, a trustee in bankruptcy is appointed;

(g) where the registered provider is a company or partnership, a receiver, manager, liquidator or provisional liquidator is appointed; or

(h) the premises of the care home are significantly altered or extended, or additional premises are acquired.

DEFINITIONS

registered person: reg.2(1).   **4–146**
Commission: reg.2(1).
registered provider: reg.2(1).

GENERAL NOTE

A contravention or failure to comply with this regulation is an offence (reg.43(1)).   **4–147**

Notice of termination of accommodation

4–148   **40.**—(1) Subject to paragraph (2), the registered person shall not terminate the arrangements for the accommodation of a service user unless he has given reasonable notice of his intention to do so to—

(a) the service user;

(b) the person who appears to be the service user's next of kin; and

(c) where a local authority has made arrangements for the provision of accommodation, nursing or personal care to the service user at the care home, that authority.

(2) If it is impracticable for the registered person to comply with the requirement in paragraph (1)—

(a) he shall do so as soon as it is practicable to do so; and

(b) he shall provide to the Commission a statement as to the circumstances which made it impracticable for him to comply with the requirement.

<small>DEFINITIONS</small>
4–149   registered person: reg.2(1).
service user: reg.2(1).
Commission: reg.2(1).

<small>GENERAL NOTE</small>
4–150   A contravention or failure to comply with this regulation is an offence (reg.43(1)).

<small>PARA.(1)(B)</small>
4–151   *Next of kin:* The legal definition of this term, which is not appropriate in this context, is concerned with the disposal of property to blood relatives where someone dies without making a will. The service user should be asked on admission which person he or she would wish to be contacted if the need for contact arose. This person, who in the light of the Human Rights Act 1989 and associated caselaw could either be a relative, spouse or cohabiting partner of either sex, should be treated as the next of kin of the service user. If the service user is mentally incapable of making such identification, the registered person should notify the person outside of the care home who appears to be most closely involved in the service user's life.

Appointment of liquidators etc.

4–152   **41.**—(1) Any person to whom paragraph (2) applies must—

(a) forthwith notify the Commission of his appointment, indicating the reasons for it;

(b) appoint a manager to take full-time day to day charge of the care home in any case where there is no registered manager; and

(c) within 28 days of his appointment notify the Commission of his intentions regarding the future operation of the care home.

(2) This paragraph applies to any person appointed as—

(a) the receiver or manager of the property of a company or partnership which is a registered provider in respect of a care home;

(b) a liquidator or provisional liquidator of a company which is a registered provider of a care home; or

(c) the trustee in bankruptcy of a registered provider of a care home.

DEFINITIONS

Commission: reg.2(1).   **4–153**
registered provider: reg.2(1).

GENERAL NOTE

There is no requirement for a person appointed under para.(2) to be registered with the **4–154** registration authority.

Death of registered person

42.—(1) If more than one person is registered in respect of a care home, and a **4–155** registered person dies, the surviving registered person shall without delay notify the Commission of the death in writing.

(2) If only one person is registered in respect of a care home, and he dies, his personal representatives shall notify the Commission in writing—

(a) without delay of the death; and

(b) within 28 days of their intentions regarding the future running of the home.

(3) The personal representatives of the deceased registered provider may carry on the care home without being registered in respect of it—

(a) for a period not exceeding 28 days; and

(b) for any further period as may be determined in accordance with paragraph (4).

(4) The Commission may extend the period specified in paragraph (3)(a) by such further period, not exceeding one year, as the Commission shall determine, and shall notify any such determination to the personal representatives in writing.

(5) The personal representatives shall appoint a person to take full-time day to day charge of the home during any period in which, in accordance with paragraph (3), they carry on the care home without being registered in respect of it.

DEFINITIONS

registered person: reg.2(1).   **4–156**
Commission: reg.2(1).

Offences

43.—(1) A contravention or failure to comply with any of the provisions of **4–157** regulations 4, 5, [5A,] 11, 12(1) to (4), 13(1) to (4) and (6) to (8), 14, 15, 16(1), (2)(a) to (j) and (1) to (n) and (3), 17 to 26 and 37 to 40, shall be an offence.

(2) The Commission shall not bring proceedings against a person in respect of any contravention or failure to comply with those regulations unless—

(a) subject to paragraph (4), he is a registered person;

(b) notice has been given to him in accordance with paragraph (3);

[(c) the period specified in the notice, within which the registered person may make representations to the Commission, has expired; and

(d) in a case where, in accordance with paragraph (3)(b), the notice specifies any action that is to be taken within a specified period, the period has expired and the action has not been taken within that period.]

(3) Where the Commission considers that the registered person has contravened or failed to comply with any of the provisions of the regulations mentioned in paragraph (1), it may serve a notice on the registered person specifying—

(a) in what respect in its opinion the registered person has contravened or is contravening any of the regulations, or has failed or is failing to comply with the requirements of any of the regulations;

[(b) where it is practicable for the registered person to take action for the purpose of complying with any of those regulations, the action which, in the opinion of the Commission, the registered person should take for that purpose;

(c) the period, not exceeding three months, within which the registered person should take any action specified in accordance with sub-paragraph (b);

(d) the period, not exceeding one month, within which the registered person may make representations to the Commission about the notice.]

(4) The Commission may bring proceedings against a person who was once, but no longer is, a registered person, in respect of a failure to comply with regulation 17 and for this purpose, references in paragraphs (2) and (3) to a registered person shall be taken to include such a person.

AMENDMENTS

4–158   The amendments to this regulation were made by SI 2002/865, reg.3(3) and SI 2003/1703, reg.2(4).

DEFINITIONS

4–159   registered person: reg.2(1).
Commission: reg.2(1).

GENERAL NOTE

4–160   This regulation is applied by reg.36 where a child is accommodated in the care home. Also see the General Note to these Regulations.

PARA.(3)

4–161   In *Cunningham v Lewisham LBC (Decn. No.437)*, the Registered Homes Tribunal said that the point of issuing a notice under the equivalent provision of the 1984 Act "is to secure compliance with the regulations through the threat of prosecution. If the notice is necessary and is to be effective, the threat of prosecution must be a real one." In this case the proprietor had failed to comply with six enforcement notices without being prosecuted.

Compliance with regulations

44. Where there is more than one registered person in respect of a care home, anything which is required under these regulations to be done by the registered person shall, if done by one of the registered persons, not be required to be done by any of the other registered persons. **4–162**

DEFINITION

registered person: reg.2(1). **4–163**

Adult placements

45.—(1) For the purposes of this regulation and [regulations 46 and 47], a regis- **4–164** tered provider is an adult placement carer in respect of a care home if—

(a) he is the registered provider in respect of, and manages, the care home;

(b) no person other than the registered provider manages the care home;

(c) the care home is, or forms part of—

    (i) the registered provider's home; or

    (ii) if the registered provider has more than one home, the home where he ordinarily resides;

(d) no more than three service users are accommodated in the care home;

(e) a placement agreement has been made in respect of each of the service users;

(f) each service user is over the age of 18.

(2) In this regulation [and in regulation 47], "placement agreement" means an agreement that—

(a) has been made between—

    (i) the registered provider;

    (ii) the service user;

    (iii) the local authority or other body which manages a scheme ("adult placement scheme") under which it has arranged or proposes to arrange for the service user to be accommodated in a care home;

(b) makes provision for the following matters—

    (i) the aims of the arrangements under which the service user is accommodated in the care home;

    (ii) the room to be occupied by the service user;

    (iii) the services to be provided to the service user;

    (iv) the fees to be charged;

    (v) the qualifications and experience of the registered provider;

    (vi) the terms and conditions in respect of the accommodation and services to be provided;

    (vii) services and assistance to be provided under the adult placement scheme under which the accommodation is or has been arranged.

4–165   The amendments to this regulation were made by SI 2003/1845, reg.3.

DEFINITIONS
4–166   registered provider: reg.2(1).
service user: reg.2(1).

GENERAL NOTE
4–167   In July 2002, the Department of Health issued "Policy Guidance and supplementary practice guidance for Adult Placement Schemes".

General information about adult placements can be found on the National Association for Adult Placement Services website: *www.naaps.co.uk*.

Modification of regulations in respect of adult placement carers
4–168   **46.**—(1) The following provisions of this regulation shall apply where the registered provider is an adult placement carer in respect of a care home.

(2) Regulations 4, 8, 18, 19, 21, 24, 26 to 36 and 41 (statement of purpose; appointment of manager; staffing; fitness of workers; staff views as to conduct of care home; review of quality of care home; visits by registered provider; children; appointment of liquidators etc.) and Schedules 1 and 5 to 7 (information to be included in the statement of purpose; additional information to be included in the statement of purpose where children are accommodated; additional information and documents to be obtained in respect of persons working at a care home where children are accommodated; and matters to be monitored at a care home where children are accommodated) shall not apply.

(3) Regulation 5 (service user's guide) shall have effect as if sub-paragraph (a) of paragraph (1) of that regulation were omitted.

(4) Regulation 6 (review of statement of purpose and service user's guide) shall have effect as if in paragraph (a) of that regulation the words "the statement of purpose and" were omitted.

(5) Regulation 16 (facilities and services) shall have effect as if in sub-paragraph (j) of paragraph (2) of that regulation the words "after consultation with the environmental health authority" were omitted.

(6) Regulation 23 (fitness of premises) shall have effect as if sub-paragraphs (a), (f), (g), (h), (j), (k) and (n) of paragraph (2) and paragraphs (3) to (5) of that regulation were omitted.

(7) Regulation 25 (financial position) shall have effect as if—

(a) paragraph (1) of that regulation were omitted;

(b) in paragraph (2) of that regulation, sub-paragraphs (a) to (d) were omitted;

(c) paragraphs (3) and (4) of that regulation were omitted.

(8) […]
[(9) Schedule 4 (other records to be kept in a care home) shall have effect as if paragraphs 1 to 7, 13 and 14 were omitted.]

4–169   The amendments to this paragraph were made by SI 2003/1845, reg.4.

DEFINITION
registered provider: reg.2(1).   **4–170**

Modification of regulations in respect of adult placement carer providing short term break for service user

47.—(1) The following provisions of this regulation shall apply where an adult **4–171** placement carer in respect of a care home is providing a short term break for a service user.

(2) Regulation 13 (further requirements as to health and welfare) shall have effect as if—

(a) in paragraph (1), at the beginning, the words "Subject to paragraph (1A)," were inserted; and

(b) after paragraph (1), the following paragraph was inserted—

"(1A) Where the registered provider is an adult placement carer in respect of a care home providing a short term break for a service user the registered provider shall ensure that satisfactory arrangements are made to meet the service user's medical needs."

(3) Regulation 16(2)(d) (facilities and services) shall not apply in relation to a service user who is being provided with a short term break by an adult placement carer in respect of a care home.

(4) Where the adult placement carer in respect of a care home provides only short term breaks for each of the service users, regulation 38 (notice of absence) shall not apply at any time when the care home is not providing accommodation for any service user.

(5) For the purposes of this regulation an adult placement carer in respect of a care home provides a short term break for a service user where—

(a) the service user does not ordinarily reside with the adult placement carer; and

(b) the placement agreement in respect of that service user is for a period no longer than 6 months in any 12 month period.]

AMENDMENT
This regulation was inserted by SI 2003/1845, reg.5.   **4–172**

GENERAL NOTE
This regulation is inserted in order to modify certain Regulations in relation to an adult **4–173** placement carer providing a short-term break for a service user. In this situation, a registered provider does not have to ensure that the service user is registered with a general practitioner of his choice, but instead has to ensure that satisfactory arrangements are made to meet the service user's medical needs. In addition, reg.16(2)(d) (facilities and services) does not apply to a service user being accommodated by an adult placement carer on a short-term break, and reg.38 (notice of absence) does not apply to a registered provider who provides only short-term breaks for service users at any time where no service user is accommodated in the care home. A "short-term break" is defined as occurring where the service user does not normally reside with the adult placement carer and the placement agreement in respect of a service user is for no longer than six months in any 12-month period.

Regulation 4(1)(c)   SCHEDULE 1

4–174   INFORMATION TO BE INCLUDED IN THE STATEMENT OF PURPOSE

1. The name and address of the registered provider and of any registered manager.

2. The relevant qualifications and experience of the registered provider and any registered manager.

3. The number, relevant qualifications and experience of the staff working at the care home.

4. The organisational structure of the care home.

5. The age-range and sex of the service users for whom it is intended that accommodation should be provided.

6. The range of needs that the care home is intended to meet.

7. Whether nursing is to be provided.

8. Any criteria used for admission to the care home, including the care home's policy and procedures (if any) for emergency admissions.

9. The arrangements for service users to engage in social activities, hobbies and leisure interests.

10. The arrangements made for consultation with service users about the operation of the care home.

11. The fire precautions and associated emergency procedures in the care home.

12. The arrangements made for service users to attend religious services of their choice.

13. The arrangements made for contact between service users and their relatives, friends and representatives.

14. The arrangements made for dealing with complaints.

15. The arrangements made for dealing with reviews of the service user's plan referred to in regulation 15(1).

16. The number and size of rooms in the care home.

17. Details of any specific therapeutic techniques used in the care home and arrangements made for their supervision.

18. The arrangements made for respecting the privacy and dignity of service users.

DEFINITIONS

4–175   registered provider: reg.2(1).
registered manager: reg.2(1).
service user: reg.2(1).

Regulation 7, 9, 19   SCHEDULE 2

4–176   INFORMATION AND DOCUMENTS IN RESPECT OF PERSONS CARRYING ON,
MANAGING OR WORKING AT A CARE HOME

1. Proof of the person's identity, including a recent photograph.

2. The person's birth certificate.

3. The person's current passport (if any).

4. Documentary evidence of any relevant qualifications of the person.

5. Two written references relating to the person.

6. Evidence that the person is physically and mentally fit for the purposes of the work which he is to perform at the care home or, where it is impracticable for the person to obtain such evidence, a declaration signed by the person that he is so fit.

7. Either—

(a) where the certificate is required for a purpose relating to section 115(5)(ea) of the Police Act 1997 (registration under Part II of the Care Standards Act 2000), or the position falls within section 115(3) or (4) of that Act, an enhanced criminal record certificate issued under section 115 of that Act; or

(b) in any other case, a criminal record certificate issued under section 113 of that Act,

including, where applicable, the matters specified in [sections 113(3A) and 116(6A) of that Act and the following provisions once they are in force, namely section 113(3C)(a) and (b) and section 115(6B)(a) and (b) of that Act.]

AMENDMENTS
The amendments to this Schedule were made by SI 2002/865, reg.2(5).   **4–177**

GENERAL NOTE
PARA.7
Certificates under this paragraph are obtained from the Criminal Records Bureau which **4–178** is an Executive Agency of the Home Office which carries out criminal records checks in England and Wales. These checks are called "disclosures" and have taken the place of the previous system of police checks. The CRB has a website at *www.crb.gov.uk* and has two telephone contacts: one for information (0870 90 90 822) and one for registration applications (0870 90 90 822).

There are currently two levels of CRB disclosures:

Standard Disclosures: These are primarily for positions that involve working with children or regular contact with vulnerable adults. They contain all convictions held on the Police National Computer (including "spent" convictions, *i.e.* those that happened some time ago and which normally do not need to be revealed under the terms of the Rehabilitation of Offenders Act 1974) plus details of any cautions, reprimands or warnings. The standard disclosure also includes information contained on government departments' lists of people considered unsuitable to work with children, and vulnerable adults. With regard to services regulated under the Act, a standard disclosure is required where the job entails regular contact with children or vulnerable adults, but does not involve directly working with, caring for, or supervising these categories or service users. Jobs that would fall into this category include domestic, catering or maintenance posts.

Enhanced Disclosures: These are for posts which involve regularly caring for, training, supervising, or being in sole charge of children or vulnerable adults. The disclosure involves an extra level of checking with local police force records in addition to the checks with the Police National Computer and government departments' lists. It is up to the Chief Constable of the local police force to decide what, if any, information held by that force is disclosed to the applicant.

A person who needs a disclosure from the CRB must have their disclosure application form countersigned by a person authorised to do so by a body which is registered with the CRB (a "registered body"). This person will receive a copy of the disclosure, as will the person to whom the disclosure relates. The person countersigning the form is required to verify the identity and address of the applicant. An application made in respect of a provider or manager newly applying for registration must be countersigned by the registration authority. All other applications must be countersigned in accordance with arrangements made by the providers, *i.e.* by the provider becoming a registered body or by arranging with another organisation which is already a registered body for it to countersign application forms on their behalf. The CRB calls organisations that are available to do this "Umbrella Bodies". Detailed guidance on making an application can be found on the CRB website.

The NCSC published a "Guide to Criminal Records Bureau Checks on service providers, managers and staff" (revised January 14, 2004). This sets out a table which shows who needs which level of disclosure and by when. The guidance makes the following statement about the implications of a criminal conviction:

"If an offence or other information is disclosed, this does not necessarily mean that a registration or other NCSC approval or consent will be refused. We will consider fairly in each individual case whether the offence or other information indicates a significant risk to children or vulnerable adults. We will take into account the nature of the offence or other information disclosed, the role of the person concerned is to fulfil, the type of service for children or vulnerable adults involved, and the nature and needs of the children or vulnerable adults likely to use the service. Decisions are to be made on the basis of an assessment of any possible risk to children or vulnerable adults, rather than the simple fact of a conviction or other information disclosed. Where there is significant doubt, the decision will however always favour the welfare of children or vulnerable adults."

Falls within s.115(3) or (4): A position falls within s.115(3) if it involves regularly caring for, training, supervising or being in sole charge of persons under 18. A position is within s.115(4) if it is of a kind specified in regulations and involves regularly caring for, training, supervising or being in sole charge of persons under 18 or over.

Regulation 17(1)(a)   **SCHEDULE 3**

4–179   RECORDS TO BE KEPT IN A CARE HOME IN RESPECT OF EACH SERVICE USER

1. The following documents in respect of each service user—

(a) the assessment referred to in regulation 14(1);

(b) the service user's plan referred to in regulation 15(1).

2. A photograph of the service user.

3. A record of the following matters in respect of each service user—

(a) the name, address, date of birth and marital status of each service user;

(b) the name, address and telephone number of the service user's next of kin or of any person authorised to act on his behalf;

(c) the name, address and telephone number of the service user's general practitioner and of any officer of a local social services authority whose duty it is to supervise the welfare of the service user;

(d) the date on which the service user entered the care home;

(e) the date on which the service user left the care home;

(f) if the service user is transferred to another care home or to a hospital, the name of the care home or hospital and the date on which the service user is transferred;

(g) if the service user died at the care home, the date, time and cause of death;

(h) the name and address of any authority, organisation or other body, which arranged the service user's admission to the care home;

(i) a record of all medicines kept in the care home for the service user, and the date on which they were administered to the service user;

(j) a record of any accident affecting the service user in the care home and of any other incident in the care home which is detrimental to the health or welfare of the service user, which record shall include the nature, date and time of the accident or incident, whether medical treatment was required and the name of the persons who were respectively in charge of the care home and supervising the service user;

(k) a record of any nursing provided to the service user, including a record of his condition and any treatment or surgical intervention;

(l) details of any specialist communications needs of the service user and methods of communication that may be appropriate to the service user;

(m) details of any plan relating to the service user in respect of medication, nursing, specialist health care or nutrition;

(n) a record of incidence of pressure sores and of treatment provided to the service user;

(o) a record of falls and of treatment provided to the service user;

(p) a record of any physical restraint used on the service user;

(q) a record of any limitations agreed with the service user as to the service user's freedom of choice, liberty of movement and power to make decisions.

4. A copy of correspondence relating to each service user.

DEFINITIONS
service user: reg.2(1).   **4–180**
general practitioner: reg.2(1).

GENERAL NOTE
PARA.2
A photograph of a mentally capable service user should not be taken in the absence of the **4–181**
service user's consent as this would constitute of beach of that person's rights under Art.8 of
the European Convention on Human Rights. A justification for taking a photograph of a
mentally incapable service user must be found in Art.8(2) which authorises an interference
with a persons right to respect for his private and family if it is required for the prevention of
disorder or crime, for the protection of health or morals or for the protection of the rights
and freedoms of others.

PARA.3(G)
Under s.46(1) of the Public Health (Control of Disease) Act 1984 it is the duty of the **4–182**
relevant district or London borough council "to cause to be buried or cremated the body
of any person who has died or been found dead in their area, in any case where it appears
to the authority that no suitable arrangements for the disposal of the body have been or are
being made otherwise than by the authority." A power to claim re-imbursement is contained in s.46(5).

PARA.(3)(I)
Note *Ruggee v The Registered Homes Tribunal and Bradford Health Authority*, **4–183**
December 1, 1999 (CO/3925/98) which is considered in the note on reg.15(5) of the
Private and Voluntary Healthcare (England) Regulations 2001.

Regulation 17(2)   **SCHEDULE 4**

OTHER RECORDS TO BE KEPT IN A CARE HOME   **4–184**

1. A copy of the statement of purpose.
2. A copy of the service user's guide.
3. A record of all accounts kept in the care home.
4. A copy of all inspection reports.
5. A copy of any report made under regulation 26(4)(c).
6. A record of all persons employed at the care home, including in respect of each person
[employed—]

(a) his full name, address, date of birth, qualifications and experience;

(b) a copy of his birth certificate and passport;

(c)   a copy of each reference obtained in respect of him;

(d)   the dates on which he commences and ceases to be so employed;

(e)   the position he holds at the care home, the work that he performs and the number of hours for which he is employed each week;

(f)   correspondence, reports, records of disciplinary action and any other records in relation to his employment.

7. A copy of the duty roster of persons working at the care home, and a record of whether the roster was actually worked.

8. A record of the care home's charges to service users, including any extra amounts payable for additional services not covered by those charges, and the amounts paid by or in respect of each service user.

9. A record of all money or other valuables deposited by a service user for safekeeping or received on the service user's behalf, which—

(a)   shall state the date on which the money or valuables were deposited or received, the date on which any money or valuables were returned to a service user or used, at the request of the service user, on his behalf and, where applicable, the purpose for which the money or valuables were used; and

(b)   shall include the written acknowledgement of the return of the money or valuables.

10. A record of furniture brought by a service user into the room occupied by him.

11. A record of all complaints made by service users or representatives or relatives of service users or by persons working at the care home about the operation of the care home, and the action taken by the registered person in respect of any such complaint.

12. A record of any of the following events that occur in the care home—

(a)   any accident;

(b)   any incident which is detrimental to the health or welfare of a service user, including the outbreak of infectious disease in the care home;

(c)   any injury or illness;

(d)   any fire;

(e)   except where a record to which paragraph 14 refers is to be made, any occasion on which the fire alarm equipment is operated;

(f)   any theft or burglary.

13. Records of the food provided for service users in sufficient detail to enable any person inspecting the record to determine whether the diet is satisfactory, in relation to nutrition and otherwise, and of any special diets prepared for individual service users.

14. A record of every fire practice, drill or test of fire equipment (including fire alarm equipment) conducted in the care home and of any action taken to remedy defects in the fire equipment.

15. A statement of the procedure to be followed in the event of a fire, or where a fire alarm is given.

16. A statement of the procedure to be followed in the event of accidents or in the event of a service user becoming missing.

17. A record of all visitors to the care home, including the names of visitors.

<small>AMENDMENTS</small>

4–185   The amendments to this Schedule were made by SI 2002/865, reg.3(3).

DEFINITIONS
statement of purpose: reg.2(1).
service users guide: reg.2(1).
inspection report: reg.2(1).
employed: reg.2(1).
service user: reg.2(1).
representative: reg.2(1).
relative: reg.2(1).

GENERAL NOTE
PARA.6(B)

It is difficult to ascertain a legitimate reason to explain why the registered person should **4–187** be required to keep copies of the birth certificates and passports of staff at the home.

Regulations 4 and 29 **SCHEDULE 5**

ADDITIONAL INFORMATION TO BE INCLUDED IN THE STATEMENT OF PURPOSE **4–188**
WHERE CHILDREN ARE ACCOMMODATED

1. The following details about the children for whom it is intended that accommodation should be provided—

(a) their age-range;

(b) their sex;

(c) the number of children;

(d) whether they are disabled, have special needs or any other special characteristics; and

(e) the range of needs that the care home is intended to meet.

2. Any criteria used for admission to the care home, including the care home's policy and procedures for emergency admissions, if applicable.

3. If the care home provides or is intended to provide accommodation for more than six children, a description of the positive outcomes intended for children in a care home of such a size, and of the care home's strategy for counteracting any adverse effects arising from its size, on the children accommodated there.

4. A description of the care home's underlying ethos and philosophy, and where this is based on any theoretical or therapeutic model, a description of that model.

5. The facilities and services to be provided or made available, within and outside the care home, for the children accommodated there.

6. The arrangements made to protect and promote the health of the children accommodated there.

7. The arrangements for the promotion of the education of the children accommodated there, including the facilities for private study.

8. The arrangements to promote children's participation in hobbies and recreational, sporting and cultural activities.

9. The arrangements made for consultation with the children accommodated there about the operation of the care home.

10. The policy on behaviour management and the use of restraint in the care home, including in particular the methods of control and discipline and the disciplinary measures which may be used, the circumstances in which any such measures will be used and who will be permitted to use and authorise them.

11. The arrangements for child protection and to counter bullying.

12. The fire precautions and associated emergency procedures in the care home.

13. The arrangements made for the children's religious instruction and observance.

14. The arrangements made for contact between a child accommodated there and his parents, relatives and friends.

15. The procedure for dealing with any unauthorised absence of a child from the care home.

16. The arrangements for dealing with complaints.

17. The arrangements for dealing with reviews of the placement plans of children accommodated there.

18. The type of accommodation and sleeping arrangements provided, and, where applicable, how children are to be grouped, and in what circumstances they are to share bedrooms.

19. Details of any specific therapeutic techniques used in the care home and arrangements for their supervision.

20. A description of the care home's policy on anti-discriminatory practice in relation to children and children's rights.

Regulations 19 and 33(b)　　　　**SCHEDULE 6**

4–189 Additional Information and Documents to be Obtained in Respect of Persons Working at a Care Home where Children are Accommodated

1. Two written references, including a reference from the last employer.

2. Where a person has previously worked in a position whose duties involved work with children or vulnerable adults, so far as reasonably practicable, verification of the reason why the employment or position ended.

3. A full employment history, together with a satisfactory written explanation of any gaps in employment.

Regulations 24 and 35(a)　　　　**SCHEDULE 7**

4–190　　Matters to be Monitored at a Care Home where Children are Accommodated

1. Compliance with any plan for the care of the child prepared by the placing authority and the placement plan of each child accommodated in the care home.

2. The deposit and issue of money and other valuables handed in for safekeeping.

3. Daily menus.

4. All accidents and injuries sustained in the care home or by children accommodated there.

5. Any illnesses of children accommodated in the care home.

6. Complaints in relation to children accommodated in the care home and their outcomes.

7. Any allegations or suspicions of abuse in respect of children accommodated in the care home and the outcome of any investigation.

8. Staff recruitment records and conduct of required checks for new workers in the care home.

9. Visitors to the care home and to children in the care home.

10. Notifications of the events listed in Schedule 5 to the Children's Homes Regulations 2001.

11. Any unauthorised absence from the care home of a child accommodated there.

12. The use of disciplinary measures in respect of children accommodated in the care home.

13. The use of physical restraint in respect of children accommodated in the care home.

THE PRIVATE AND VOLUNTARY HEALTH CARE (ENGLAND) REGULATIONS 2001

(SI 2001/3968)

*Dated December 11, 2001, and made by the Secretary of State for Health under
the Care Standards Act 2000 (c.14), ss.2(4), (7)(f) and (8), 22(1), (2)(a) to (d), (f)
to (j), (5)(a) and (7)(a) to (h), (j) and (k), 25(1), 34(1), 35(1) and 118(5) to (7).*

GENERAL NOTE

These Regulations apply to England only.   **4–191**

PART VI

PART VII

SCHEDULES

PART I

GENERAL

Citation, commencement and extent

1.—(1) These Regulations may be cited as the Private and Voluntary Health **4–193** Care (England) Regulations 2001 and shall come into force on 1st April 2002.

(2) These Regulations extend to England only.

Interpretation

2.—(1) In these Regulations—   **4–194**

"the Act" means the Care Standards Act 2000;

"agency" means an independent medical agency;

["Commission" means the Commission for Healthcare Audit and Inspection;]

"dentist" means a person registered in the dentists register under the Dentists Act 1984;

"establishment" means an independent hospital, including an independent hospital in which treatment or nursing (or both) are provided for persons liable to be detained under the Mental Health Act 1983, or an independent clinic;

"general practitioner" means a medical practitioner who—

   (a) provides general medical services within the meaning of Part II of the NHS Act;
   (b) performs personal medical services in connection with a pilot scheme under the National Health Service (Primary Care) Act 1997; or
   (c) provides services which correspond to services provided under Part II of the NHS Act, otherwise than in pursuance of that Act;

"health care professional" means a person who is registered as a member of any profession to which section 60(2) of the Health Act 1999 applies, or who is a clinical psychologist or child psychotherapist, and "health care profession" shall be construed accordingly;

"medical device" has the same meaning as in the Medical Devices Regulations 1994;

"medical practitioner" means a registered medical practitioner;

"midwife" means a registered midwife who has notified her intention to practise to the local supervisory authority in accordance with any rules made under section 14(1)(b) of the Nurses, Midwives and Health Visitors Act 1997;

"the NHS Act" means the National Health Service Act 1977;

"organisation" means a body corporate or any unincorporated association other than a partnership;

"patient", in relation to any establishment or agency, means a person for whom treatment is provided in or for the purposes of the establishment, or for the purposes of the agency;

"patients' guide" means the guide compiled in accordance with regulation 7;

"practising privileges" in relation to a medical practitioner, refers to the grant to a person who is not employed in an independent hospital of permission to practise in that hospital;

"registered manager", in relation to an establishment or agency, means a person who is registered under Part II of the Act as the manager of the establishment or agency;

"registered person", in relation to an establishment or agency, means any person who is the registered provider or the registered manager of the establishment or agency;

"registered provider", in relation to an establishment or agency, means a person who is registered under Part II of the Act as the person carrying on the establishment or agency;

"responsible individual" shall be construed in accordance with regulation 10(2)(b)(i);

"statement of purpose" means the written statement compiled in accordance with regulation 6;

"treatment" includes palliative care and nursing and listed services within the meaning of section 2 of the Act.

(2) In these Regulations, a reference—

(a) to a numbered regulation or Schedule is to the regulation in, or Schedule to, these Regulations bearing that number;

(b) in a regulation or Schedule to a numbered paragraph, is to the paragraph in that regulation or Schedule bearing that number;

(c) in a paragraph to a lettered or numbered sub-paragraph is to the sub-paragraph in that paragraph bearing that letter or number.

(3) In these Regulations, references to employing a person include employing a person whether under a contract of service or a contract for services, and references to an employee or to a person being employed shall be construed accordingly.

AMENDMENT
The definition of "Commission" was inserted by SI 2004/664, art.1, para.4.   **4–195**

Prescribed techniques or technology and exceptions to the definition of independent hospital

3.—(1) Subject to paragraph (2), for the purposes of section 2 of the Act, "listed **4–196** services" include treatment using any of the following techniques or technology—

(a) a Class 3B or Class 4 laser product, as defined in Part I of British Standard EN 60825-1 (Radiation safety of laser products and systems);

(b) an intense light, being broadband non-coherent light which is filtered to produce a specified range of wavelengths; such filtered radiation being delivered to the body with the aim of causing thermal, mechanical or chemical damage to structures such as hair follicles and skin blemishes while sparing surrounding tissues;

(c) haemodialysis or peritoneal dialysis;

(d) endoscopy;

(e) hyperbaric oxygen therapy, being the administration of pure oxygen through a mask to a patient who is in a sealed chamber which is gradually pressurised with compressed air, except where the primary use of that chamber is—

 (i) pursuant to regulation 6(3)(b) of the Diving at Work Regulations 1997 or regulation 8 or 12 of the Work in Compressed Air Regulations 1996; or

 (ii) otherwise for the treatment of workers in connection with the work which they perform; and

(f) in vitro fertilisation techniques, being treatment services for which a licence may be granted under paragraph 1 of Schedule 2 to the Human Fertilisation and Embryology Act 1990.

(2) Listed services shall not include treatment using the following techniques or technology—

(a) treatment for the relief of muscular and joint pain using an infra-red heat treatment lamp;

(b) treatment using a Class 3B laser where such treatment is carried out by or under the supervision of a health care professional; and

(c) the use of an apparatus (not being an apparatus falling within paragraph (1)(b)), for acquiring an artificial suntan, consisting of a lamp or lamps emitting ultraviolet rays.

(3) For the purposes of section 2 of the Act, establishments of the following descriptions are excepted from being independent hospitals—

(a) an establishment which is a hospital by virtue of section 2(3)(a)(i) of the Act solely because its main purpose is to provide medical or psychiatric treatment for illness or mental disorder but which provides no overnight beds for patients;

(b) an establishment which is a service hospital within the meaning of section 13(9) of the Armed Forces Act 1981;

(c) an establishment which is, or forms part of, a prison, remand centre, young offender institution or secure training centre within the meaning of the Prison Act 1952;

(d) an establishment which is an independent clinic by virtue of regulation 4;

(e) an establishment (not being a health service hospital) which has as its sole or main purpose the provision by a general practitioner of general medical services within the meaning of Part II of the NHS Act or personal medical services in connection with a pilot scheme under the National Health Service (Primary Care) Act 1997; and such an establishment shall not become an independent hospital as a result of the provision of listed services to a patient by such a general practitioner;

(f) the private residence of a patient or patients in which treatment is provided to such patient or patients, but to no-one else;

(g) sports grounds and gymnasia where health professionals provide treatment to persons taking part in sporting activities and events; and

(h) a surgery or consulting room, not being part of a hospital, where a medical practitioner provides medical services solely under arrangements made on behalf of the patients by their employer or another person.

(4)   *[Amends s.2(7) of the Care Standards Act 2000.]*

DEFINITIONS

4–197   treatment: reg.2(1).
establishment: reg.2(1).
NHS Act: reg.2(1).
general practitioner: reg.2(1).
patient: reg.2(1).
medical practitioner: reg.2(1).

GENERAL NOTE

PARA.(1)(A)

4–198   Copies of EN 60825-1 may be obtained from BSI Customer Services, 389 Chiswick High Road, London W4 4AL.

PARA.(2)(B)
  Under the supervision of: The health care professional must be present in order to supervise **4–199**
the treatment.

PARA.(3)(A)
  This exclusion does not apply to hospitals which provide palliative care.   **4–200**

PARA.(3)(E)
  An establishment which is not a NHS hospital is not registerable as an independent hos- **4–201**
pital because NHS medical services, which may include listed services, are provided to
patients on the establishment by a GP.

PARA.(3)(G)
  Health professionals: See the definition of health care professional in reg.2.

PARA.(3)(H)
  This exclusion covers occupational health schemes where the employer refers the patient **4–202**
to the medical practitioner.

Meaning of independent clinic

4.—(1) For the purposes of section 2(4) of the Act, establishments of the fol- **4–203**
lowing kinds are prescribed—

  (a) a walk-in centre, in which one or more medical practitioners provide ser-
      vices of a kind which, if provided in pursuance of the NHS Act, would
      be provided as general medical services under Part II of that Act; and

  (b) a surgery or consulting room in which a medical practitioner who provides
      no services in pursuance of the NHS Act provides medical services of any
      kind (including psychiatric treatment) otherwise than under arrangements
      made on behalf of the patients by their employer or another person.

  (2) Where two or more medical practitioners use different parts of the same
premises as a surgery or consulting room, or use the same surgery or consulting
room at different times, each of the medical practitioners shall be regarded as carrying on a separate independent clinic unless they are in practice together.

DEFINITIONS
  establishment: reg.2(1).   **4–204**
  medical practitioner: reg.2(1).
  patient: reg.2(1).

GENERAL NOTE
PARA.(1)(A)
  As an establishment cannot be an independent clinic if it provides NHS services (s.2(4)), **4–205**
a walk-in centre cannot provide services to NHS patients.

PARA.(1)(B)
  This covers surgeries and consulting rooms where private medical practice is conducted, **4–206**
but excludes an occupational health scheme where the employer refers the patient to the
medical practitioner.

Exception of undertaking from the definition of independent medical agency

4–207   **5.** For the purposes of the Act, any undertaking which consists of the provision of medical services by a medical practitioner solely under arrangements made on behalf of the patients by their employer or another person shall be excepted from being an independent medical agency.

DEFINITIONS

4–208   medical practitioner: reg.2(1).
patient: reg.2(1).

Statement of purpose

4–209   **6.**—(1)The registered person shall compile in relation to the establishment or agency a written statement (in these Regulations referred to as "the statement of purpose") which shall consist of a statement as to the matters listed in Schedule 1.

(2) The registered person shall supply a copy of the statement of purpose to the Commission and shall make the statement available for inspection by every patient and any person acting on behalf of a patient.

(3) Nothing in regulation 15(1) or 25(1) and (2) shall require or authorise the registered person to contravene, or not to comply with—

(a) any other provision of these Regulations; or

(b) the conditions for the time being in force in relation to the registration of the registered person under Part II of the Act.

DEFINITIONS

4–210   registered person: reg.2(1).
establishment: reg.2(1).
agency: reg.2(1).
patient: reg.2(1).
Commission: reg.2(1).

GENERAL NOTE

4–211   The statement of purpose must be kept under review and, where appropriate, revised (reg.8).

Patients' guide

4–212   **7.**—(1) The registered person shall produce a written guide to the establishment or agency (in these Regulations referred to as "the patients' guide") which shall consist of—

(a) a summary of the statement of purpose;

(b) the terms and conditions in respect of services to be provided for patients, including as to the amount and method of payment of charges for all aspects of their treatment;

(c) a standard form of contract for the provision of services and facilities by the registered provider to patients;

(d) a summary of the complaints procedure established under regulation 23;

(e) a summary of the results of the consultation conducted in accordance with regulation 17(3);

(f) the address and telephone number of the Commission; and

(g) the most recent inspection report prepared by the Commission or information as to how a copy of that report may be obtained.

(2) The registered person shall supply a copy of the patients' guide to the Commission, and shall make the patients' guide available for inspection by every patient and any person acting on behalf of a patient.

DEFINITIONS

registered person: reg.2(1).   **4–213**
establishment: reg.2(1).
agency: reg.2(1).
statement of purpose: reg.2(1).
Commission: reg.2(1).
patient: reg.2(1).
registered provider: reg.2(1).
inspection report: reg.2(1).

GENERAL NOTE

The patient's guide must be kept under review and, where appropriate, revised (reg.8). **4–214**

Review of statement of purpose and patients' guide

8. The registered person shall—   **4–215**

(a) keep under review and, where appropriate, revise the statement of purpose and the content of the patients' guide; and

(b) notify the Commission of any such revision.

DEFINITIONS

registered person: reg.2(1).   **4–216**
statement of purpose: reg.2(1).
patient's guide: reg.2(1).
Commission: reg.2(1).

Policies and procedures

9. The registered person shall prepare and implement written statements of the **4–217** policies to be applied and the procedures to be followed in or for the purposes of an establishment in relation to—

(a) the arrangements for admission or acceptance of patients, their transfer to a hospital where required and, in the case of an establishment which admits in-patients, their discharge;

(b) the arrangements for assessment, diagnosis and treatment of patients;

(c) ensuring that the premises used by or for the purposes of an establishment are at all times fit for the purpose for which they are used;

(d) monitoring the quality and suitability of facilities and equipment;

(e) identifying, assessing and managing risks to employees, patients and visitors associated with the operation of the establishment;

(f) the creation, management, handling and storage of records and other information;

(g) the provision of information to patients and others;

(h) the recruitment, induction and retention of employees and their employment conditions;

(i) the grant and withdrawal of practising privileges to medical practitioners in establishments where such privileges are granted; and

(j) ensuring that, where research is carried out in an establishment, it is carried out with the consent of any patient or patients involved, is appropriate for the establishment concerned and is conducted in accordance with up-to-date and authoritative published guidance on the conduct of research projects.

(2) The registered person shall prepare and implement a written statement of the policies to be applied and the procedures to be followed for the purposes of an agency in relation to—

(a) the arrangements for transfer to a hospital, where required; and

(b) each of the matters specified in sub-paragraphs (b), (f), (g) and (h) of paragraph (1).

(3) The registered person shall prepare and implement written statements of policies to be applied and procedures to be followed in or for the purposes of an establishment, or for the purpose of an agency, which ensure that—

(a) the competence of each patient to consent to treatment is assessed;

(b) in the case of a competent patient, properly informed consent to treatment is obtained;

(c) in the case of a patient who is not competent, he is, so far as practicable, consulted before any treatment proposed for him is administered; and

(d) information about a patient's health and treatment is disclosed only to those persons who need to be aware of that information in order to treat the patient effectively or minimise any risk of the patient harming himself or another person, or for the purposes of the proper administration of the establishment or agency.

(4) The registered person shall review the operation of each policy and procedure implemented under—

(a) this regulation;

(b) regulation 23; and

(c) in so far as they apply to him, regulations 35, 41(10), 45 and 46, at intervals of not more than three years and shall, where appropriate, prepare and implement revised policies and procedures.

(5) The registered person shall make a copy of all written statements prepared in accordance with this regulation available for inspection by the Commission.

DEFINITIONS

    registered person: reg.2(1).   **4–218**
    establishment: reg.2(1).
    patient: reg.2(1).
    treatment: reg.2(1).
    employment: reg.2(3).
    practising privileges: reg.2(1).
    agency: reg.2(1).
    Commission: reg.2(1).

GENERAL NOTE

PARA.(3)(A)

The competence of the patient to consent to every proposed treatment must be assessed. **4–219**

PART II

REGISTERED PERSONS

Fitness of registered provider

10.—(1) A person shall not carry on an establishment or agency unless he is fit **4–220** to do so.

(2) A person is not fit to carry on an establishment or agency unless the person—

  (a) is an individual, who carries on the establishment or agency—

      (i) otherwise than in partnership with others, and he satisfies the requirements set out in paragraph (3);
      (ii) in partnership with others, and he and each of his partners satisfies the requirements set out in paragraph (3);

  (b) is a partnership, and each of the partners satisfies the requirements set out in paragraph (3);

  (c) is an organisation and—

      (i) the organisation has given notice to the Commission of the name, address and position in the organisation of an individual (in these Regulations referred to as "the responsible individual") who is a director, manager, secretary or other officer of the organisation and is responsible for supervising the management of the establishment or agency; and
      (ii) that individual satisfies the requirements set out in paragraph (3).

(3) The requirements are that—

  (a) he is of integrity and good character;

  (b) he is physically and mentally fit to carry on the establishment or agency; and

(c) full and satisfactory information is available [in relation to him in respect of each of the matters specified in Schedule 2.]

(4) [...]

(5) A person shall not carry on an establishment or agency if—

(a) he has been adjudged bankrupt or sequestration of his estate has been awarded and (in either case) he has not been discharged and the bankruptcy order has not been annulled or rescinded; or

(b) he has made a composition or arrangement with his creditors and has not been discharged in respect of it.

AMENDMENTS

4–221   The amendments to this Regulation were made by SI 2002/865, reg.10(2).

DEFINITIONS

4–222   establishment: reg.2(1).
agency: reg.2(1).
organisation: reg.2(1).
Commission: reg.2(1).

GENERAL NOTE

4–223   The notion of fitness is considered in the note on reg.7 of the Care Homes Regulations 2001.

Appointment of manager

4–224   **11.**—(1) The registered provider shall appoint an individual to manage an establishment or agency if—

(a) there is no registered manager in respect of the establishment or agency; and

(b) the registered provider—

   (i) is an organisation or a partnership;
   (ii) is not a fit person to manage an establishment or agency; or
   (iii) is not, or does not intend to be, in full-time day to day charge of the establishment or agency.

(2) Where the registered provider appoints a person to manage the establishment or agency, he shall forthwith give notice to the Commission of—

(a) the name of the person so appointed; and

(b) the date on which the appointment is to take effect.

DEFINITIONS

4–225   registered provider: reg.2(1).
establishment: reg.2(1).
agency: reg.2(1).
organisation: reg.2(1).
Commission: reg.2(1).

A person cannot manages an establishment or agency unless he is fit to do so (reg.12)   **4–226**

Fitness of registered manager
12.—(1) A person shall not manage an establishment or agency unless he is fit   **4–227**
to do so.
   (2) A person is not fit to manage an establishment or agency unless—

   (a) he is of integrity and good character;
   (b) having regard to the size of the establishment or agency and the number and
         needs of the patients—

      (i) he has the qualifications, skills and experience necessary to manage the
            establishment or agency; and
      (ii) he is physically and mentally fit to do so; and

   (c) full and satisfactory information is available [in relation to him in respect of
         each of the matters specified in Schedule 2.]

   (3) [...]

AMENDMENTS
   The amendments to this regulation were made by SI 2002/865, reg.10(3).   **4–228**

DEFINITIONS
   establishment: reg.2(1).   **4–229**
   agency: reg.2(1).
   patient: reg.2(1).

GENERAL NOTE
   The notion of fitness is considered in the note on reg.7 of the Care Homes Regulations **4–230**
2001. The interviewing of potential managers is considered in the note on reg.9 of the 2001
Regulations.

Registered person—general requirements
13.—(1) The registered provider and the registered manager shall, having **4–231**
regard to the size of the establishment or agency and the number and needs of
the patients, carry on or (as the case may be) manage the establishment or agency
with sufficient care, competence and skill.
   (2) If the registered provider is—

   (a) an individual, he shall undertake;
   (b) an organisation, it shall ensure that the responsible individual undertakes;
   (c) a partnership, it shall ensure that one of the partners undertakes,

from time to time such training as is appropriate to ensure that he has the skills
necessary for carrying on the establishment or agency.
   (3) The registered manager shall undertake from time to time such training as is
appropriate to ensure that he has the skills necessary for managing the establishment or agency.

DEFINITIONS
4–232   registered provider: reg.2(1).
registered manager: reg.2(1).
establishment: reg.2(1).
agency: reg.2(1).
patient: reg.2(1).
organisation: reg.2(1).
responsible individual: reg.2(1).

Notification of offences
4–233   **14.** Where the registered person or the responsible individual is convicted of any criminal offence, whether in England and Wales or elsewhere, he shall forthwith give notice in writing to the Commission of—

(a) the date and place of the conviction;

(b) the offence of which he was convicted; and

(c) the penalty imposed on him in respect of the offence.

DEFINITIONS
4–234   registered person: reg.2(1).
responsible individual: reg.2(1).

PART III

CONDUCT OF HEALTH CARE ESTABLISHMENTS AND AGENCIES

Chapter 1—Quality of Service Provision

Quality of treatment and other service provision
4–235   **15.**—(1) Subject to regulation 6(3), the registered person shall provide treatment and any other services to patients in accordance with the statement of purpose, and shall ensure that the treatment and any other services provided to each patient—

(a) meet his individual needs;

(b) reflect published research evidence and guidance issued by the appropriate professional and expert bodies, as to good practice in the treatment of the condition from which the patient is suffering; and

(c) are (where necessary) provided by means of appropriate equipment.

(2) The registered person shall ensure that all equipment used in or for the purposes of the establishment, or for the purposes of the agency is—

(a) suitable for the purposes for which it is to be used; and

(b) properly maintained and in good working order.

(3) Where reusable medical devices are used in an establishment or agency, the registered person shall ensure that appropriate procedures are implemented in relation to cleaning, disinfection, inspection, packaging, sterilisation, transportation and storage of such devices.

(4) The procedures implemented in accordance with paragraph (3) shall be such as to ensure that reusable medical devices are handled safely and decontaminated effectively prior to re-use.

(5) The registered person shall make suitable arrangements for the ordering, recording, handling, safe keeping, safe administration and disposal of medicines used in or for the purposes of the establishment, or for the purposes of the agency.

(6) The registered person shall make suitable arrangements to minimise the risk of infection and toxic conditions and the spread of infection between patients and staff (including medical practitioners with practising privileges).

(7) If an establishment provides food for patients, the registered provider shall ensure that it is—

(a) provided in adequate quantities and at appropriate intervals;

(b) properly prepared, wholesome and nutritious; and

(c) suitable for the needs of patients,

and that the menu is varied at suitable intervals.

DEFINITIONS

registered person: reg.2(1).   **4–236**
patient: reg.2(1).
treatment: reg.2(1).
statement of purpose: reg.2(1).
establishment: reg.2(1).
agency: reg.2(1).
medical devices: reg.2(1).
practicing privileges: reg.2(1).

GENERAL NOTE
PARA.(5)

In *Ruggee v The Registered Homes Tribunal and Bradford Health Authority*, December **4–237** 1, 1999 (CO/3925/98), Sullivan J. considered a similar provision in the 1984 Act and said that there was nothing illogical in the Registered Homes Tribunal saying that one breach of the provision would not of itself a finding of unfitness, but then going on to consider the attitude of the appellant appearing before it to the breach. His Lordship considered that there might be a considerable difference between an appellant who promptly acknowl-edged his or her error, recorded it in a proper manner and thus showed his or her determination that it would never happen again, and an appellant who shrugged off the error, failed to report it and then sought to minimise it, thus appearing to be unaware of its significance.

Care and welfare of patients

16.—(1) The registered person shall, so far as practicable, enable each patient **4–238** to make decisions about matters affecting the way in which he is cared for and his general welfare.

(2) The registered person shall ensure that patients are permitted to control their own money, except where a patient does not wish, or lacks the capacity, to do so, in which case the registered person shall ensure that patient monies are properly held and recorded and that receipts are issued as appropriate.

(3) The registered person shall, so far as practicable, ascertain and take into account the wishes and feelings of all patients in determining the manner in which they are cared for and services are provided to them.

(4) The registered person shall make suitable arrangements to ensure that the establishment or agency is conducted—

(a) in a manner which respects the privacy and dignity of patients; and

(b) with due regard to the sex, religious and spiritual needs, racial origin, and cultural and linguistic background and any disability of patients.

(5) The registered provider and the registered manager (if any) shall each take all reasonable steps to ensure that the establishment or agency is conducted on the basis of good personal and professional relationships—

(a) between each other; and

(b) between each of them and the patients and staff.

DEFINITIONS
4–239   registered person: reg.2(1).
          patient: reg.2(1).
          establishment: reg.2(1).
          agency: reg.2(1).
          registered manager: reg.2(1).
          patient: reg.2(1).
          treatment: reg.2(1).

Review of quality of treatment and other services
4–240   **17.**—(1) The registered person shall introduce and maintain a system for reviewing at appropriate intervals the quality of treatment and other services provided in or for the purposes of an establishment or for the purposes of an agency.

(2) The registered person shall supply to the Commission a report in respect of any review conducted by him for the purposes of paragraph (1) and make a copy of the report available to patients.

(3) The system referred to in paragraph (1) shall provide for consultation with patients and their representatives.

DEFINITIONS
4–241   registered person: reg.2(1).
          treatment: reg.2(1).
          establishment: reg.2(1).
          agency: reg.2(1).
          Commission: reg.2(1).

GENERAL NOTE
4–242   There is no equivalent to reg.14 of the Care Homes Regulations 2001 requiring the assessment of the patient prior to admission.

Staffing
4–243   **18.**—(1) The registered person shall, having regard to the nature of the establishment or agency and the number and needs of patients, ensure that there is at all

166

times an appropriate number of suitably qualified, skilled and experienced persons employed in or for the purposes of the establishment or, as the case may be, for the purposes of the agency.

(2) The registered person shall ensure that each person employed in or for the purposes of the establishment or, for the purposes of the agency—

(a) receives appropriate training, supervision and appraisal;

(b) is enabled from time to time to obtain further qualifications appropriate to the work he performs; and

(c) is provided with a job description outlining his responsibilities.

(3) The registered person shall ensure that each person employed in or for the purposes of the establishment, or for the purposes of the agency and any medical practitioner with practising privileges, receives regular and appropriate appraisal and shall take such steps as may be necessary to address any aspect of—

(a) a health care professional's clinical practice; or

(b) the performance of a member of staff who is not a health care professional,

which is found to be unsatisfactory.

(4) The registered person shall take reasonable steps to ensure that any person working in an establishment or agency who is not employed by him and to whom paragraph (2) does not apply, is appropriately supervised while carrying out his duties.

DEFINITIONS
    registered person: reg.2(1).   **4–244**
    establishment: reg.2(1).
    agency: reg.2(1).
    patient: reg.2(1).
    employed: reg.2(3).
    medical practitioner: reg.2(1).
    practising privileges: reg.2(1).
    health care professional: reg.2(1).

Fitness of workers

19.—(1) The registered person shall ensure that—   **4–245**

(a) no person is employed to work in or for the purposes of the establishment or for the purposes of the agency; and

(b) no medical practitioner is granted consulting or practising privileges,

unless that person is fit to work in or for the purposes of the establishment, or for the purposes of the agency.

(2) A person is not fit to work in or for the purposes of an establishment, or for the purposes of an agency unless—

(a) he is of integrity and good character;

    (b) he has the qualifications, skills and experience which are necessary for the work which he is to perform;

    (c) he is physically and mentally fit for that work; and

    (d) full and satisfactory information is available [in relation to him in respect of each of the matters specified in Schedule 2.]

    (3) [...]

AMENDMENTS

4–246   The amendments to this regulation were made by SI 2002/865, reg.10(4).

DEFINITIONS

4–247   registered person: reg.2(1).
establishment: reg.2(1).
agency: reg.2(1).
medical practitioner: reg.2(1).
practising privileges: reg.2(1).

GENERAL NOTE

4–248   See the notes on reg.7 of the Care Homes Regulations 2001.

Guidance for health care professionals

4–249   **20.** The registered person shall ensure that any code of ethics or professional practice prepared by a body which is responsible for regulation of members of a health care profession is made available in the establishment or agency to members of the health care profession in question.

DEFINITIONS

4–250   registered person: reg.2(1).
health care professional: reg.2(1).
establishment: reg.2(1).
agency: reg.2(1).

Records

4–251   **21.**—(1) The registered person shall ensure that except in cases to which regulation 40(5) applies—

    (a) a comprehensive medical record is maintained in relation to each patient, which includes—

        (i) a contemporaneous note of all treatment provided to him;
        (ii) his medical history and all other notes prepared by a health care professional about his case; and

    (b) the record is retained for a period which is not less than that specified in Part I of Schedule 3 in relation to the type of patient in question or, where more than one such period could apply, the longest of them.

    (2) The registered person shall ensure that—

(a) the medical record for a person who is currently a patient is kept in a secure place in the establishment or the agency premises; and

(b) the medical record for a person who is not currently a patient is stored securely (whether in the establishment or the agency premises or elsewhere) and that it can be located if required.

(3) The registered person shall ensure that the records specified in Part II of Schedule 3 are maintained and that they are—

(a) kept up to date;

(b) at all times available for inspection in the establishment or the agency premises by any person authorised by the Commission to enter and inspect the establishment or agency premises; and

(c) retained for a period of not less than three years beginning on the date of the last entry.

DEFINITIONS

    registered person: reg.2(1).   **4–252**
    treatment: reg.2(1).
    health care professional: reg.2(1).
    patient: reg.2(1).
    establishment: reg.2(1).
    agency: reg.2(1).
    Commission: reg.2(1).

GENERAL NOTE
PARA.(3)(B)
    An authorised person has a power to inspect the establishment or agency under s.31.   **4–253**

Staff views as to conduct of establishment or agency

22.—(1) This regulation applies to any matter relating to the conduct of the **4–254** establishment or agency so far as it may affect the health and welfare of patients.

(2) The registered person shall make arrangements to enable any person employed in or for the purposes of the establishment, or for the purposes of the agency, and any medical practitioner with practising privileges to inform the registered person and the Commission of their views about any matter to which this regulation applies.

DEFINITIONS

    establishment: reg.2(1).   **4–255**
    agency: reg.2(1).
    patient: reg.2(1).
    Commission: reg.2(1).
    registered person: reg.2(1).
    employed: reg.2(3).
    medical practitioner: reg.2(1).
    practising privileges: reg.2(1).

GENERAL NOTE
    See the note on reg.21 of the Care Homes Regulations 2001 for comment on the Public **4–256** Interest Disclosure Act 1998.

Complaints

4–257   **23.**—(1) The registered person shall establish a procedure (in these Regulations referred to as "the complaints procedure") for considering complaints made to the registered person by a patient or a person acting on behalf of a patient.

(2) The registered person shall ensure that any complaint made under the complaints procedure is fully investigated.

(3) The registered person shall supply a written copy of the complaints procedure to every patient and, upon request, to—

(a) any person acting on behalf of a patient; and

(b) any person who is considering whether to become a patient.

(4) The written copy of the complaints procedure shall include—

(a) the name, address and telephone number of the Commission; and

(b) the procedure (if any) which has been notified by the Commission to the registered person for making complaints to the Commission relating to the establishment or agency.

(5) The registered person shall maintain a record of each complaint, including details of the investigations made, the outcome and any action taken in consequence and the requirements of regulation 21(3)(b) and (c) shall apply to that record.

(6) The registered person shall supply to the Commission annually a statement containing a summary of the complaints made during the preceding twelve months and the action taken in response.

DEFINITIONS
4–258   registered person: reg.2(1).
patient: reg.2(1).
Commission: reg.2(1).

GENERAL NOTE
4–259   The complaints procedure must be reviewed at intervals of not more than three years (reg.9(4)(b)).

Research

4–260   **24.**—(1) The registered person shall ensure that—

(a) before any research involving patients, information about patients, or bodily material and organs is undertaken in or for the purposes of an establishment, or for the purposes of an agency, a research proposal is prepared and approval is obtained from the appropriate Research Ethics Committee; and

(b) all such research projects include adequate safeguards for patients and employees.

(2) For the purposes of paragraph (1)(a), "the appropriate Research Ethics Committee" means a research ethics committee established in accordance with guidance issued from time to time by the Department of Health.

registered person: reg.2(1).   **4–261**
patient: reg.2(1).
establishment: reg.2(1).
agency: reg.2(1).

Chapter 2—Premises

Fitness of premises
25.—(1) Subject to regulation 6(3), the premises used as an establishment or **4–262**
agency must be in a location, and of a physical design and layout, which are suitable for the purpose of achieving the aims and objectives set out in the statement
of purpose.
(2) The registered person shall ensure that—

(a) the premises are of sound construction and kept in a good state of repair
externally and internally;

(b) the size and layout of rooms are suitable for the purposes for which they are
to be used and are suitably equipped and furnished;

(c) all parts of the establishment or agency are kept clean and meet appropriate
standards of hygiene;

(d) all parts of the establishment or agency to which patients have access are so
far as reasonably practicable free from hazards to their safety; and

(e) if surgical procedures are undertaken, life support systems are used, or
obstetric services and, in connection with childbirth, medical services, are
provided in the establishment or agency, such electrical supply is provided
during the interruption of public supply as is needed to safeguard the lives of
the patients.

(3) The registered person shall provide for employees and medical practitioners
with practising privileges—

(a) suitable facilities and accommodation, other than sleeping accommodation,
including—

(i) facilities for the purpose of changing; and
(ii) storage facilities; and

(b) where the provision of such accommodation is needed by employees in connection with their work, sleeping accommodation.

(4) The registered person shall, after consultation with the fire authority—

(a) take adequate precautions against the risk of fire, including the provision
and maintenance of suitable fire equipment;

(b) provide adequate means of escape in the event of a fire;

(c) make arrangements for persons employed in the establishment or for the
purposes of the agency and medical practitioners to whom practising privileges have been granted to receive suitable training in fire prevention;

(d) ensure, by means of fire drills and practices at suitable intervals, that the persons employed in the establishment or for the purposes of the agency and, so far as practicable, patients and medical practitioners to whom practising privileges have been granted, are aware of the procedure to be followed in case of fire; and

(e) review fire precautions, the suitability of fire equipment and the procedure to be followed in case of fire at intervals not exceeding twelve months.

(5) In this regulation "fire authority", in relation to an establishment or agency, means the authority discharging in the area in which the establishment or agency is situated, the function of fire authority under the Fire Services Act 1947.

DEFINITIONS

4–263   establishment: reg.2(1).
agency: reg.2(1).
statement of purpose: reg.2(1).
registered person: reg.2(1).
patient: reg.2(1).
medical practitioner: reg.2(1).
practising privileges: reg.2(1).
fire authority: para.(5).
employed: reg.2(3).

Chapter 3—Management

Visits by registered provider

4–264   **26.**—(1) Where the registered provider is an individual, but is not in day to day charge of the establishment or agency, he shall visit the establishment or agency premises in accordance with this regulation.

(2) Where the registered provider is an organisation or a partnership, the establishment or agency shall be visited in accordance with this regulation by—

(a) the responsible individual or one of the partners, as the case may be;

(b) another of the directors or other persons responsible for the management of the organisation or partnership; or

(c) an employee of the organisation or partnership who is not directly concerned with the conduct of the establishment or agency.

(3) Visits under paragraph (1) or (2) shall take place at least once every six months and shall be unannounced.

(4) The person carrying out the visit shall—

(a) interview, with their consent and in private (if necessary, by telephone), such of the patients and their representatives and such employees as appears to him to be necessary in order to form an opinion of the standard of treatment and other services provided in or for the purposes of the establishment, or for the purposes of the agency;

(b) inspect records of any complaints and, in the case of an establishment, its premises; and

(c) prepare a written report on the conduct of the establishment or agency.

(5) The registered provider shall supply a copy of the report required to be made under paragraph (4)(c) to—

(a) the Commission;

(b) the registered manager; and

(c) in the case of a visit under paragraph (2)—

> (i) where the registered provider is an organisation, to each of the directors or other persons responsible for the management of the organisation; and
>
> (ii) where the registered provider is a partnership, to each of the partners.

DEFINITIONS

    registered provider: reg.2(1).   **4–265**
    establishment: reg.2(1).
    agency: reg.2(1).
    organisation: reg.2(1).
    responsible individual: reg.2(1).
    patient: reg.2(1).
    treatment: reg.2(1).
    registered manager: reg.2(1).
    registered provider: reg.2(1).
    Commission: reg.2(1).

Financial position

27.—(1) The registered provider shall carry on the establishment or agency in **4–266** such manner as is likely to ensure that the establishment or agency will be financially viable for the purpose of achieving the aims and objectives set out in the statement of purpose.

(2) The registered person shall, if the Commission so requests, provide the Commission with such information and documents as it may require for the purpose of considering the financial viability of the establishment or agency, including—

(a) the annual accounts of the establishment or agency, certified by an accountant; or

(b) the annual accounts of the organisation which is the registered provider of the establishment or agency, certified by an accountant, together with accounts relating to the establishment or agency itself.

(3) The registered person shall also provide the Commission with such other information as it may require in order to consider the financial viability of the establishment or agency, including—

(a) a reference from a bank expressing an opinion as to the registered provider's financial standing;

(b) information as to the financing and financial resources of the establishment or agency;

(c) where the registered provider is a company, information as to any of its associated companies; and

(d) a certificate of insurance for the registered provider in respect of liability which may be incurred by him in relation to the establishment or agency in respect of death, injury, public liability, damage or other loss.

(4) In this regulation, one company is associated with another if one of them has control of the other, or both are under the control of the same person.

DEFINITIONS

4–267   registered provider: reg.2(1).
establishment: reg.2(1).
agency: reg.2(1).
statement of purpose: reg.2(1).
registered person: reg.2(1).
organisation: reg.2(1).
Commission: reg.2(1).

GENERAL NOTE

4–268   Regulation 13 of the National Care Standards Commission (Registration) Regulations 2001 requires the registered person to notify the registration authority if the establishment or agency is likely to become financially unviable.

Chapter 4—Notices to be given to the Commission

Notification of events

4–269   **28.**—(1) The registered person shall give notice to the Commission of—

(a) the death of a patient—

 (i) in an establishment;
 (ii) during treatment provided by an establishment or agency; or
 (iii) as a consequence of treatment provided by an establishment or agency within the period of seven days ending on the date of the death, and the circumstances of his death;

(b) any serious injury to a patient;

(c) the outbreak in an establishment of any infectious disease, which in the opinion of any medical practitioner employed in the establishment is sufficiently serious to be so notified;

(d) any allegation of misconduct resulting in actual or potential harm to a patient by the registered person, any person employed in or for the purposes of the establishment or for the purposes of the agency, or any medical practitioner with practising privileges.

(2) Notice under paragraph (1) shall be given within the period of 24 hours beginning with the event in question and, if given orally, shall be confirmed in writing as soon as practicable.

DEFINITIONS
    registered person: reg.2(1).   **4–270**
    Commission: reg.2(1).
    patient: reg.2(1).
    establishment: reg.2(1).
    treatment: reg.2(1).
    agency: reg.2(1).
    medical practitioner: reg.2(1).
    employed: reg.2(3).
    practising privileges: reg.2(1).

Notice of absence
    29.—(1) Where—   **4–271**

(a) the registered provider, if he is the person in day to day charge of the establishment or agency; or

(b) the registered manager,

proposes to be absent from the establishment or agency for a continuous period of 28 days or more, the registered person shall give notice in writing to the Commission of the proposed absence.

    (2) Except in the case of an emergency, the notice referred to in paragraph (1) shall be given no later than one month before the proposed absence commences or within such shorter period as may be agreed with the Commission and the notice shall specify with respect to the proposed absence—

(a) its length or expected length;

(b) the reason for it;

(c) the arrangements which have been made for running the establishment or agency;

(d) the name, address and qualifications of the person who will be responsible for the establishment or agency during that absence; and

(e) in the case of the absence of the registered manager, the arrangements that have been, or are proposed to be, made for appointing another person to manage the establishment or agency during that absence, including the proposed date by which the appointment is to be made.

    (3) Where the absence arises as a result of an emergency, the registered person shall give notice of the absence within one week of its occurrence specifying the matters set out in sub-paragraphs (a) to (e) of paragraph (2).
    (4) Where—

(a) the registered provider, if he is the person in day to day charge of the establishment or agency; or

(b) the registered manager,

has been absent from the establishment or agency for a continuous period of 28 days or more, and the Commission has not been given notice of the absence, the registered person shall, without delay, give notice in writing to the Commission of the absence, specifying the matters set out in paragraph (2)(a) to (e).

(5) The registered person shall notify the Commission of the return to duty of the registered provider or (as the case may be) the registered manager not later than 7 days after the date of his return.

<small>DEFINITIONS</small>

4–272   registered provider: reg.2(1).
establishment: reg.2(1).
agency: reg.2(1).
registered manager: reg.2(1).
registered person: reg.2(1).
Commission: reg.2(1).

Notice of changes

4–273   **30.** The registered person shall give notice in writing to the Commission as soon as it is practicable to do so if any of the following events take place or are proposed to take place—

(a) a person other than the registered person carries on or manages the establishment or agency;

(b) a person ceases to carry on or manage the establishment or agency;

(c) where the registered person is an individual, he changes his name;

(d) where the registered provider is a partnership, there is any change in the membership of the partnership;

(e) where the registered provider is an organisation—

   (i) the name or address of the organisation is changed;
   (ii) there is any change of director, manager, secretary or other similar officer of the organisation;
   (iii) there is any change in the identity of the responsible individual;

(f) where the registered provider is an individual, a trustee in bankruptcy is appointed;

(g) where the registered provider is a company or partnership, a receiver, manager, liquidator or provisional liquidator is appointed; or

(h) the premises of the establishment or agency are significantly altered or extended, or additional premises are acquired.

<small>DEFINITIONS</small>

4–274   registered person: reg.2(1).
Commission: reg.2(1).
establishment: reg.2(1).
agency: reg.2(1).
organisation: reg.2(1).
registered provider: reg.2(1).

Appointment of liquidators etc.

31.—(1) Any person to whom paragraph (2) applies must—   **4–275**

(a) forthwith notify the Commission of his appointment indicating the reasons for it;

(b) appoint a manager to take full-time day to day charge of the establishment or agency in any case where there is no registered manager; and

(c) before the end of the period of 28 days beginning on the date of his appointment, notify the Commission of his intentions regarding the future operation of the establishment or agency.

(2) This paragraph applies to any person appointed as—

(a) the receiver or manager of the property of a company or partnership which is a registered provider of an establishment or agency;

(b) liquidator or provisional liquidator of a company which is the registered provider of an establishment or agency;

(c) the trustee in bankruptcy of a registered provider of an establishment or agency.

DEFINITIONS
Commission: reg.2(1).   **4–276**
establishment: reg.2(1).
agency: reg.2(1).
registered manager: reg.2(1).
registered provider: reg.2(1).

Death of registered person

32.—(1) If more than one person is registered in respect of an establishment or **4–277**
agency, and a registered person dies, the surviving registered person shall without
delay notify the Commission of the death in writing.

(2) If only one person is registered in respect of an establishment or agency, and
he dies, his personal representatives must notify the Commission in writing—

(a) without delay of the death; and

(b) within 28 days of their intentions regarding the future running of the establishment or agency.

(3) The personal representatives of the deceased registered provider may carry
on the establishment or agency without being registered in respect of it—

(a) for a period not exceeding 28 days; and

(b) for any further period as may be determined in accordance with paragraph (4).

(4) The Commission may extend the period specified in paragraph (3)(a) by such further period, not exceeding one year, as the Commission shall determine, and shall notify any such determination to the personal representatives in writing.

(5) The personal representatives shall appoint a person to take full-time day to day charge of the establishment or agency during any period in which, in accordance with paragraph (3), they carry on the establishment or agency without being registered in respect of it.

DEFINITIONS

4–278   establishment: reg.2(1).
agency: reg.2(1).
registered person: reg.2(1).
Commission: reg.2(1).

PART IV

ADDITIONAL REQUIREMENTS APPLYING TO INDEPENDENT HOSPITALS

Chapter 1—Pathology Services, Resuscitation and Treatment of Children in Independent Hospitals

Application of regulations 34 to 36
4–279   **33.**—(1) Regulations 34 to 36 apply to independent hospitals of the following kinds—

(a) those defined in section 2(3)(a)(i) of the Act except establishments excepted by regulation 3(2); and

(b) those in which medical treatment, including cosmetic surgery, is provided under anaesthesia or sedation.

(2) Regulation 34 also applies to any establishment or agency which provides pathology services.

DEFINITIONS

4–280   treatment: reg.2(1).
establishment: reg.2(1).
agency: reg.2(1).

Pathology services
4–281   **34.** The registered person shall ensure that—

(a) an adequate range of pathology services is available to meet the needs of the independent hospital;

(b) those services are provided to an appropriate standard;

(c) appropriate arrangements are made for the collection, and (where pathology services are provided outside the hospital) transportation of pathology specimens; and

(d) the patient from whom a specimen was taken, and such specimen, is identifiable at all times.

DEFINITIONS
registered person: reg.2(1).
patient: reg.2(1).

4–282

Resuscitation

35.—(1) The registered person shall prepare and implement a written statement **4–283** of the policies to be applied and the procedures to be followed in the hospital in relation to resuscitation of patients, and shall review such statement annually.

(2) The registered person shall ensure that the policies and procedures implemented in accordance with paragraph (1)—

(a) take proper account of the right of all patients who are competent to do so to give or withhold consent to treatment;

(b) are available on request to every patient and any person acting on behalf of a patient; and

(c) are communicated to and understood by all employees and all medical practitioners with practising privileges who may be involved in decisions about resuscitation of a patient.

DEFINITIONS
registered person: reg.2(1).   **4–284**
patient: reg.2(1).
employee: reg.2(3).
medical practitioner: reg.2(1).
practicing privileges: reg.2(1).

GENERAL NOTE
The policies on resuscitation must be reviewed at intervals of not more than three years **4–285** (reg.9(4)(c)).

Treatment of children

36. The registered person shall ensure that, where a child is treated in an inde- **4–286** pendent hospital—

(a) he is treated in accommodation which is separate from accommodation in which adult patients are treated;

(b) particular medical, physical, psychological, social, educational and supervision needs arising from his age are met;

(c) his treatment is provided by persons who have appropriate qualifications, skills and experience in the treatment of children;

(d) his parents are kept fully informed of his condition and so far as is practicable consulted about all aspects of his treatment, except where the child is himself competent to consent to treatment and does not wish his parents to be so informed and consulted.

DEFINITIONS
registered person: reg.2(1).   **4–287**
treated: reg.2(1).
agency: reg.2(1).

organisation: reg.2(1).
registered provider: reg.2(1).

GENERAL NOTE
4–288   Compare the absolute requirement in this regulation that children should be treated separately from adults with reg.31 of the Care Homes Regulations 2001 which states that there should be separate provision for children in a care home "so far as it is practicable to do so".

PARA.(D)
4–289   *Parents:* This means the person(s) who has parental responsibility for the child (Children Act 1989, ss.2,12). If a care order is in force with respect to the child, the local authority shall have parental responsibility for the child (*ibid.*, s.33(3)).
    Competent: In *Re C (Detention: Medical Treatment)* [1997] 2 F.L.R. 180, Wall J. used the test of capacity established by the Court of Appeal in *Re M.B.* (see reg.37(2), below) to determine whether a child was "*Gillick* competent" to refuse medical treatment.

Chapter 2—Independent Hospitals in Which Certain Listed Services are Provided

Surgical procedures
4–290   **37.**—(1) Where medical treatment (including cosmetic surgery) is provided under anaesthesia or sedation in an independent hospital, the registered person shall ensure that—

(a) each operating theatre is designed, equipped and maintained to an appropriate standard for the purposes for which it is to be used;

(b) all surgery is carried out by, or under the direction of, a suitably qualified, skilled and experienced medical practitioner;

(c) an appropriate number of suitably qualified, skilled and experienced employees are in attendance during each surgical procedure; and

(d) the patient receives appropriate treatment—

   (i) before administration of an anaesthetic or sedation;
   (ii) whilst undergoing a surgical procedure;
   (iii) during recovery from general anaesthesia; and
   (iv) post-operatively.

(2) The registered person shall ensure that before a patient consents to any surgery offered by the independent hospital, he has received clear and comprehensive information about the procedure and any risks associated with it.

(3) In the case of a patient who is not competent to consent to surgery, the information mentioned in paragraph (2) shall, wherever possible, be provided to his representatives.

DEFINITIONS
4–291   treatment: reg.2(1).
registered person: reg.2(1).
medical practitioner: reg.2(1).

PARA.(2)

An adult patient is assumed to have the mental capacity to decide whether or not he or **4–292** she will accept medical treatment. However the presumption of capacity to decide is rebut-table. The test of capacity was set out by Butler-Sloss P. in *Re M.B. (Medical Treatment)* [1997] 2 F.L.R. 426, CA, at 437:

> "A person lacks capacity if some impairment or disturbance of mental functioning renders the person unable to make a decision whether to consent to or refuse treatment. The inability to make a decision will occur when;
>
> (a) the patient is unable to comprehend and retain information which is material to the decision, especially as to the likely consequences of having or not having the treatment in question;
> (b) the patient is unable to use the information and weigh it in the balance as part of the process of arriving at a decision ..."

PARA.(3)

Representatives: It is not clear which people would come into this category. It is suggested **4–293** that the information should be given to the person who is most closely involved with the patient's welfare.

Dental treatment under general anaesthesia

38. Where the treatment provided in an independent hospital includes dental **4–294** treatment under general anaesthesia, the registered person shall ensure that—

(a) the dentist and any employees assisting him are suitably qualified, skilled and experienced to deal with any emergency which occurs during or as a result of the general anaesthesia or treatment; and

(b) adequate facilities, drugs and equipment are available to deal with any such emergency.

DEFINITIONS
   treatment: reg.2(1).   **4–295**
   registered person: reg.2(1).
   dentist: reg.2(1).

Obstetric services—staffing

39.—(1) This regulation and regulation 40 apply to an independent hospital in **4–296** which obstetric services and, in connection with childbirth, medical services are provided.

(2) The registered person shall appoint a Head of Midwifery Services who is responsible for managing the provision of midwifery services in an independent hospital and, except in cases where obstetric services are provided in the hospital primarily by midwives, a Head of Obstetric Services whose name is included in the specialist medical register in respect of a specialty in obstetrics and who is responsible for managing the provision of obstetric services.

(3) The registered person shall ensure that the health care professional who is primarily responsible for caring for pregnant women and assisting at childbirth is a midwife, an appropriately qualified general practitioner, or a medical practitioner whose name is included in the specialist medical register in respect of a specialty in obstetrics.

(4) Where obstetric services are provided in an independent hospital primarily by midwives, the registered person shall ensure that the services of a medical practitioner who is competent to deal with obstetric emergencies are available at all times.

(5) The registered person shall ensure that a health care professional who is competent to undertake resuscitation of a new born baby is available in the hospital at all times and that his skills are regularly reviewed and, if necessary, updated.

DEFINITIONS

4–297   registered person: reg.2(1).
health care professional: reg.2(1).
general practitioner: reg.2(1).
medical practitioner: reg.2(1).

Obstetric services—further requirements

4–298   **40.**—(1) The registered person shall ensure that—

(a) any death of a patient in an independent hospital during, or as a result of, pregnancy or childbirth; and

(b) any still-birth or neonatal death in an independent hospital,

are reported to any person undertaking an enquiry into such deaths on behalf of the Secretary of State.

(2) The registered person shall ensure that facilities are available within the hospital to provide adequate treatment to patients who have undergone a delivery requiring surgical intervention or the use of forceps and that such patients are cared for by an appropriately experienced midwife.

(3) The registered person shall ensure that appropriate arrangements are in place for the immediate transfer, where necessary, of a patient and her new born child to critical care facilities within the hospital or elsewhere in the near vicinity.

(4) The registered person shall ensure that appropriate arrangements are in place for the treatment and, if necessary transfer to a specialist care facility, of a very sick patient or new born child.

(5) The registered person shall ensure that a maternity record is maintained for each patient receiving obstetric services and each child born in the hospital, which—

(a) includes the details specified in regulation 21(1)(a) and in Parts I and II of Schedule 4; and

(b) is retained for a period of not less than 25 years beginning on the date of the last entry,

and the requirements of regulation 21(2) shall apply to that record.

(6) In this regulation—

"still-birth" has the meaning given to it in the Births and Deaths Registration Act 1953;

"neonatal death" means the death of a child before the end of the period of 28
days beginning with the date of the child's birth.

DEFINITIONS
registered person: reg.2(1).   **4–299**
patient: reg.2(1).
treatment: reg.2(1).

GENERAL NOTE
PARA.(6)
"Still-birth" is defined in s.41 of the Births and Deaths Registration Act 1953 (as **4–300**
amended by s.1 of the Still-Birth (Definition) Act 1992).

Termination of pregnancies

41.—(1) This regulation applies to an independent hospital in which termina- **4–301**
tion of pregnancies takes place.

(2) The registered person shall ensure that no patient is admitted to the hospital
for termination of a pregnancy, and that no fee is demanded or accepted from a
patient in respect of a termination, unless two certificates of opinion have been
received in respect of the patient.

(3) The registered person shall ensure that a certificate of opinion in respect of a
patient undergoing termination of a pregnancy is completed and included with the
patient's record, within the meaning of regulation 21.

(4) The registered person shall ensure that no termination of a pregnancy is
undertaken after the 20th week of gestation, unless—

(a) the patient is treated by persons who are suitably qualified, skilled and
   experienced in the late termination of pregnancy; and

(b) appropriate procedures are in place to deal with any medical emergency
   which occurs during or as a result of the termination.

(5) The registered person shall ensure that no termination of a pregnancy is
undertaken after the 24th week of gestation.

(6) The registered person shall ensure that a register of patients undergoing termination of a pregnancy in the hospital is maintained, which is—

(a) separate from the register of patients which is to be maintained under paragraph 1 of Schedule 3;

(b) completed in respect of each patient at the time the termination is undertaken; and

(c) retained for a period of not less than three years beginning on the date of the
   last entry.

(7) The registered person shall ensure that a record is maintained of the total
numbers of terminations undertaken in the hospital; and the requirements of regulation 21(3) shall apply to that record.

(8) The registered person shall ensure that notice in writing is sent to the Chief
Medical Officer of the Department of Health of each termination of pregnancy
which takes place in the hospital.

(9) If the registered person—

(a) receives information concerning the death of a patient who has undergone termination of a pregnancy in the hospital during the period of 12 months ending on the date on which the information is received; and

(b) has reason to believe that the patient's death may be associated with the termination,

he shall give notice in writing to the Commission of that information, within the period of 14 days beginning on the day on which the information is received.

(10) The registered person shall prepare and implement appropriate procedures in the hospital to ensure that fetal tissue is treated with respect.

(11) In this regulation, "certificate of opinion" means a certificate required by regulations made under section 2(1) of the Abortion Act 1967.

DEFINITIONS
4–302   registered person: reg.2(1).
        patient: reg.2(1).
        certificate of opinion: para.(11).
        Commission: reg.2(1).

GENERAL NOTE
PARA.(10)
4–303   *Procedures:* These must be reviewed at intervals of not more than three years (reg.9(4)(c)).

GENERAL NOTE
PARA.(8)
4–304   See SI 1991/499, which requires such notice to be given by the medical practitioner carrying out the termination.

Use of certain techniques or technology
4–305   42.—(1) The registered person shall ensure that no Class 3B or Class 4 laser or intense light source (within the meaning of regulation 3(1)), is used in or for the purposes of an independent hospital unless that hospital has in place a professional protocol drawn up by a trained and experienced medical practitioner or dentist from the relevant discipline in accordance with which treatment is to be provided, and is so provided.

(2) The registered person shall ensure that such a laser or intense light source is used in or for the purposes of the hospital only by a person who has undertaken appropriate training and has demonstrated an understanding of—

(a) the correct use of the equipment in question;

(b) the risks associated with using a laser or intense light source;

(c) its biological and environmental effects;

(d) precautions to be taken before and during use of a laser or intense light source; and

(e) action to be taken in the event of an accident, emergency, or other adverse incident.

DEFINITIONS
    registered person: reg.2(1).
    medical practitioner: reg.2(1).
    dentist: reg.2(1).
    treatment: reg.2(1).

4–306

GENERAL NOTE
    This regulation will apply where the hospital is not exempt from registration by virtue of **4–307**
the exemption contained in reg.3(2)(a).

Chapter 3—Mental Health Hospitals

Application of regulations 44 to 47

43. Regulations 44 to 47 apply to independent hospitals of the following **4–308**
kinds—

(a) those, the main purpose of which, is to provide medical or psychiatric treat-
    ment for mental disorder; and

(b) those in which treatment or nursing (or both) are provided for persons liable
    to be detained under the Mental Health Act 1983.

Safety of patients and others

44.—(1) The statement of policies and procedures which is to be prepared and **4–309**
implemented by the registered person in accordance with regulation 9(1)(e) shall
include policies and procedures in relation to—

(a) assessment of a patient's propensity to violence and self harm;

(b) the provision of information to employees as to the outcome of such an
    assessment;

(c) assessment of the effect of the layout of the hospital premises, and its poli-
    cies and procedures, on the risk of a patient harming himself or another
    person; and

(d) the provision of training to enable employees to minimise the risk of a
    patient harming himself or another person.

    (2) The registered person shall in particular prepare and implement a suicide
protocol in the hospital which requires—

(a) a comprehensive examination of the mental condition of each patient;

(b) an evaluation of the patient's history of mental disorder, including identifi-
    cation of suicidal tendencies;

(c) an assessment of the patient's propensity to suicide; and

(d) if necessary, appropriate action to reduce the risk of the patient committing
    suicide.

DEFINITIONS
    registered person: reg.2(1).
    patient: reg.2(1).

4–310

Management of disturbed behaviour

4–311   **45.** The registered person shall prepare and implement a written policy setting out—

(a) how disturbed behaviour exhibited by a patient is to be managed;

(b) permitted measures of restraint and the circumstances in which they may be used;

(c) requirements for employees to report serious incidents of violence or self harm, including guidance as to how those incidents should be classified; and

(d) the procedure for review of such incidents and determination of the action which is to be taken subsequently.

DEFINITION

4–312   registered person: reg.2(1).

GENERAL NOTE

4–313   The policy on the management of disturbed behaviour must be reviewed at intervals of not more than three years (reg.9(4)(b)).

Visitors

4–314   **46.** The registered person shall prepare and implement written policies and pro-cedures in the hospital in relation to patients receiving visitors.

DEFINITIONS

4–315   registered person: reg.2(1).
         patient: reg.2(1).

GENERAL NOTE

4–316   The policies and procedures on visitors must be reviewed at intervals of not more than three years (reg.9(4)(b)).

Mental health records

4–317   **47.** The registered person shall ensure that any records which are required to be made under the Mental Health (Hospital, Guardianship and Consent to Treatment) Regulations 1983, and which relate to the detention or treatment of a patient in an independent hospital, are kept for a period of not less than five years beginning on the date on which the person to whom they relate ceases to be a patient in the hospital.

DEFINITIONS

4–318   registered person: reg.2(1).
         patient: reg.2(1).

PART V

ADDITIONAL REQUIREMENTS APPLYING TO INDEPENDENT CLINICS

Independent clinics

4–319   **48.** Where an independent clinic provides antenatal care to patients, the regis-tered person shall ensure that the health care professional who is primarily

186

responsible for providing that care is a midwife, an appropriately qualified general practitioner, or a medical practitioner with a specialist qualification in obstetrics.

DEFINITIONS

health care professional: reg.2(1).   **4–320**
general practitioner: reg.2(1).
medical practitioner: reg.2(1).

PART VI

ADDITIONAL REQUIREMENTS APPLYING TO INDEPENDENT MEDICAL AGENCIES

Independent medical agencies
49. The registered person shall ensure that the register of patients to be main- **4–321**
tained in relation to an independent medical agency under paragraph 1 of
Schedule 3 includes the name of the medical practitioner by whom each patient
is treated.

DEFINITIONS

registered person: reg.2(1).   **4–322**
medical practitioner: reg.2(1).

PART VII

MISCELLANEOUS

Compliance with regulations
50. Where there is more than one registered person in respect of an establish- **4–323**
ment or agency, anything which is required under these Regulations to be done by
the registered person shall, if done by one of the registered persons, not be
required to be done by any of the other registered persons.

DEFINITIONS

registered person: reg.2(1).   **4–324**
establishment: reg.2(1).
agency: reg.2(1).

Offences
51.—(1) A contravention, or failure to comply with, any of the provisions of **4–325**
regulations 6, 7, 9, 14, 15, 16(1) to (4), [17 to 30] 34 to 42 and 44 to 49 shall
be an offence.
(2) The Commission shall not bring proceedings against a person in respect of
any contravention or failure to comply with those regulations unless—

(a) subject to paragraph (4), he is a registered person;

(b) notice has been given to him in accordance with paragraph (3);

[(c) the period specified in the notice, within which the registered person may
make representations to the Commission, has expired; and

(d) in a case where, in accordance with paragraph (3)(b), the notice specifies
any action that is to be taken within a specified period, the period has
expired and the action has not been taken within that period.]

(3) Where the Commission considers that the registered person has contravened or failed to comply with any of the provisions of the regulations mentioned in paragraph (1), it may serve a notice on the registered person specifying—

(a) in what respect in its opinion the registered person has contravened or is contravening any of the regulations, or has failed or is failing to comply with the requirements of any of the regulations;

[(b) where it is practicable for the registered person to take action for the purpose of complying with any of those regulations, the action which, in the opinion of the Commission, the registered person should take for that purpose;

(c) the period, not exceeding three months, within which the registered person should take any action specified in accordance with sub-paragraph (b);

(d) the period, not exceeding one month, within which the registered person may make representations to the Commission about the notice.]

(4) The Commission may bring proceedings against a person who was once, but no longer is a registered person, in respect of a failure to comply with regulation 21 and for this purpose, references in paragraphs (2) and (3) to a registered person shall be taken to include such a person.

AMENDMENTS

4–326   The amendments to this regulation were made by SI 2002/865, reg.11(2).

DEFINITIONS

4–327   Commission: reg.2(1).
registered person: reg.2(1).

Regulation 6   **SCHEDULE 1**

4–328   INFORMATION TO BE INCLUDED IN THE STATEMENT OF PURPOSE

1. The aims and objectives of the establishment or agency.

2. The name and address of the registered provider and of any registered manager.

3. The relevant qualifications and experience of the registered provider and any registered manager.

4. The number, relevant qualifications and experience of the staff working in the establishment, or for the purposes of the agency.

5. The organisational structure of the establishment or agency.

6. The kinds of treatment and any other services provided for the purposes of the establishment or agency, the range of needs which those services are intended to meet and the facilities which are available for the benefit of patients.

7. The arrangements made for consultation with patients about the operation of the establishment or agency.

8. The arrangements made for contact between any in-patients and their relatives, friends and representatives.

9. The arrangements for dealing with complaints.

10. The arrangements for respecting the privacy and dignity of patients.

DEFINITIONS

4–329   establishment: reg.2(1).
agency: reg.2(1).

registered provider: reg.2(1).
registered manager: reg.2(1).
treatment: reg.2(1).
patient: reg.2(1).

**Regulations 10(3), 12(2)
and 19(2) 6**   **SCHEDULE 2**

INFORMATION REQUIRED IN RESPECT OF PERSONS SEEKING TO CARRY ON, MANAGE OR WORK AT AN
ESTABLISHMENT OR AGENCY

1. Positive proof of identity including a recent photograph.   **4–330**
2. Either—

(a) where the certificate is required for a purpose relating to section 115(5)(ea) of the
Police Act 1997 (registration under Part II of the Care Standards Act 2000), or
the position falls within section 115(3) or (4) of that Act, an enhanced criminal
record certificate issued under section 115 of that Act; or

(b) in any other case, a criminal record certificate issued under section 113 of that Act,

including, where applicable, the matters specified in [sections 113(3A) and 115(6A) of that
Act and the following provisions once they are in force, namely section 113(3C)(a) and (b)
and section 115(6B)(a) and (b) of that Act.]
3. Two written references, being references from the person's most recent employers, if
any.
4. Where a person has previously worked in a position which involved work with children or vulnerable adults, verification, so far as reasonably practicable, of the reason why
he ceased to work in that position.
5. Documentary evidence of any relevant qualifications.
6. A full employment history, together with a satisfactory written explanation of any gaps
in employment.
7. Where he is a health care professional, details of his registration with the body (if any)
responsible for regulation of members of the health care profession in question.
8. [...]

AMENDMENTS
The amendments to this Schedule were made by SI 2002/865, reg.10(5).   **4–331**

DEFINITIONS
employer: reg.2(3).   **4–332**
health care professional: reg.2(1).

GENERAL NOTE
See the notes on para.7 of Sch.2 to the Care Homes Regulations 2001.   **4–333**

PARA.(2)(A)
A position falls within s.115(3) if it involves regularly caring for, training, supervising or   **4–334**
being in sole charge of persons aged under 18. A position falls within s.115(4) if it is of a
kind specified in regulations and involves regularly caring for, training, supervising or
being in sole charge of persons aged 18 or over.

Regulations 21(1), (3)   **SCHEDULE 3**

PART I

4–335 **Period for which medical records must be retained**

Type of patient	Minimum period of retention
(a) Patient who was under the age of 17 at the date on which the treatment to which the records refer was concluded.	Until the patient's 25th birthday.
(b) Patient who was aged 17 at the date on which the treatment to which the records refer was concluded.	Until the patient's 26th birthday.
(c) Patient who died before attaining the age of 18.	A period of 8 years beginning on the date of the patient's death.
(d) Patient who was treated for mental disorder during the period to which the records refer.	A period of 20 years beginning on the date of the last entry in the record.
(e) Patient who was treated for mental disorder during the period to which the records refer and who died whilst receiving that treatment.	A period of 8 years beginning on the date of the patient's death.
(f) Patient whose records relate to treatment by a general practitioner.	A period of 10 years beginning on the date of the last entry.
(g) Patient who has received an organ transplant.	A period of 11 years beginning on the date of the patient's death or discharge whichever is the earlier.
(h) All other cases.	A period of 8 years beginning on the date of the last entry in the record.

PART II

Records to be maintained for inspection

4–336 **1.** A register of patients, including—

    (a) the name, address, telephone number, date of birth and marital status of each patient;

    (b) the name, address and telephone number of the patient's next of kin or any person authorised by the patient to act on his behalf;

    (c) the name, address and telephone number of the patient's general practitioner;

    (d) where the patient is a child, the name and address of the school which he attends or attended before admission to an establishment;

    (e) where a patient has been received into guardianship under the Mental Health Act 1983, the name, address and telephone number of the guardian;

(f) the name and address of any body which arranged the patient's admission or treatment;

(g) the date on which the patient was admitted to an establishment or first received treatment provided for the purposes of an establishment or agency;

(h) the nature of the treatment for which the patient was admitted or which he received;

(i) where the patient has been an in-patient in an independent hospital, the date of his discharge;

(j) if the patient has been transferred to a hospital (including a health service hospital), the date of the transfer, the reasons for it and the name of the hospital to which the patient was transferred;

(k) if the patient dies whilst in an establishment or during treatment provided for the purposes of an establishment or agency, the date, time and cause of his death.

2. A register of all surgical operations performed in an establishment or by an agency, including—

(a) the name of the patient on whom the operation was performed;

(b) the nature of the surgical procedure and the date on which it took place;

(c) the name of the medical practitioner or dentist by whom the operation was performed;

(d) the name of the anaesthetist in attendance;

(e) the name and signature of the person responsible for checking that all needles, swabs and equipment used during the operation have been recovered from the patient;

(f) details of all implanted medical devices, except where this would entail the disclosure of information contrary to the provisions of section 33(5) of the Human Fertilisation and Embryology Act 1990 (restrictions on disclosure of information).

3. A register of each occasion on which a technique or technology to which regulation 42 applies has been used; including—

(a) the name of the patient in connection with whose treatment the technique or technology was used;

(b) the nature of the technique or technology in question and the date on which it was used; and

(c) the name of the person using it.

4. A register of all mechanical and technical equipment used for the purposes of treatment provided by the establishment or agency including—

(a) the date of purchase of the equipment;

(b) the date of installation of the equipment;

(c) details of maintenance of the equipment and the dates on which maintenance work was carried out.

5. A register of all events which must be notified to the Commission in accordance with regulation 28.

6. A record of the rostered shifts for each employee and a record of the hours actually worked by each person.

7. A record of each person employed in or for the purposes of the establishment, or for the purposes of the agency and each medical practitioner to whom practising privileges have been granted, including—

(a) his name and date of birth;

(b) details of his position in the establishment or agency;

(c) dates of employment; and

(d) in respect of a health care professional, details of his professional qualifications and registration with his professional regulatory body.

DEFINITIONS

4–337   patient: reg.2(1).
treatment: reg.2(1).
general practitioner: reg.2(1).
establishment: reg.2(1).
agency: reg.2(1).
medical practitioner: reg.2(1).
dentist: reg.2(1).
employed: reg.2(3).
practising privileges: reg.2(1).
healthcare professional: reg.2(1)

Regulation 40(5)(a)   **SCHEDULE 4**

PART I

Details to be recorded in respect of patients receiving obstetric services

4–338   **1.** The date and time of delivery of each patient, the number of children born to the patient, the sex of each child and whether the birth was a live birth or a stillbirth.
2. The name and qualifications of the person who delivered the patient.
3. The date and time of any miscarriage occurring in the hospital.
4. The date on which any child born to a patient left the hospital.
5. If any child born to a patient died in the hospital, the date and time of death.

PART II

Details to be recorded in respect of a child born in an independent hospital

4–339   **1.** Details of the weight and condition of the child at birth.
2. A daily statement of the child's health.
3. If any paediatric examination is carried out involving any of the following procedures—

(a) examination for congenital abnormalities including congenital dislocation of the hip;

(b) measurement of the circumference of the head of the child;

(c) measurement of the length of the child;

(d) screening for phenylketonuria,

details of such examination and the result.

NURSES AGENCIES REGULATIONS 2002

(SI 2002/3212)

Dated December 21, 2002, and made by the Secretary of State for Health under the Care Standards Act 2000 (c.14), ss.4(6), 22(1), (2)(a) to (c), (f) to (j) and 7(a) to (h) and (j), 25, 34(1), 35 and 118(5) to (7).

GENERAL NOTE

These Regulations apply in relation to nurses agencies in England only. **4–340**

ARRANGEMENT OF REGULATIONS **4–341**

PART I

GENERAL

PART II

REGISTERED PERSONS

PART III

CONDUCT OF NURSES AGENCIES

Chapter 1—Quality of Service Provision

Chapter 2—Premises

PART I

GENERAL

Citation, commencement and application

4–342   **1.**—(1) These Regulations may be cited as the Nurses Agencies Regulations 2002 and shall come into force on 1st April 2003.

(2) These Regulations apply to nurses agencies in England only.

Interpretation

4–343   **2.**—(1) In these Regulations—

"the Act" means the Care Standards Act 2000;

["Commission" means the Commission for Social Care Inspection;]

"agency" means a nurses agency;

"nurse" means a registered nurse, registered midwife or registered health visitor;

"NHS trust" has the same meaning as in the National Health Service and Community Care Act 1990;

"organisation" means a body corporate or any unincorporated association other than a partnership;

"patient" means a person to whom nursing is provided by a nurse supplied by an agency;

"registered manager", in relation to an agency, means a person who is registered under Part II of the Act as the manager of that agency;

"registered person", in relation to an agency, means any person who is the registered provider or the registered manager of that agency;

"registered provider", in relation to an agency, means a person who is registered under Part II of the Act as the person carrying on that agency;

"responsible individual" shall be construed in accordance with regulation 7;

"service user" means a person to whom an agency—

(a) supplies a nurse who is employed by the agency; or
(b) provides services for the purpose of supplying the service user with a nurse for employment by that service user;

"service user's guide" means the written guide produced in accordance with regulation 5;

"statement of purpose" means the written statement compiled in accordance with regulation 4.

(2) In these Regulations, references to the supply of a nurse mean—

(a) the supply of a nurse who is employed for the purposes of an agency to act for and under the control of another person; and
(b) the introduction of a nurse by an agency to a service user for employment by that service user.

(3) In the definition of "service user" in paragraphs (1) and (2), the terms "employed" and "employment" include employment under a contract for services.

AMENDMENT
The reference to the Commission was inserted by SI 2004/664, art.3, Sch.2. **4–344**

Excepted agencies

[3. For the purposes of the Act— **4–345**

(a) a Special Health Authority which supplies staff, including nurses, to work for another National Health Service body;

(b) an NHS trust which supplies nurses to work solely for another National Health Service body; and

(c) an NHS foundation trust, which supplies nurses to work solely for another National Health Service body,

shall be excepted from being a nurses agency.]

AMENDMENT
This regulation was substituted by SI 2004/1269, reg.2.

DEFINITIONS
the Act: reg.2(1). **4–346**
NHS trust: reg.2(1).
nurse: reg.2(1).

Statement of purpose

4–347   **4.**—(1) The registered person shall compile in relation to the agency a written statement (in these Regulations referred to as "the statement of purpose") which shall consist of a statement as to the matters listed in Schedule 1.

(2) The registered person shall supply a copy of the statement of purpose to the Commission and shall make a copy of it available on request for inspection by every service user and any person acting on behalf of a service user.

(3) Nothing in regulation 20 shall require or authorise the registered person to contravene, or not to comply with—

(a) any other provision of these Regulations; or

(b) the conditions for the time being in force in relation to the registration of the registered person under Part II of the Act.

DEFINITIONS

4–348   registered person: reg.2(1).
Commission: reg.2(1).
service user: reg.2(1).

GENERAL NOTE

4–349   The statement of purpose must be kept under review (reg.6). Guidance on the statement of purpose is contained in Appendix 3 to *Choice, Power, Performance: The Need for Information on Care Services in England* which was published by the NCSC in March 2004.

It is an offence to contravene or fail to comply with this regulation (reg.27).

PARA.(2)

4–350   *Acting on behalf of a service user:* The registered person would need to be satisfied as to the legitimacy of a claim made by a person who states that he or she is so acting.

Service user's guide

4–351   **5.**—(1) The registered person shall prepare a service user's guide which shall include—

(a) a summary of the statement of purpose;

(b) the terms and conditions in respect of the services to be provided to service users, including as to the amount and method of payment of fees;

(c) a summary of the complaints procedure established in accordance with regulation 18; and

(d) the address and telephone number of the Commission.

(2) The registered person shall make a copy of the service user's guide available on request for inspection at the agency premises by every service user and any person acting on behalf of a service user.

DEFINITIONS

4–352   registered person: reg.2(1).
statement of purpose: reg.4(1).
service user: reg.2(1).
Commission: reg.2(1).

The service user's guide must be kept under review (reg.6). **4–353**
It is an offence to contravene or fail to comply with this regulation (reg.27).

PARA.(2)
Acting on behalf of a service user: See the note on reg.4, above. **4–354**

Review of statement of purpose and service user's guide
6. The registered person shall— **4–355**

(a) keep under review and, where appropriate, revise the statement of purpose and the service user's guide; and

(b) notify the Commission of any material revision within 28 days.

DEFINITIONS
registered person: reg.2(1). **4–356**
statement of purpose: reg.4(1).
Commission: reg.2(1).

PART II

REGISTERED PERSONS

Fitness of registered provider
7.—(1) A person shall not carry on an agency unless she is fit to do so. **4–357**
(2) A person is not fit to carry on an agency unless the person—

(a) is an individual, who carries on the agency—

(i) otherwise than in partnership with others, and she satisfies the requirements set out in paragraph (3);
(ii) in partnership with others, and she and each of her partners satisfies the requirements set out in paragraph (3);

(b) is a partnership, and each of the partners satisfies the requirements set out in paragraph (3);

(c) is an organisation and—

(i) the organisation has given notice to the Commission of the name, address and position in the organisation of an individual (in these Regulations referred to as "the responsible individual") who is a director, manager, secretary or other officer of the organisation and is responsible for supervising the management of the agency; and
(ii) that individual satisfies the requirements set out in paragraph (3).

(3) The requirements are that—

(a) she is of integrity and good character;

(b) she is physically and mentally fit to carry on the agency; and

(c) full and satisfactory information is available in relation to her in respect of each of the matters specified in Schedule 2.

(4) A person shall not carry on an agency if—

(a) she has been adjudged bankrupt or sequestration of her estate has been awarded and (in either case) she has not been discharged and the bankruptcy order has not been annulled or rescinded; or

(b) she has made a composition or arrangement with her creditors and has not been discharged in respect of it.

DEFINITIONS

4–358   registered provider: reg.2(1).
agency: reg.2(1).
organisation: reg.2(1).
Commission: reg.2(1).

GENERAL NOTE

4–359   The notion of fitness is considered in the note on reg.7 of the Care Homes Regulations 2001.

Appointment of manager

4–360   **8.**—(1) The registered provider shall appoint an individual to manage the agency where—

(a) there is no registered manager in respect of the agency; and

(b) the registered provider—

(i) is an organisation or a partnership; or
(ii) is not a fit person to manage an agency; or
(iii) is not, or does not intend to be, in full-time day to day charge of the agency.

(2) Where the registered provider appoints a person to manage the agency, she shall forthwith give notice to the Commission of—

(a) the name of the person so appointed; and

(b) the date on which the appointment is to take effect.

DEFINITIONS

4–361   registered provider: reg.2(1).
agency: reg.2(1).
registered manager: reg.2(1).
organisation: reg.2(1).
Commission: reg.2(1).

GENERAL NOTE

4–362   A person shall not be appointed as a manager unless he or she is fit to manage the agency (reg.9). The registered provider can also manage the agency if he or she is in full-time day-to-day charge of the agency (para.(b)(iii)).

Fitness of manager

4–363   **9.**—(1) A person shall not manage an agency unless she is fit to do so.
(2) A person is not fit to manage an agency unless—

(a) she is of integrity and good character;

(b) having regard to the size of the agency, its statement of purpose and the number and needs of the service users—

(i) she has the qualifications, skills and experience necessary to manage the agency; and

(ii) she is physically and mentally fit to do so; and

(c) full and satisfactory information is available in relation to her in respect of each of the matters specified in Schedule 2.

DEFINITIONS
    agency: reg.2(1).   **4–364**
    statement of purpose: reg.4(1).
    service user: reg.2(1).

GENERAL NOTE
    The notion of fitness is considered in the note on reg.7 of the Care Homes Regulations **4–365**
2001.
    The interviewing of potential managers is considered in the note on reg.9 of the 2001
Regulations.

Registered person—general requirements and training

    10.—(1) The registered provider and the registered manager shall, having **4–366**
regard to the size of the agency, its statement of purpose and the number and
needs of the service users, carry on or (as the case may be) manage the agency
with sufficient care, competence and skill.

    (2) If the registered provider is—

(a) an individual, she shall undertake;

(b) an organisation, it shall ensure that the responsible individual undertakes; or

(c) a partnership, it shall ensure that one of the partners undertakes,

from time to time such training as is appropriate to ensure that she has the experience and skills necessary for carrying on the agency.

    (3) The registered manager shall undertake from time to time such training as is
appropriate to ensure that she has the experience and skills necessary for managing the agency.

DEFINITIONS
    registered provider: reg.2(1).   **4–367**
    registered manager: reg.2(1).
    agency: reg.2(1).
    statement of purpose: reg.4(1).
    service user: reg.2(1).
    organisation: reg.2(1).
    responsible individual; reg.2(1).

Notification of offences

4–368   **11.** Where the registered person or the responsible individual is convicted of any criminal offence, whether in England and Wales or elsewhere, she shall forthwith give notice in writing to the Commission of—

(i)   the date and place of the conviction;

(ii) the offence of which she was convicted; and

(iii) the penalty imposed on her in respect of the offence.

DEFINITIONS

4–369   registered person: reg.2(1).
responsible individual: reg.2(1).
Commission: reg.2(1).

GENERAL NOTE

4–370   *Conviction:* Cautions need not be notified.
Offence: Even if the offence is not related to the carrying on of an agency.

PART III

CONDUCT OF NURSES AGENCIES

Chapter 1—Quality of Service Provision

Fitness of nurses supplied by an agency

4–371   **12.**—(1) The registered person shall ensure that no nurse is supplied by the agency unless—

(a) she is of integrity and good character;

(b) she has the qualifications, skills and experience which are necessary for the work which she is to perform;

(c) she is physically and mentally fit for that work; and

(d) full and satisfactory information is available in relation to her in respect of each of the matters specified in Schedule 3.

(2) The registered person shall ensure that the selection of a nurse for supply is made by or under the supervision of a nurse and that full and satisfactory information in respect of each of the matters listed in Schedule 2 is available in relation to the nurse carrying out the selection.

(3) The registered person shall ensure that every nurse supplied by the agency acting as an employment business is instructed that when working for a service user she must at all times wear identification showing her name, the name of the agency and a recent photograph.

[(4) Paragraph (1)(d), in so far as it relates to paragraph 13 of Schedule 3, shall not apply in respect of a nurse who, at any time during the period from 1st October 2002 to 30th September 2003, has been supplied by the agency.]

AMENDMENT

4–372   Paragraph 4 was added by SI 2003/2323, reg.3(2).

    registered person: reg.2(1).   **4–373**
    nurse: reg.2(1).
    agency: reg.2(1).
    service user: reg.2(1).

GENERAL NOTE
    It is an offence to contravene or fail to comply with this regulation (reg.27).   **4–374**

PARA.*(1)*
    Supplied: See reg.2(2).   **4–375**

Policies and procedures

13.—(1) Paragraphs (2) and (3) apply where an agency acting as an employ- **4–376**
ment business supplies a nurse to provide nursing care in the private residence
of a service user or patient.

    (2) The registered person shall prepare and implement written policies in
relation to—

(a) ensuring that the services provided to each patient are in accordance with
      the statement of purpose and meet that patient's individual needs;

(b) the circumstances in which nurses may administer or assist in the adminis-
      tration of a patient's medication;

(c) the other tasks which nurses may or may not perform in connection with a
      patient's care, and the tasks which may only be performed if the nurse has
      received specialist training;

(d) arrangements to assist patients with mobility in their homes, where
      required;

(e) measures to protect the safety and property of the patient;

(f) arrangements to ensure that the privacy, dignity and wishes of the patient are
      respected;

(g) measures to safeguard the patient against abuse or neglect;

(h) measures to safeguard nurses against abuse or other harm;

(i) the procedure to be followed after an allegation of abuse, neglect or other
      harm has been made.

    (3) The procedure referred to in paragraph (2)(i) shall in particular provide
for—

(a) written records to be kept of any allegation of abuse, neglect or other harm
      and of the action taken in response; and

(b) the Commission to be notified of any incident reported to the police, not
      later than 24 hours after the registered person—

      (i) has reported the matter to the police; or
      (ii) is informed that the matter has been reported to the police.

(4) The registered person shall ensure that any personal information about a patient for whom a nurse is supplied by the agency is not disclosed to any member of the agency's staff unless it is necessary to do so in order to provide an effective service to the patient.

DEFINITIONS
4–377   agency: reg.2(1).
nurse: reg.2(1).
service user: reg.2(1).
patient: reg.2(1).
registered person: reg.2(1).
statement of purpose: reg.4(1).
Commission: reg.2(1).

GENERAL NOTE
4–378   It is an offence to contravene or fail to comply with this regulation (reg.27).

PARA.(1)
4–379   *Employment business:* Is defined in s.121(1) of the Act.

PARA.(4)
4–380   *Supplied:* See reg.2(2).

Staffing
4–381   **14.**—(1) Where an agency is acting as an employment business, the registered person shall, having regard to the size of the agency, its statement of purpose and the number and needs of the service users, take all reasonable measures to ensure that there is at all times an appropriate number of suitably qualified, skilled and experienced persons employed for the purposes of the agency.

(2) The registered person shall ensure that each employee of the agency—

(a) receives appropriate supervision; and

(b) is provided with a job description outlining her responsibilities.

(3) The registered person shall establish a procedure for collecting information from service users about the performance of nurses employed for the purposes of the agency, and shall take such steps as may be necessary to address any aspect of a nurse's clinical practice.

(4) The registered person shall provide to each nurse who is employed for the purposes of the agency a written statement of the terms and conditions on which she will be supplied to work for, and under the control of, a service user.

(5) The statement of terms and conditions provided under paragraph (4) shall, in particular, specify the employment status of the nurse.

DEFINITIONS
4–382   agency: reg.2(1).
registered person: reg.2(1).
statement of purpose: reg.4(1).
service user: reg.2(1).
nurse: reg.2(1).

GENERAL NOTE
It is an offence to contravene or fail to comply with this regulation (reg.27).   **4–383**
See the note on reg.21 of the Care Homes Regulations 2001 for comment on the Public Interest Disclosure Act 1998.

PARA.*(1)*
Employment business: Is defined in s.121(1) of the Act.   **4–384**

Staff handbook

15.—(1) Where the agency is acting as an employment business, the registered **4–385** person shall prepare a staff handbook and provide a copy to every member of staff.

(2) The handbook prepared in accordance with paragraph (1) shall include a statement as to—

(a) the conduct expected of staff, and disciplinary action which may be taken against them;

(b) the role and responsibilities of nurses and other staff;

(c) record keeping requirements;

(d) recruitment procedures; and

(e) training and development requirements and opportunities.

DEFINITIONS
agency: reg.2(1).   **4–386**
registered person: reg.2(1).
nurse: reg.2(1).

GENERAL NOTE
It is an offence to contravene or fail to comply with this regulation (reg.27).   **4–387**

PARA.*(1)*
Employment business: Is defined in s.121(1) of the Act.   **4–388**

Provision of information to service users

16.—(1) The registered person shall ensure that before a nurse is supplied, the **4–389** service user is informed of—

(a) the name of the nurse who is to be supplied and the means of contacting her;

(b) the name of the member of staff of the agency who is responsible for the supply of that nurse; and

(c) where the agency is acting as an employment business, details of how the service user may contact the registered person, or a person nominated to act on behalf of the registered person.

(2) Where the service user is also the patient, the registered person shall ensure that the information specified in paragraph (1) is, where appropriate, provided to the person acting on behalf of the patient.

DEFINITIONS
registered person: reg.2(1).   **4–390**

nurse: reg.2(1).
service user: reg.2(1).
agency: reg.2(1).
patient: reg.2(1).

GENERAL NOTE

4–391   It is an offence to contravene or fail to comply with this regulation (reg.27).

Records
4–392   **17.** The registered person shall ensure that the records specified in Schedule 4 are maintained and that they are—

(a) kept up to date, in good order and in a secure manner; and

(b) retained for a period of not less than three years beginning on the date of the last entry.

DEFINITION

4–393   registered person: reg.2(1).

GENERAL NOTE

4–394   It is an offence to contravene or fail to comply with this regulation (reg.27).

Complaints
4–395   **18.**—(1) The registered person shall establish a procedure ("the complaints procedure") for considering complaints made to the registered person by a service user or a person acting on behalf of the service user.

(2) The registered person shall supply a written copy of the complaints procedure to every service user and, upon request, to any person acting on behalf of a service user.

(3) The written copy of the complaints procedure shall include—

(a) the address and telephone number of the Commission; and

(b) the procedure (if any) which has been notified by the Commission to the registered person for making complaints to the Commission relating to the agency.

(4) The registered person shall ensure that every complaint made under the complaints procedure is fully investigated.

(5) The registered person shall, within the period of 28 days beginning on the date on which the complaint is made, or such shorter period as may be reasonable in the circumstances, inform the person who made the complaint of the action (if any) that is to be taken in response.

(6) The registered person shall maintain a record of each complaint, including details of the investigation made, the outcome and any action taken in consequence and the requirements of regulation 17 shall apply to that record.

(7) The registered person shall supply to the Commission annually a statement containing a summary of the complaints made during the preceding twelve months and the action taken in response.

(8) The registered person shall ensure that any evidence of misconduct by a nurse is reported promptly and in writing to the Nursing and Midwifery Council.

    registered person: reg.2(1).   **4–396**
    service user: reg.2(1).
    nurse: reg.2(1).
    Commission: reg.2(1).

GENERAL NOTE
    It is an offence to contravene or fail to comply with this regulation (reg.27).   **4–397**

PARA.*(1)*
    Acting on behalf of the service user: See the note on reg.16(2), above.   **4–398**

PARA.*(8)*
    Evidence: As opposed to an allegation of misconduct.   **4–399**

Review of quality of service provision

    19.—(1) The registered person shall introduce and maintain a system for **4–400**
reviewing at appropriate intervals the quality of services provided by the agency.

    (2) The registered person shall supply to the Commission a report in respect of
any review conducted by her for the purposes of paragraph (1) and shall make a
copy of the report available upon request for inspection by service users and persons acting on behalf of service users.

    (3) The system referred to in paragraph (1) shall provide for consultation with
service users and persons acting on behalf of service users.

DEFINITIONS
    registered person: reg.2(1).   **4–401**
    agency: reg.2(1).
    service user: reg.2(1).
    Commission: reg.2(1).

GENERAL NOTE
    It is an offence to contravene or fail to comply with this regulation (reg.27).   **4–402**

PARA.*(1)*
    Reviewing: This review is in addition to the procedure established under reg.14(3).   **4–403**

Chapter 2—Premises

Fitness of premises

    20. The registered person shall not use premises for the purposes of an agency **4–404**
unless the premises are suitable for the purpose of achieving the aims and objectives of the agency set out in the statement of purpose.

DEFINITIONS
    registered person: reg.2(1).   **4–405**
    agency: reg.2(1).
    statement of purpose: reg.4(1).

GENERAL NOTE
    It is an offence to contravene or fail to comply with this regulation (reg.27).   **4–406**

Financial position

4–407   **21.**—(1) The registered provider shall carry on the agency in such manner as is likely to ensure that the agency will be financially viable for the purpose of achieving the aims and objectives set out in the statement of purpose.

(2) The registered person shall, if the Commission so requests, provide the Commission with such information and documents as it may require in order to consider the financial viability of the agency, including—

(a) the annual accounts of the agency certified by an accountant; and

(b) a certificate of insurance for the registered provider in respect of liability which may be incurred by her in relation to the agency in respect of death, injury, public liability, damage or other loss.

Definitions

4–408   registered provider: reg.2(1).
agency: reg.2(1).
statement of purpose: reg.2(1).
registered person: reg.2(1).
Commission: reg.2(1).

Chapter 4—Notices to be Given to the Commission

Notice of absence

4–409   **22.**—(1) Where—

(a) the registered provider, being an individual in full-time day to day charge of the agency; or

(b) the registered manager,

proposes to be absent from the agency for a continuous period of 28 days or more, the registered person shall give notice in writing to the Commission of the proposed absence.

(2) Except in the case of an emergency, the notice referred to in paragraph (1) shall be given no later than one month before the proposed absence commences or within such shorter period as may be agreed with the Commission and the notice shall specify—

(a) the length or expected length of the absence;

(b) the reason for the absence;

(c) the arrangements which have been made for running the agency during that absence;

(d) the name, address and qualifications of the person who will be responsible for the agency during that absence; and

(e) in the case of the absence of the registered manager, the arrangements that have been, or are proposed to be, made for appointing another person to manage the agency during that absence, including the proposed date by which the appointment is to be made.

(3) Where the absence arises as a result of an emergency, the registered person shall give notice of the absence within one week of its occurrence specifying the matters set out in paragraph (2)(a) to (e).

(4) Where—

(a) the registered provider, being an individual in full-time day to day charge of the agency; or

(b) the registered manager,

has been absent from the agency for a continuous period of 28 days or more, and the Commission has not been given notice of the absence, the registered person shall, without delay, give notice in writing to the Commission of the absence, specifying the matters set out in paragraph (2)(a) to (e).

(5) The registered person shall notify the Commission of the return to duty of the registered provider or (as the case may be) the registered manager not later than 7 days after the date of her return.

DEFINITIONS

registered provider: reg.2(1).   **4–410**
agency: reg.2(1).
registered manager: reg.2(1).
registered person: reg.2(1).
Commission: reg.2(1).

GENERAL NOTE

It is an offence to contravene or fail to comply with this regulation (reg.27).   **4–411**

PARA.(3)

Notification under this provision is only required if the absence is likely to last more than **4–412**
28 days.

Notice of changes

23. The registered person shall give notice in writing to the Commission as soon **4–413** as it is practicable to do so if any of the following events takes place or is proposed to take place—

(a) a person other than the registered person carries on or manages the agency;

(b) a person ceases to carry on or manage the agency;

(c) where the registered person is an individual, she changes her name;

(d) where the registered provider is a partnership, there is any change in the membership of the partnership;

(e) where the registered provider is an organisation—

   (i) the name or address of the organisation is changed;
   (ii) there is any change of director, manager, secretary or other similar offi-cer of the organisation;

(iii) there is any change in the identity of the responsible individual;

(f) where the registered provider is an individual, a trustee in bankruptcy is appointed;

(g) where the registered provider is a company or partnership, a receiver, manager, liquidator or provisional liquidator is appointed; or

(h) where the registered provider acquires additional premises for the purposes of the agency.

DEFINITIONS

4–414   registered person: reg.2(1).
Commission: reg.2(1).
registered provider: reg.2(1).
organisation: reg.2(1).
responsible individual: reg.2(1).

Appointment of liquidators etc.

4–415   24.—(1) Any person to whom paragraph (2) applies must—

(a) forthwith notify the Commission of his appointment indicating the reasons for it;

(b) appoint a manager to take full-time day to day charge of the agency in any case where there is no registered manager; and

(c) not more than 28 days after his appointment, notify the Commission of his intentions regarding the future operation of the agency.

(2) This paragraph applies to any person appointed as—

(a) the receiver or manager of the property of a company or partnership which is a registered provider in respect of an agency;

(b) the liquidator or provisional liquidator of a company which is the registered provider in respect of an agency;

(c) the trustee in bankruptcy of a registered provider in respect of an agency.

DEFINITIONS

4–416   Commission: reg.2(1).
registered provider: reg.2(1).
agency: reg.2(1).

Death of registered person

4–417   25.—(1) If more than one person is registered in respect of an agency, and a registered person dies, the surviving registered person shall without delay notify the Commission of the death in writing.

(2) If only one person is registered in respect of an agency, and she dies her personal representatives must notify the Commission in writing—

(a) without delay of the death; and

(b) within 28 days of their intentions regarding the future running of the agency.

(3) The personal representatives of the deceased registered provider may carry on the agency without being registered in respect of it—

(a) for a period not exceeding 28 days; and

(b) for any further period as may be determined in accordance with paragraph (4).

(4) The Commission may extend the period specified in paragraph (3)(a) by such further period, not exceeding one year, as the Commission shall determine, and shall notify any such determination to the personal representatives in writing.

(5) The personal representatives shall appoint a person to take full-time day to day charge of the agency during any period in which, in accordance with paragraph (3), they carry on the agency without being registered in respect of it.

DEFINITIONS
  agency: reg.2(1).   **4–418**
  registered person: reg.2(1).
  Commission: reg.2(1).

PART IV

MISCELLANEOUS

Compliance with regulations
26. Where there is more than one registered person in respect of an agency, any- **4–419** thing which is required under these Regulations to be done by the registered person shall, if done by one of the registered persons, not be required to be done by any of the other registered persons.

DEFINITIONS
  registered person: reg.2(1).   **4–420**
  agency: reg.2(1).

Offences
27.—(1) A contravention or failure to comply with any of the provisions of **4–421** regulations 4 to 6 and 11 to 23 shall be an offence.

(2) The Commission shall not bring proceedings against a person in respect of any contravention or failure to comply with those regulations unless—

(a) subject to paragraph (4), she is a registered person;

(b) notice has been given to her in accordance with paragraph (3);

(c) the period specified in the notice, within which the registered person may make representations to the Commission, has expired; and

(d) in a case where, in accordance with paragraph (3)(b), the notice specifies any action that is to be taken within a specified period, the period has expired and the action has not been taken within that period.

(3) Where the Commission considers that the registered person has contravened or failed to comply with any of the provisions of the regulations mentioned in paragraph (1), it may serve a notice on the registered person specifying—

(a) in what respect in its opinion the registered person has contravened any of the regulations, or has failed, or is failing, to comply with the requirements of any of those regulations;

(b) where it is practicable for the registered person to take action for the purpose of complying with any of those regulations, the action which, in the opinion of the Commission, the registered person should take for that purpose;

(c) the period, not exceeding three months, within which the registered person should take any action specified in accordance with sub-paragraph (b);

(d) the period, not exceeding one month, within which the registered person may make representations to the Commission about the notice.

(4) The Commission may bring proceedings against a person who was once, but no longer is, a registered person, in respect of a failure to comply with regulation 17 and for this purpose, references in paragraphs (2) and (3) to a registered person shall be taken to include such a person.

DEFINITIONS
4–422   Commission: reg.2(1).
registered person: reg.2(1).

Regulation 4   **SCHEDULE 1**

INFORMATION TO BE INCLUDED IN THE STATEMENT OF PURPOSE

4–423   **1.** The aims and objectives of the agency.
2. The nature of the services which the agency provides.
3. The name and address of the registered provider and of any registered manager.
4. The relevant qualifications and experience of the registered provider and any registered manager.
5. The range of qualifications of nurses supplied by the agency, and the types of settings in which they are supplied to work.
6. The complaints procedure established in accordance with regulation 18.

DEFINITIONS
4–424   agency: reg.2(1).
registered provider: reg.2(1).
registered manager: reg.2(1).

PARA.5
4–425   *Supplied to the agency:* See reg.2(2).

Regulations 7(3), 9(2) and 12(2)   **SCHEDULE 2**

INFORMATION REQUIRED IN RESPECT OF REGISTERED PROVIDERS AND MANAGERS OF AN AGENCY AND NURSES RESPONSIBLE FOR SELECTING NURSES FOR SUPPLY TO SERVICE USERS

4–426   **1.** Proof of identity, including a recent photograph.
2. Either—

(a) where the certificate is required for a purpose relating to section 115(5)(ea) of the Police Act 1997 (registration under Part II of the Care Standards Act 2000), or the position falls within section 115(3) or (4) of that Act, an enhanced criminal record certificate issued under section 115 of that Act; or

(b) in any other case, a criminal record certificate issued under section 113 of that Act,

including, where applicable, the matters specified in sections 113(3A) and 115(6A) of that Act and the following provisions once they are in force, namely section 113(3C)(a) and (b) and section 115(6B)(a) and (b) of that Act.

3. Two written references, including a reference relating to the last period of employment of not less than three months duration.

4. Where a person has previously worked in a position which involved work with children or vulnerable adults, verification of the reason why she ceased to work in that position, unless it is not reasonably practicable to obtain such verification.

5. Documentary evidence of any relevant qualifications and training.

6. A full employment history, together with a satisfactory written explanation of any gaps in employment.

7. Details of health record.

8. In respect of a nurse to whom regulation 12(3) applies, confirmation of current registration with the Nursing and Midwifery Council, including details of the Part of the register in which the nurse is registered.

9. Details of any professional indemnity insurance.

DEFINITION
nurse: reg.2(1).   **4–427**

GENERAL NOTE
PARA.2
    For a note on disclosure checks from the Criminal Records Bureaux, see para.7 of Sch.2 **4–428** to the Care Homes Regulations 2001.

Regulation 12(1)   **SCHEDULE 3**

INFORMATION REQUIRED IN RESPECT OF NURSES TO BE SUPPLIED BY AN AGENCY

1. Name, address, date of birth and telephone number.   **4–429**
2. Name, address and telephone number of next of kin.
3. Proof of identity, including a recent photograph.
4. Details of any criminal offences—

(a) of which the person has been convicted, including details of any convictions which are spent within the meaning of section 1 of the Rehabilitation of Offenders Act 1974 and which may be disclosed by virtue of the Rehabilitation of Offenders (Exceptions) Order 1975; or

(b) in respect of which she has been cautioned by a constable and which, at the time the caution was given, she admitted.

5. Two written references from nurses or other health professionals, including a reference relating to the last period of employment as a nurse of not less than three months duration.

6. Where a nurse has previously worked in a position which involved work with children or vulnerable adults, verification of the reason why she ceased to work in that position, unless it is not reasonably practicable to obtain such verification.

7. Evidence of a satisfactory knowledge of the English language, where the nurse's nursing qualifications were obtained outside the United Kingdom.

8. Documentary evidence of any relevant qualifications and training.

9. A full employment history, together with a satisfactory written explanation of any gaps in employment and details of any current employment other than for the purposes of the agency.

10. Details of health record, including immunisation status.

11. Confirmation of current registration with the Nursing and Midwifery Council, including details of the Part of the register in which the nurse is registered.

12. Details of any professional indemnity insurance.

13. Either—

(a) where the position falls within section 115(3) or (4) of the Police Act 1997 (registration under Part 2 of the Care Standards Act 2000), an enhanced criminal record certificate issued under section 115 of that Act; or

(b) in any other case, a criminal record certificate issued under section 113 of that Act,

including, where applicable, the matters specified in section 113(3A) or 115(6A) of that Act and, once they are in force, section 113(3C)(a) and (b) or section 115(6B)(a) and (b) of that Act.

AMENDMENT

4–430   Paragraph 13 was added by SI 2003/2323, reg.3(3).

DEFINITION

4–431   nurse: reg.2(1).

GENERAL NOTE

PARA.2

4–432   *Next of kin:* See the note on reg.40(1)(b) of the Care Homes Regulations 2001.

Regulation 17   **SCHEDULE 4**

RECORDS TO BE MAINTAINED FOR INSPECTION

Records relating to supply of nurses

4–433   **1.** Copies of all agreements between the agency and nurses supplied or to be supplied by the agency and evidence that a copy of any standard terms and conditions has been supplied by the agency to each nurse.

2. Details of the remuneration payable to each nurse who is employed by the agency and her conditions of employment.

3. Copies of any statement given to a service user setting out the qualifications and relevant experience of a nurse supplied to that service user.

4. An alphabetical index of service users, including the full name, address and telephone number of each of them and any serial numbers assigned to them.

5. An alphabetical index of nurses supplied or available for supply by the agency, including any serial numbers assigned to them.

6. Details of each supply of a nurse to a service user.

7. Where the agency is acting as an employment business and a nurse is supplied to provide nursing care in the private residence of a service user or patient, details of—

(a) the illness or disability from which the patient is suffering;

(b) the name and address of the patient's general medical practitioner;

(c) other health professionals from whom the patient is receiving treatment;

(d) the patient's next of kin;

(e) the patient's religion;

(f) other occupants at the property where nursing will be provided; and

(g) the nursing plan devised for the patient and a detailed record of the nursing care provided.

Other records

1. All information provided to the Commission for the purposes of registration in relation to the agency. **4–434**

2. Details of every allegation of abuse—

(a) against a nurse; or

(b) by a nurse (which is not the subject of a complaint made under regulation 18),

who is employed by the agency, including details of the investigations made, the outcome and any action taken in consequence.

Definitions

agency: reg.2(1). **4–435**
nurse: reg2(1).
service user: reg.2(1).
Commission: reg.2(1).

General Note
Para.1
Supplied: See reg.2(2). **4–436**

Para.7
Employment business: Is defined in s.121(1) of the Act. **4–437**

THE DOMICILIARY CARE AGENCIES REGULATIONS 2002

(SI 2002/3214)

Dated December 21, 2002, and made by the Secretary of State for Health under the Care Standards Act 2000 (c.14), ss.4(6), 22(1), (2)(a) to (d), and (f) to (j), (5)(a) and (7)(a) to (h) and (j), 25, 34(1), 35 and 118(5) to (7).

GENERAL NOTE

4–438   These Regulations apply in relation to dommiciliary care agencies in England only.

4–439   ARRANGEMENT OF REGULATIONS

PART I

GENERAL

PART II

REGISTERED PERSONS

PART III

CONDUCT OF DOMICILIARY CARE AGENCIES

Chapter 1—Quality of Service Provision

Chapter 2—Premises

PART 1

GENERAL

Citation, commencement and application

1.—(1) These Regulations may be cited as the Domiciliary Care Agencies **4–440** Regulations 2002 and shall come into force on 1st April 2003.

(2) These Regulations apply to domiciliary care agencies in England only.

Interpretation

2.—(1) In these Regulations—   **4–441**

"the Act" means the Care Standards Act 2000;

"agency" means a domiciliary care agency;

"agency premises" means the premises from which the activities of an agency are carried on;

["Commission" means the Commission for Social Care Inspection;]

"direct service provider" means a provider who supplies a domiciliary care worker who is employed by, and who acts for and under the control of, the provider;

"domiciliary care worker" means a person who—

(a) is employed by the agency to act for, and under the control of, another person;

(b) is introduced by an agency to a service user for employment by him; or

(c) is employed by a direct service provider,

215

in a position which is concerned with the provision of personal care in their own homes for persons who by reason of illness, infirmity or disability are unable to provide it for themselves without assistance;

"organisation" means a body corporate or any unincorporated association other than a partnership;

"registered manager", in relation to an agency, means a person who is registered under Part II of the Act as the manager of the agency;

"registered person", in relation to an agency, means any person who is registered as the provider or the manager of the agency;

"registered provider", in relation to an agency, means a person who is registered under Part II of the Act as the person carrying on the agency;

"responsible individual" shall be construed in accordance with regulation 7(2);

"service user" means any person for whom an agency—

(a) supplies a domiciliary care worker who is employed by the agency (including domiciliary care workers supplied by a direct service provider); or

(b) provides services for the purpose of supplying him with a domiciliary care worker for employment by him;

"service user's guide" means the guide produced in accordance with regulation 5(1);

"statement of purpose" means the written statement compiled in accordance with regulation 4(1).

(2) In these Regulations, references to the supply of a domiciliary care worker mean—

(a) the supply of a domiciliary care worker who is employed by an agency to act for and under the control of another person;

(b) the introduction of a domiciliary care worker by an agency to a service user for employment by him; and

(c) the supply of a domiciliary care worker employed by a direct service provider to a service user.

(3) In these Regulations, the terms "employed" and "employment" include employment under a contract of service or a contract for services, or otherwise than under a contract and whether or not for payment.

Amendment

4–442   The reference to the Commission was inserted by SI 2004/664, art.3, Sch.2.

Excepted undertakings
4–443   **3.** For the purposes of the Act, an undertaking is excepted from the definition of "domiciliary care agency" in section 4(3) of the Act if the undertaking is carried on by an individual who—

(a) carries it on otherwise than in partnership with others;

(b) is not employed by an organisation to carry it on; and

(c) does not employ any other person for the purpose of the undertaking.

DEFINITIONS
    employed: s.2(3).   **4–444**
    organisation: s.2(1).

GENERAL NOTE
    This regulation exempts a sole self employed provider of domiciliary care services from   **4–445**
registration as an agency.

Statement of purpose

    4.—(1) The registered person shall compile in relation to the agency a written   **4–446**
statement (in these Regulations referred to as "the statement of purpose") which
shall consist of a statement as to the matters listed in Schedule 1.

    (2) The registered person shall supply a copy of the statement of purpose to the
Commission and shall make a copy of it available on request for inspection at the
agency premises by every service user and any person acting on behalf of a service
user.

    (3) Nothing in regulation 22 shall require or authorise the registered person to
contravene, or not to comply with—

(a) any other provision of these Regulations; or

(b) the conditions for the time being in force in relation to the registration of the
    registered person under Part II of the Act.

DEFINITIONS
    registered person: reg.2(1).   **4–447**
    agency: reg.2(1).
    service user: reg.2(1).

GENERAL NOTE
    The statement of purpose, which must include the information listed in Sched.1, must be   **4–448**
kept under review by the registered person (reg.6). Guidance on the statement of purpose is
contained in Appendix 3 to *Choice, Power, Performance: The Need for Information on
Care Services in England* which was published by the NCSC in March 2004.
    A contravention or failure to comply with this regulation is an offence (reg.29).

PARA.2
    Acting on behalf of a service user: The registered person would need to be satisfied as to the   **4–449**
legitimacy of a claim made by a person who states that he or she is so acting.

PARA.3
    Nothing in reg.22: This places an obligation on the registered person to provide suitable   **4–450**
premises for the agency.

Service user's guide

    5.—(1) The registered person shall produce a service user's guide which shall   **4–451**
include—

(a) a summary of the statement of purpose;

(b) the terms and conditions in respect of the services to be provided to service users, including as to the amount and method of payment of fees;

(c) a summary of the complaints procedure established in accordance with regulation 20; and

(d) the address and telephone number of the Commission.

(2) The registered person shall make a copy of the service user's guide available on request for inspection at the agency premises by every service user and any person acting on behalf of a service user.

DEFINITIONS

4–452   registered person: reg.2(1).
service user's guide: reg.2(1).
statement of purpose: reg.2(1).
service user: reg.2(1).
agency premises: reg.2(1).
Commission; reg.2(1).

GENERAL NOTE

4–453   The service user's guide must be kept under review by the registered person (reg.6). A contravention or failure to comply with this regulation is an offence (reg.29).

PARA.2

4–454   *Acting on behalf of a service user:* See reg.4(2), above.

Review of statement of purpose and service user's guide
4–455   **6.** The registered person shall—

(a) keep under review and, where appropriate, revise the statement of purpose and the service user's guide; and(b) notify the Commission of any material revision within 28 days.

DEFINITIONS

4–456   registered person: reg.2(1).
statement of purpose: reg.2(1).
service user's guide: reg.2(1).
Commission: reg.2(1).

GENERAL NOTE

4–457   A contravention or failure to comply with this regulation is an offence (reg.29).

PART II

REGISTERED PERSONS

Fitness of registered provider
4–458   **7.**—(1) A person shall not carry on an agency unless he is fit to do so.
(2) A person is not fit to carry on an agency unless the person—

(a) is an individual, who carries on the agency—

    (i) otherwise than in partnership with others, and he satisfies the requirements set out in paragraph (3);

    (ii) in partnership with others, and he and each of his partners satisfies the requirements set out in paragraph (3);

(b) is a partnership, and each of the partners satisfies the requirements set out in paragraph (3);

(c) is an organisation and—

    (i) the organisation has given notice to the Commission of the name, address and position in the organisation of an individual (in these Regulations referred to as "the responsible individual") who is a director, manager, secretary or other officer of the organisation and is responsible for supervising the management of the agency; and

    (ii) that individual satisfies the requirements set out in paragraph (3).

(3) The requirements are that—

(a) he is of integrity and good character;

(b) he is physically and mentally fit to carry on the agency; and

(c) full and satisfactory information is available in relation to him in respect of each of the matters specified in Schedule 2.

(4) A person shall not carry on an agency if—

(a) he has been adjudged bankrupt or sequestration of his estate has been awarded and (in either case) he has not been discharged and the bankruptcy order has not been annulled or rescinded; or

(b) he has made a composition or arrangement with his creditors and has not been discharged in respect of it.

DEFINITIONS
    agency: reg.2(1).
    organisation: reg.2(1).
    Commission: reg.2(1).

4–459

GENERAL NOTE
    The notion of fitness is considered in the note on reg.7 of the Care Homes Regulations **4–460** 2001.

PARA.(7)(B)
    As this provision is mandatory, an appeal against the decision of the registration authority to refuse an application for registration of a company that was the subject of a Creditors' Voluntary Arrangement is bound to fail *(Company Care (Whitney) Ltd v CSCI* [2004] 0263 EA).

Appointment of manager

    8.—(1) The registered provider shall appoint an individual to manage the **4–461** agency where—

(a) there is no registered manager in respect of the agency; and(b) the registered provider—

(i) is an organisation or a partnership; or
(ii) is not a fit person to manage an agency; or
(iii) is not, or does not intend to be, in full-time day to day charge of the agency.

(2) Where the registered provider appoints a person to manage the agency, he shall forthwith give notice to the Commission of—

(a) the name of the person so appointed; and

(b) the date on which the appointment is to take effect.

DEFINITIONS

4–462   registered provider: reg.2(1).
agency: reg.2(1).
organisation: reg.2(1).: reg.2(1).
Commission: reg.2(1).

GENERAL NOTE

4–463   This regulation identifies when a registered provider is required to appoint a manager.

Fitness of manager

4–464   **9.**—(1) A person shall not manage an agency unless he is fit to do so.
(2) A person is not fit to manage an agency unless—

(a) he is of integrity and good character;

(b) having regard to the size of the agency, the statement of purpose and the number and needs of the service users—

(i) he has the qualifications, skills and experience necessary to manage the agency; and
(ii) he is physically and mentally fit to do so; and

(c) full and satisfactory information is available in relation to him in respect of each of the matters specified in Schedule 2.

DEFINITIONS

4–465   agency: reg.2(1).
statement of purpose: reg.2(1).
service user: reg.2(1).

GENERAL NOTE

4–466   The notion of fitness is considered in the note on reg.7 of the Care Homes Regulations 2001.

The interviewing of potential managers is considered in the note on reg.9 of the 2001 Regulations.

Registered person—general requirements and training

4–467   **10.**—(1) The registered provider and the registered manager shall, having regard to the size of the agency, the statement of purpose and the number and needs of the service users, carry on or (as the case may be) manage the agency with sufficient care, competence and skill.

(2) If the registered provider is—

(a) an individual, he shall undertake;

(b) an organisation, it shall ensure that the responsible individual undertakes; or

(c) a partnership, it shall ensure that one of the partners undertakes,

from time to time such training as is appropriate to ensure that he has the experience and skills necessary for carrying on the agency.

(3) The registered manager shall undertake from time to time such training as is appropriate to ensure that he has the experience and skills necessary for managing the agency.

DEFINITIONS   **4–468**
   registered provider: reg.2(1).
   registered manager: reg.2(1).
   agency: reg.2(1).
   statement of purpose: reg.2(1).
   service user: reg.2(1)

Notification of offences

11. Where the registered person or the responsible individual is convicted of **4–469** any criminal offence, whether in England and Wales or elsewhere, he shall forthwith give notice in writing to the Commission of—

(a) the date and place of the conviction;

(b) the offence of which he was convicted; and

(c) the penalty imposed on him in respect of the offence.

DEFINITIONS   **4–470**
   registered person: reg.2(1).
   responsible individual: reg.2(1).
   Commission: reg.2(1).

GENERAL NOTE   **4–471**
   Convicted: A police caution does involve a conviction.

PART III

CONDUCT OF DOMICILIARY CARE AGENCIES

Chapter 1—Quality of service provision

Fitness of domiciliary care workers supplied by an agency

12. [—(1)] The registered person shall ensure that no domiciliary care worker is **4–472** supplied by the agency unless—

(a) he is of integrity and good character;

(b) he has the experience and skills necessary for the work that he is to perform;

(c) he is physically and mentally fit for the purposes of the work which he is to perform; and

(d) full and satisfactory information is available in relation to him in respect of each of the matters specified in Schedule 3.

[(2) Paragraph (1)(d), in so far as it relates to paragraph 13 of Schedule 3, shall not apply until 31st October 2004 in respect of a domiciliary care worker who has been supplied by the agency at any time during the period from 1st October 2002 to 30th September 2003.]

DEFINITIONS

4–473   registered person: reg.2(1).
agency: reg.2(1).
domiciliary care worker: reg.2(1).

AMENDMENT

4–474   Paragraph (2) was inserted by SI 2003/2323, reg.2(3).

GENERAL NOTE

4–475   The notion of fitness is considered in the note on reg.7 of the Care Homes Regulations 2001.
A contravention or failure to comply with this regulation is an offence (reg.29).

PARA.1

4–476   *Supplied:* See reg.2(2).

Conduct of agency

4–477   **13.** Where the agency is acting otherwise than as an employment agency, the registered person shall make suitable arrangements to ensure that the agency is conducted, and the personal care arranged by the agency, is provided—

(a) so as to ensure the safety of service users;

(b) so as to safeguard service users against abuse or neglect;

(c) so as to promote the independence of service users;

(d) so as to ensure the safety and security of service users' property, including their homes;

(e) in a manner which respects the privacy, dignity and wishes of service users, and the confidentiality of information relating to them; and

(f) with due regard to the sex, religious persuasion, racial origin, and cultural and linguistic background and any disability of service users, and to the way in which they conduct their lives.

DEFINITIONS

4–478   agency: reg.2(1).
registered person: reg.2(1).
service user: reg.2(1).

GENERAL NOTE

A contravention or failure to comply with this regulation is an offence (reg.29). There is **4–479** no equivalent in these regulations to the requirement in reg.37 of the Care Homes Regulations 2001 for the registered person to inform the registration authority of "any allegation of misconduct" by either the registered person or an employee.

Employment agency: Is defined in s.121(1) of the Act.

Arrangements for the provision of personal care

14.—(1) Paragraphs (2) to (12) apply only to the supply of domiciliary care **4–480** workers to service users by an agency which is acting otherwise than as an employment agency.

(2) The registered person shall, after consultation with the service user, prepare a written plan ("the service user plan") which shall specify—

(a) the service user's needs in respect of which personal care is to be provided;

(b) how those needs are to be met by the provision of personal care.

(3) The registered person shall—

(a) make the service user plan available to the service user;

(b) keep the service user plan under review;

(c) where appropriate, and after consultation with the service user, or if consultation with the service user is not practicable, after consultation with a person acting on behalf of the service user, revise the service user plan; and

(d) notify the service user or, where applicable, the person acting on his behalf, of any such revision.

(4) The registered person shall, so far as is practicable, ensure that the personal care which the agency arranges to be provided to any service user meets the service user's needs specified in the service user plan prepared in respect of him.

(5) The registered person shall, for the purpose of providing personal care to service users, so far as is practicable—

(a) ascertain and take into account their wishes and feelings;

(b) provide them with comprehensive information and suitable choices as to the personal care that may be provided to them; and

(c) encourage and enable them to make decisions with respect to such personal care.

(6) The registered person shall ensure that where the agency arranges the provision of personal care to a service user, the arrangements shall—

(a) specify the procedure to be followed after an allegation of abuse, neglect or other harm has been made;

(b) specify the circumstances in which a domiciliary care worker may administer or assist in the administration of the service user's medication, or any other tasks relating to the service user's health care, and the procedures to be adopted in such circumstances;

(c) include arrangements to assist the service user with mobility in his home, where required; and

(d) specify the procedure to be followed where a domiciliary care worker acts as agent for, or receives money from, a service user.

(7) The registered person shall make arrangements for the recording, handling, safe keeping, safe administration and disposal of medicines used in the course of the provision of personal care to service users.

(8) The registered person shall make suitable arrangements, including training, to ensure that domiciliary care workers operate a safe system of working, including in relation to lifting and moving service users.

(9) The registered person shall make arrangements, by training or by other measures, to prevent service users being harmed or suffering abuse or being placed at risk of harm or abuse.

(10) The registered person shall ensure that no service user is subject to physical restraint unless restraint of the kind employed is the only practicable means of securing the welfare of that or any other service user and there are exceptional circumstances.

(11) On any occasion on which a service user is subject to physical restraint by a person who works as a domiciliary care worker for the purposes of the agency, the registered person shall record the circumstances, including the nature of the restraint.

(12) The procedure referred to in paragraph (6)(a) shall in particular provide for—

(a) written records to be kept of any allegation of abuse, neglect or other harm and of the action taken in response; and

(b) the Commission to be notified of any incident reported to the police, not later than 24 hours after the registered person—

(i) has reported the matter to the police; or
(ii) is informed that the matter has been reported to the police.

(13) The registered person shall ensure that any personal information about a service user for whom a domiciliary care worker is supplied by the agency is not disclosed to any member of the agency's staff unless it is necessary to do so in order to provide an effective service to the service user.

DEFINITIONS

4–481   domiciliary care worker: reg.2(1).
service user: reg.2(1).
agency: reg.2(1).
registered person: reg.2(1).
Commission: reg.2(1).

GENERAL NOTE

4–482   A contravention or failure to comply with this regulation is an offence (reg.29).

Supply: See reg.2(2).   **4–483**
Employment agency: Is defined in s.121(1) of the Act.

Para.2
Service user plan: Unlike the service user's guide which is produced under reg.5, this docu- **4–484**
ment relates to the needs of individual service users.

Para.6
Allegation: A written record of each allegation must be made (para.12(a)).   **4–485**

Para.(9)
The NCSC, the Association of Directors of Social Services and the Association of Chief **4–486**
Police Officers have agreed an "Adult Protection Protocol" (December, 2003) which sets
out the processes and procedures to be followed by the three parties when protecting vulnerable adults from abuse.

Staffing

15.—(1) Where an agency is acting otherwise than as an employment agency, **4–487**
the registered person shall, having regard to the size of the agency, the statement
of purpose and the number and needs of the service users, ensure that—

(a) there is at all times an appropriate number of suitably skilled and experi-
    enced persons employed for the purposes of the agency;

(b) appropriate information and advice are provided to persons employed for
    the purposes of the agency, and are made available to them at their request,
    in respect of—

    (i) service users and their needs in respect of personal care; and
    (ii) the provision of personal care to service users;

(c) suitable assistance and where necessary, appropriate equipment, is provided
    to persons working for the purposes of the agency, and is made available to
    them at their request, in respect of the provision of personal care to service
    users;

(d) suitably qualified and competent persons are available to be consulted dur-
    ing any period of the day in which a person is working for the purposes of
    the agency; and

(e) neither of the following circumstances, that is—

    (i) the employment of any persons on a temporary basis for the purposes
        of the agency; and
    (ii) any arrangements made for persons to work as domiciliary care
        workers on a temporary basis for those purposes,

will prevent service users from receiving such continuity of care as is reasonable
to meet their needs for personal care.

(2) The registered person shall ensure that each employee of the agency—

(a) receives training and appraisal which are appropriate to the work he is to perform;

(b) receives suitable assistance, including time off, for the purpose of obtaining qualifications appropriate to such work;

(c) is provided with a job description outlining his responsibilities.

(3) The registered person shall take such steps as may be necessary to address any aspect of the performance of a domiciliary care worker which is found to be unsatisfactory.

(4) The registered person shall ensure that each employee receives appropriate supervision.

DEFINITIONS

4–488   agency: reg.2(1).
registered person: reg.2(1).
service user: reg.2(1).
employed: reg.2(3).
domiciliary care worker: reg.2(1).

GENERAL NOTE

4–489   A contravention or failure to comply with this regulation is an offence (reg.29).
See the note on reg.21 of the Care Homes Regulations 2001 for comment on the Public Interest Disclosure Act 1998.

PARA.1

4–490   *Employment agency:* Is defined in s.121(1) of the Act.

Staff handbook

4–491   **16.**—(1) Where the agency is acting otherwise than as an employment agency, the registered person shall prepare a staff handbook and provide a copy to every member of staff.

(2) The handbook prepared in accordance with paragraph (1) shall include a statement as to—

(a) the conduct expected of members of staff, and disciplinary action which may be taken against them;

(b) the role and responsibilities of domiciliary care workers and other staff;

(c) record keeping requirements;

(d) recruitment procedures; and

(e) training and development requirements and opportunities.

DEFINITIONS

4–492   agency: reg.2(1).
registered person: reg.2(1).
domiciliary care worker: reg.2(1).

GENERAL NOTE

4–493   A contravention or failure to comply with this regulation is an offence (reg.29).

Para.1
Employment agency: Is defined in s.121(1) of the Act.   **4–494**

Provision of information to service users

17.—(1) The registered person shall ensure that before a domiciliary care **4–495**
worker is supplied to a service user, the service user is informed of—

(a) the name of the domiciliary care worker to be supplied, and the means of
contacting him;

(b) the name of the member of staff of the agency who is responsible for the
supply of that domiciliary care worker; and

(c) where the agency is acting otherwise than as an employment agency, details
of how he may contact the registered person, or a person nominated to act on
behalf of the registered person.

(2) The registered person shall ensure that the information specified in paragraph (1) is, where appropriate, provided to the service user's relatives or carers.

DEFINITIONS
registered person: reg.2(1).   **4–496**
domiciliary care worker: reg.2(1).
service user: reg.2(1).

GENERAL NOTE
A contravention or failure to comply with this regulation is an offence (reg.29).   **4–497**

Para.1
Supplied: See reg.2(2).   **4–498**

Identification of workers

18. Where the agency is acting otherwise than as an employment agency, the **4–499**
registered person shall ensure that every domiciliary care worker supplied by
the agency is instructed that, while attending on a service user for the purposes
of the provision of personal care, he must present the service user with identification showing his name, the name of the agency and a recent photograph.

DEFINITIONS
agency: reg.2(1).   **4–500**
registered person: reg.2(1).
domiciliary care worker: reg.2(1).
service user: reg.2(1).

GENERAL NOTE
A contravention or failure to comply with this regulation is an offence (reg.29).   **4–501**
Employment agency: Is defined in s.121(1) of the Act.
Supplied: See reg.2(2).

Records

19.—(1) The registered person shall ensure that the records specified in **4–502**
Schedule 4 are maintained and that they are—

(a) kept up to date, in good order and in a secure manner; and

(b) retained for a period of not less than three years beginning on the date of the last entry.

(2) The registered person shall ensure that, in addition to the records referred to in paragraph (1), a copy of the service user plan and a detailed record of the personal care provided to the service user are kept at the service user's home and that they are kept up to date, in good order and in a secure manner.

DEFINITIONS
4–503   registered person: reg.2(1).
service user: reg.2(1).

GENERAL NOTE
4–504   A contravention or failure to comply with this regulation is an offence (reg.29).

PARA.2
4–505   *Service user plan:* See reg.14(2).

Complaints

4–506   **20.**—(1) The registered person shall establish a procedure ("the complaints procedure") for considering complaints made to the registered person by a service user or a person acting on behalf of a service user.

(2) The registered person shall supply a written copy of the complaints procedure to every service user and, upon request, to any person acting on behalf of a service user.

(3) The written copy of the complaints procedure shall include—

(a) the address and telephone number of the Commission; and

(b) the procedure (if any) which has been notified by the Commission to the registered person for making complaints to the Commission relating to the agency.

(4) The registered person shall ensure that every complaint made under the complaints procedure is fully investigated.

(5) The registered person shall, within the period of 28 days beginning on the date on which the complaint is made, or such shorter period as may be reasonable in the circumstances, inform the person who made the complaint of the action (if any) that is to be taken in response.

(6) The registered person shall maintain a record of each complaint, including details of the investigations made, the outcome and any action taken in consequence and the requirements of regulation 19(1) shall apply to that record.

(7) The registered person shall supply to the Commission at its request a statement containing a summary of the complaints made during the twelve months ending on the date of the request and the action taken in response.

DEFINITIONS
4–507   registered person: reg.2(1).
service user: reg.2(1).
Commission: reg.2(1).

A contravention or failure to comply with this regulation is an offence (reg.29).   **4–508**

Review of quality of service provision

21.—(1) The registered person shall introduce and maintain a system for **4–509** reviewing at appropriate intervals the quality of personal care which the agency arranges to be provided.

(2) The registered person shall supply to the Commission a report in respect of any review conducted by him for the purposes of paragraph (1) and shall make a copy of the report available on request for inspection at the agency premises by service users and persons acting on behalf of service users.

(3) The system referred to in paragraph (1) shall provide for consultation with service users and persons acting on behalf of service users.

DEFINITIONS
registered person: reg.2(1).   **4–510**
agency: reg.2(1).
agency premises: reg.2(1).
service user: reg.2(1).
Commission: reg.2(1).

GENERAL NOTE
A contravention or failure to comply with this regulation is an offence (reg.29).   **4–511**

Chapter 2—Premises

Fitness of premises

22. Subject to regulation 4(3), the registered person shall not use the premises **4–512** for the purpose of an agency unless the premises are suitable for the purpose of achieving the aims and objectives of the agency set out in the statement of purpose.

DEFINITIONS
registered person: reg.2(1).   **4–513**
agency: reg.2(1).
statement of purpose: reg.2(1).

GENERAL NOTE
A contravention or failure to comply with this regulation is an offence (reg.29).   **4–514**

Chapter 3—Financial Position

Financial position

23.—(1) The registered provider shall carry on the agency in such manner as is **4–515** likely to ensure that the agency will be financially viable for the purpose of achieving the aims and objectives of the agency set out in the statement of purpose.

(2) The registered person shall, if the Commission so requests, provide the Commission with such information and documents as it may require in order to consider the financial viability of the agency, including—

(a) the annual accounts of the agency, certified by an accountant; and

(b) a certificate of insurance for the registered provider in respect of liability which may be incurred by him in relation to the agency in respect of death, injury, public liability, damage or other loss.

DEFINITIONS

4–516   registered provider: reg.2(1).
agency: reg.2(1).
statement of purpose: reg.2(1).
Commission: reg.2(1).

GENERAL NOTE

4–517 A contravention or failure to comply with this regulation is an offence (reg.29).

Chapter 4—Notices to be given to the Commission

Notice of absence
4–518   **24.**—(1) Where—

(a) the registered provider, being an individual in full-time day to day charge of the agency; or

(b) the registered manager,

proposes to be absent from the agency for a continuous period of 28 days or more, the registered person shall give notice in writing to the Commission of the proposed absence.

(2) Except in the case of an emergency, the notice referred to in paragraph (1) shall be given no later than one month before the proposed absence commences, or within such shorter period as may be agreed with the Commission and the notice shall specify—

(a) the length or expected length of the absence;

(b) the reason for the absence;

(c) the arrangements which have been made for running the agency during that absence;

(d) the name, address and qualifications of the person who will be responsible for the agency during that absence; and

(e) in the case of the absence of the registered manager, the arrangements that have been, or are proposed to be, made for appointing another person to manage the agency during that absence, including the proposed date by which the appointment is to be made.

(3) Where the absence arises as a result of an emergency, the registered person shall give notice of the absence within one week of its occurrence specifying the matters set out in paragraph (2)(a) to (e).
(4) Where—

(a) the registered provider, being an individual in full-time day to day charge of the agency; or

(b) the registered manager,

has been absent from the agency for a continuous period of 28 days or more, and the Commission has not been given notice of the absence, the registered person shall, without delay, give notice in writing to the Commission of the absence, specifying the matters set out in paragraph (2)(a) to (e).

(5) The registered person shall notify the Commission of the return to duty of the registered provider or (as the case may be) the registered manager not later than 7 days after the date of his return.

DEFINITIONS
    registered provider: reg.2(1).   **4–519**
    agency: reg.2(1).
    registered manager: reg.2(1).
    registered person: reg.2(1).
    Commission: reg.2(1).

GENERAL NOTE
    A contravention or failure to comply with this regulation is an offence (reg.29).   **4–520**

Notice of changes
    25. The registered person shall give notice in writing to the Commission as soon **4–521** as it is practicable to do so if any of the following events takes place or are proposed to take place—

(a) a person other than the registered person carries on or manages the agency;

(b) a person ceases to carry on or manage the agency;

(c) where the registered person is an individual, he changes his name;

(d) where the registered provider is a partnership, there is any change in the membership of that partnership;

(e) where the registered provider is an organisation—

  (i) the name or address of the organisation is changed;
  (ii) there is any change of director, manager, secretary or other similar officer of the organisation; and
  (iii) there is any change in the identity of the responsible individual;

(f) where the registered provider is an individual, a trustee in bankruptcy is appointed;

(g) where the registered provider is a company or partnership, a receiver, manager, liquidator or provisional liquidator is appointed; or

(h) the registered provider acquires additional premises for the purposes of the agency.

DEFINITIONS
    registered person: reg.2(1).   **4–522**
    Commission: reg.2(1).
    registered provider: reg.2(1).
    organisation: reg.2(1).

4–523 A contravention or failure to comply with this regulation is an offence (reg.29).
Responsible individual: See reg.7(2)(c).

Appointment of liquidators etc.
4–524 **26.**—(1) Any person to whom paragraph (2) applies must—

    (a) forthwith notify the Commission of his appointment indicating the reasons for it;

    (b) appoint a manager to take full-time day to day charge of the agency in any case where there is no registered manager; and

    (c) not more than 28 days after his appointment, notify the Commission of his intentions regarding the future operation of the agency.

(2) This paragraph applies to any person appointed as—

    (a) the receiver or manager of the property of a company or partnership which is a registered provider in respect of an agency;

    (b) the liquidator or provisional liquidator of a company which is the registered provider in respect of an agency;

    (c) the trustee in bankruptcy of a registered provider in respect of an agency.

4–525 Commission: reg.2(1).
registered manager: reg.2(1).
agency: reg.2(1).
registered provider: reg.2(1).

Death of registered person
4–526 **27.**—(1) If more than one person is registered in respect of an agency, and a registered person dies, the surviving registered person shall without delay notify the Commission of the death in writing.
(2) If only one person is registered in respect of an agency, and he dies, his personal representatives must notify the Commission in writing—

    (a) without delay of the death; and

    (b) within 28 days of their intentions regarding the future running of the agency.

(3) The personal representatives of the deceased registered provider may carry on the agency without being registered in respect of it—

    (a) for a period not exceeding 28 days; and

    (b) for any further period as may be determined in accordance with paragraph (4).

(4) The Commission may extend the period specified in paragraph (3)(a) by such further period, not exceeding one year, as the Commission shall determine, and shall notify any such determination to the personal representatives in writing.

(5) The personal representatives shall appoint a person to take full-time day to day charge of the agency during any period in which, in accordance with paragraph (3), they carry on the agency without being registered in respect of it.

DEFINITIONS

registered person: reg.2(1).   **4–527**
agency: reg.2(1).
registered provider: reg.2(1).
Commission: reg.2(1).

PART IV

MISCELLANEOUS

Compliance with regulations
28. Where there is more than one registered person in respect of an agency, any- **4–528**
thing which is required under these Regulations to be done by the registered person shall, if done by one of the registered persons, not be required to be done by any of the other registered persons.

DEFINITIONS

registered person: reg.2(1).   **4–529**
agency: reg.2(1).

Offences
29.—(1) A contravention or failure to comply with regulations 4 to 6 and 11 to **4–530**
25 shall be an offence.

(2) The Commission shall not bring proceedings against a person in respect of any contravention or failure to comply with those regulations unless—

(a) subject to paragraph (4), he is a registered person;

(b) notice has been given to him in accordance with paragraph (3);

(c) the period specified in the notice, within which the registered person may make representations to the Commission, has expired; and

(d) in a case where, in accordance with paragraph (3)(b), the notice specifies any action that is to be taken within a specified period, the period has expired and the action has not been taken within that period.

(3) Where the Commission considers that the registered person has contravened or failed to comply with any of the provisions of the regulations mentioned in paragraph (1), it may serve a notice on the registered person specifying—

(a) in what respect in its opinion the registered person has contravened any of the regulations, or has failed or is failing to comply with the requirements of any of those regulations;

(b) where it is practicable for the registered person to take action for the purpose of complying with any of those regulations, the action which, in the opinion of the Commission, the registered person should take for that purpose;

(c) the period, not exceeding three months, within which the registered person should take any action specified in accordance with sub-paragraph (b);

(d) the period, not exceeding one month, within which the registered person may make representations to the Commission about the notice.

(4) The Commission may bring proceedings against a person who was once, but no longer is, a registered person, in respect of a failure to comply with regulation 19, and for this purpose, references in paragraphs (2) and (3) to a registered person shall be taken to include such a person.

DEFINITIONS

4–531   registered person: reg.2(1).
agency: reg.2(1).
Commission: reg.2(1).

Regulation 4(1)   **SCHEDULE 1**

4–532   INFORMATION TO BE INCLUDED IN THE STATEMENT OF PURPOSE

1. The aims and objectives of the agency.
2. The nature of the services which the agency provides.
3. The name and address of the registered provider and of any registered manager.
4. The relevant qualifications and experience of the registered provider and any registered manager.
5. The range of qualifications of the domiciliary care workers supplied by the agency.
6. The complaints procedure established in accordance with regulation 20.

DEFINITIONS

4–533   agency: reg.2(1).
registered provider: reg.2(1).
registered manager: reg.2(1).
domiciliary care worker: reg.2(1).

PARA.5

4–534   *Supplied:* See reg.2(2).

Regulations 7(3) and 9(2)   **SCHEDULE 2**

4–535   INFORMATION REQUIRED IN RESPECT OF REGISTERED PROVIDERS AND MANAGERS OF AN AGENCY

1. Proof of identity, including a recent photograph.
2. Either—

(a) where the certificate is required for a purpose relating to section 115(5)(ea) of the Police Act 1997 (registration under Part II of the Care Standards Act 2000)[4], or the position falls within section 115(3) or (4) of that Act[5], an enhanced criminal record certificate issued under section 115 of that Act; or

(b) in any other case, a criminal record certificate issued under section 113 of that Act, including, where applicable, the matters specified in section 113(3A) and 115(6A) of that Act and the following provisions once they are in force, namely section 113(3C)(a) and (b) and section 11 5(6B)(a) and (b) of that Act[6].

3. Two written references, including a reference relating to the last period of employment of not less than three months duration.

4. Where a person has previously worked in a position which involved work with children or vulnerable adults, verification, so far as reasonably practicable, of the reason why he ceased to work in that position.

5. Documentary evidence of any relevant qualifications and training.

6. A full employment history, together with a satisfactory written explanation of any gaps in employment.

7. Details of health record.

8. Details of registration with or membership of any professional body.

9. Details of any professional indemnity insurance.

Regulation 12   **SCHEDULE 3**

INFORMATION REQUIRED IN RESPECT OF DOMICILIARY CARE WORKERS   **4–536**

1. Name, address, date of birth and telephone number.

2. Name, address and telephone number of next of kin.

3. Proof of identity, including a recent photograph.

4. Details of any criminal offences—

(a) of which the person has been convicted, including details of any convictions which are spent within the meaning of section 1 of the Rehabilitation of Offenders Act 1974 and which may be disclosed by virtue of the Rehabilitation of Offenders (Exceptions) Order 1975; or

(b) in respect of which he has been cautioned by a constable and which, at the time the caution was given, he admitted.

5. Two written references, including a reference relating to the last period of employment of not less than three months duration which involved work with children or vulnerable adults.

6. Where the person has previously worked in a position which involved work with children or vulnerable adults, verification, so far as reasonably practicable, of the reason why he ceased to work in that position.

7. Evidence of a satisfactory knowledge of the English language, where the person's qualifications were obtained outside the United Kingdom.

8. Documentary evidence of any relevant qualifications and training.

9. A full employment history, together with a satisfactory written explanation of any gaps in employment and details of any current employment other than for the purposes of the agency.

10. A statement by the person as to the state of his physical and mental health.

11. A statement by the registered provider, or the registered manager, as the case may be, that the person is physically and mentally fit for the purposes of the work which he is to perform.

12. Details of any professional indemnity insurance.

13. Either—

(a) where the position falls within section 115(3) or (4) of the Police Act 1997 (registration under Part 2 of the Care Standards Act 2000), an enhanced criminal record certificate issued under section 115 of that Act; or

(b) in any other case, a criminal record certificate issued under section 115 of that Act; or

including, where applicable, the matters specified in section 113(3A) or 115(6A) of that Act and, once they are in force, section 113(3C)(a) and (b) or section 115(6B)(a) and (b) of that Act.]

AMENDMENT
4–537   Paragraph 13 was inserted by SI 2003/2323, reg.2(4).

DEFINITIONS
4–538   registered provider: reg.2(1).
          registered manager: reg.2(1).

GENERAL NOTE
PARA.2
4–539   *Next of kin:* See the note on reg.40(1)(b) of the Care Homes Regulations 2001.

PARA.13
4–540   For a note on disclosure checks from the Criminal Records Bureaux, see para.7 of Sch.2 to the Care Homes Regulations 2001.

Regulation 19(1)   SCHEDULE 4

4–541   RECORDS TO BE MAINTAINED FOR INSPECTION

1. All information provided to the Commission for the purposes of registration in relation to the agency.

2. Details of every allegation of abuse, neglect or other harm made against an employee of, or any domiciliary care worker who works for, the agency, including details of the investigations made, the outcome and any action taken in consequence.

3. Details of any physical restraint used on a service user by a person who works as a domiciliary care worker for the purposes of the agency.

4. The service user plan devised for each service user in accordance with regulation 14, and a detailed record of the personal care provided to that service user.

PART 5

INSPECTION

The role of Inspection Units established under the Registered Homes Act 1984 was **5–001** described by the tribunal in *Heathcote v Lancashire County Council* (*Decn. No.356*) as follows:

"It is important for Registration and Inspection Units to recognise their unique position as a catalyst for the development of the quality of service as well as carrying out their regulatory role. The provision of clear and expert guidance on a personal level should help to achieve compliance with the regulations and should be an integral part of the inspection process".

Such a constructive approach was notably absent in *Joyce v NCSC* [2003] 0190 N. where the evidence that the Care Standards Tribunal received about a particular inspector gave rise to an impression of "an overbearing, intimidating and demanding individual who took a pedantic and rigorous view of her position" (para.76).

Adult placement carers and service users have expressed concern about the effect on privacy and family life of unannounced inspections and the publication of inspection reports on the internet. Following correspondence between the Minister of State for Health and the NCSC, the following approach was agreed:

"NCSC inspectors will now undertake a first announced inspection, then use a risk assessment approach, together with any other relevant information to determine if the second inspection needs to be announced or unannounced. It will only be unannounced if a concern is identified. In addition, to maintain privacy, inspection reports for adult placements will only be available in hard copy and on request, not published on the NCSC website when this facility has been developed" (NCSC Press Release 019/2003).

If an inspector considers that an offence under this Act might have been committed, the **5–002** relevant provisions of the Codes of Practice issued under the Police and Criminal Evidence Act 1984 must be complied with: see Introduction to Part 6.

It would be appropriate for a member of staff of the establishment or agency to accompany an inspector during the course of an inspection and to make a contemporaneous note of any significant event. Such an activity would not constitute an obstruction of the inspection process under s.31(9). The note could be used in the event of any dispute about what was seen or heard during the course of the inspection. The member of staff would not be able to be present if the inspector wished to interview a person in private (see s.31(3)(c), (d) and (e)).

Inspections by persons authorised by registration authority

5–003 **31.**—(1) The registration authority may at any time require a person who carries on or manages an establishment or agency to provide it with any information relating to the establishment or agency which the registration authority considers it necessary or expedient to have for the purposes of its functions under this Part.

[(1A) The power under subsection (1) to require the provision of information includes—

(a) power to require the provision of copies of any documents or records (including medical and other personal records); and

(b) in relation to records kept by means of a computer, power to require the provision of the records in legible form.]

(2) A person authorised by the registration authority may at any time enter and inspect premises which are used, or which he has reasonable cause to believe to be used, as an establishment or for the purposes of an agency.

(3) A person authorised by virtue of this section to enter and inspect premises may—

(a) make any examination into the state and management of the premises and treatment of patients or persons accommodated or cared for there which he thinks appropriate;

(b) inspect and take copies of any documents or records [(including medical and other personal records)] required to be kept in accordance with regulations under this Part, section 9(2) of the Adoption Act 1976, section 23(2)(a) or 59(2) of the 1989 Act or section 1(3) of the Adoption (Intercountry Aspects) Act 1999;

(c) interview in private the manager or the person carrying on the establishment or agency;

(d) interview in private any person [working] there;

(e) interview in private any patient or person accommodated or cared for there who consents to be interviewed.

(4) The powers under subsection (3)(b) include—

(a) power to require the manager or the person carrying on the establishment or agency to produce any documents or records, wherever kept, for inspection on the premises; and

(b) in relation to records which are kept by means of a computer, power to require the records to be produced in a form in which they are legible and can be taken away.

(5) Subsection (6) applies where the premises in question are used as an establishment and the person so authorised—

(a) is a medical practitioner or registered nurse; and

(b) has reasonable cause to believe that a patient or person accommodated or cared for there is not receiving proper care.

(6) The person so authorised may, with the consent of the person mentioned in subsection (5)(b), examine him in private [. . .].

The [power] conferred by this subsection may be exercised in relation to a person who is incapable of giving consent without that person's consent.

(7) The Secretary of State may by regulations require [the CHAI or the CSCI] to arrange for premises which are used as an establishment or for the purposes of an agency to be inspected on such occasions or at such intervals as may be prescribed.

(8) A person who proposes to exercise any power of entry or inspection conferred by this section shall if so required produce some duly authenticated document showing his authority to exercise the power.

(9) Any person who—

(a) intentionally obstructs the exercise of any power conferred by this section or section 32; or

(b) fails without a reasonable excuse to comply with any requirement under this section or that section,

shall be guilty of an offence and liable on summary conviction to a fine not exceeding level 4 on the standard scale.

AMENDMENTS

Subsection (1A) was inserted and the words in square brackets in subss.(3), (6) and (7) **5–004** were substituted by the Health and Social Care (Community Health and Standards) Act 2003, ss.108 (2)(3), 147, Sch.9, Pt 2, para.23. The words omitted in subs.(6) were repealed by s.196, Sch.14, Pt 2.

DEFINITIONS

agency: s.4(9). **5–005**
establishment: s.4(8).
registration authority: s.5.
regulations: s.121(1).
CHAI: s.121(13).
CSCI: s.121(13).

GENERAL NOTE

This section, which should be read with s.32, provides the registration authority with a **5–006** power to enter and inspect premises if they are used, or are believed to be used, as an establishment or agency (subs.(2)) and enables the authority to require a person who carries on or manages an establishment or agency to provide it with any information relevant to the discharge of its functions (subs.(1)). The registration authority, which acts through its inspectors, is also given a power to interview, in private, patients, residents and employees, and to inspect and take copies of documents and records (including computer, but not medical records) (subss.(3), (4)). A doctor or nurse can examine in private a patient or resident (with the consent of a mentally capable patient or resident) and can inspect relevant medical records, where they believe that the person concerned is not receiving proper care (subss.(5), (6). It is an offence for a person to intentionally obstruct the exercise of the powers under this section or s.32 (subs.(9)).

Apart from the power of inspection contained in the Act, the following powers contained in the Children Act 1989 and the Mental Health Act 1983 can be used to provide authorised persons with the power to inspect registered establishments.

Section 80 of the Children Act provides a person authorised by the Secretary of State (or, in relation to Wales, the National Assembly for Wales) with a power to inspect any care home or independent hospital used to accommodate children (subs.(1)((j)). This power is supplemented by a power to inspect the children (subs.(6)) and by powers to direct the person carrying on the establishment to provide specific information (subss.(4), (5)), to inspect records (subs.7)) and to enter the establishment (subs.(8)). It is an offence to intentionally obstruct the inspector (subs.(10)) and if entry is refused a warrant can be obtained under s.102 of the 1989 Act. A person carrying on a care home or an independent hospital is placed under a duty to notify the local authority if a child has been, or is likely to be, accommodated for a consecutive period of at least three months (*ibid.*, s.86). The local authority has a duty to safeguard the child's welfare (s.86(3)). The local authority is also placed under a duty by ss.24 and 24A of the 1989 Act to provide the child with advice and assistance.

Under s.120(1),(4) of the Mental Health Act 1983, the Mental Health Act Commission and persons authorised by the Commission have power to visit and interview in private patients who are detained under the provisions of that Act in registered establishments. An approved social worker has the power under s.115 of that Act to enter and inspect a registered establishment (not being a hospital), if he or she has reasonable cause to believe that a mentally disordered patient is not under proper care. An obstruction of the Commission or an approved social worker in the performance of their duties is an offence (*ibid.*, s.129).

THE HUMAN RIGHTS ACT 1998

5–007   The Commissions, as public authorities under s.6 of the Human Rights Act, must not act in a way which is incompatible with a right provided for in the European Convention on Human Rights. In particular, the Commissions must act in a manner which is compatible with the service providers rights under Art.8 of the Convention (rights to respect for home, family life and privacy). Any interference with an Art.8 right must be (1) in accordance with the law, (2) in pursuit of a legitimate aim, and (3) be proportionate to that aim. The relevant legitimate aims established by Art.8(2) are "public safety . . ., the prevention of disorder or crime, . . . the protection of health or morals, or . . . the protection of the rights and freedoms of others".

SUBS.(1)

5–008   *Information:* Medical records can only be produced under the provisions of subss.(5) and (6).

Functions under this Part: Which are the registration and inspection of establishments and agencies.

SUBS.(2)

5–009   *A person:* Who need not be an employee of the registration authority.

May: This power may be converted into a duty (subs.(7)).

At any time: An inspection carried out under this section may be made at any time of the day or night and advance notice of the inspection does not have to be given.

Enter and inspect: The authorised person is not empowered to use force in an attempt to gain entry to the premises. A person who obstructs the authorised person in the exercise of his powers under this section commits an offence under subs.(9).

Reasonable cause to believe: It is an offence under s.11 for a person to carry on or manage an establishment or agency without being registered.

SUBS.(3)

The medical examination of those being cared for in the establishment is governed by **5–010** subss.(5) and (6).

PARA.(C)

Carrying on: See s.32(4).   **5–011**

PARA.(E)

There is no power to interview a person who does not consent to be interviewed or a per- **5–012** son who lacks the mental capacity to provide consent. A mentally incapable person may be examined by either a nurse or a doctor and his or her medical records examined if it is believed that that person is not receiving proper care (subss.(5), (6)). Note that the service user does not have a right to demand an interview with the authorised person.

SUBS.(5)

Person . . . authorised: Under subs.(2).   **5–013**

SUBS.(6)

Incapable of giving consent: Incapacity should be determined by the examining doctor using **5–014** the test of capacity identified by Butler-Sloss P. in *Re M.B. (Medical Treatment)* [1997] F.L.R. 426, CA, at 437:

"A person lacks the capacity if some impairment or disturbance of mental functioning renders the person unable to make a decision whether to consent to or refuse treatment. The inability to make a decision will occur when:

(a) the patient is unable to comprehend and retain information which is material to the decision, especially as to the likely consequences of having or not having the treatment in question;

(b) the patient is unable to use the information and weigh it in the balance as part of the process of arriving at a decision . . ."

SUBS.(7)

Regulations: See the Commission for Healthcare Audit and Inspection (Fees and **5–015** Frequency of Inspections) Regulations 2004 (SI 2004/661), reg.6 and the Commission for Social Care Inspection (Fees and Frequency of Inspections) regulations 2004 (SI 2004/662), reg.6.

Inspected on such occasions: The registration authority can inspect as frequently as it thinks fit subject to the minimum requirement set out in the regulations.

SUBS.(8)

The staff of establishments and agencies should be aware of this requirement and should **5–016** always require the production of the relevant document before entry into the building is allowed.

Proposes to: The right to request production of the document is confined to the period before the commencement of the inspection.

Produce some duly authenticated document: The power to enter and inspect can be exercised even if there is nobody on the premises to whom the document can be produced; see Sommervell L.J. speaking on a similar provision in the Gas Act 1948, in *Grove v Eastern Gas Board* [1951] 2 All E.R. 1051, at 1053, CA.

SUBS.(9)

Intentionally: Mens rea is required.   **5–017**

Obstructs: Cases on the offence of obstructing a policeman in the execution of duty suggest that an offence under this section need not involve physical violence (*Hinchcliffe v Sheldon* [1955] 1 W.L.R. 1207) and might be committed if a verbal warning of an impending inspection was given (*Green v Moore* [1982] 2 W.L.R. 671). There is also authority to support the contention that an offence is committed if the defendant's conduct makes it more difficult for an inspector to carry out his duties; see the dictum of Lord Goddard C.J. in *Hinchcliffe v Sheldon*, above, at 1210 which was followed by the Divisional Court in *Lewis v Cox* [1984] 3 W.L.R. 875. In *Swallow v London County Council* [1916] 1 K.B. 224, a case under the Weights and Measures Act 1889, it was held that, in the absence of a legal duty to act, standing by and doing nothing did not amount to an obstruction.

Inspections: supplementary

5–018   **32.**—(1) A person authorised by virtue of section 31 to enter and inspect any premises may seize and remove any document or other material or thing found there which he has reasonable grounds to believe may be evidence of a failure to comply with any condition or requirement imposed by or under this Part.

(2) A person so authorised—

(a) may require any person to afford him such facilities and assistance with respect to matters within the person's control as are necessary to enable him to exercise his powers under section 31 or this section;

(b) may take such measurements and photographs and make such recordings as he considers necessary to enable him to exercise those powers.

(3) A person authorised by virtue of section 31 to inspect any records shall be entitled to have access to, and to check the operation of, any computer and any associated apparatus which is or has been in use in connection with the records in question.

(4) The references in section 31 to the person carrying on the establishment or agency include, in the case of an establishment or agency which is carried on by a company, a reference to any director, manager, secretary or other similar officer of the company.

(5) Where any premises which are used as an establishment or for the purposes of an agency have been inspected under section 31, the registration authority—

(a) shall prepare a report on the matters inspected; and

(b) shall without delay send a copy of the report to each person who is registered in respect of the establishment or agency.

(6) The registration authority shall make copies of any report prepared under subsection (5) available for inspection at its offices by any person at any reasonable time; and may take any other steps for publicising a report which it considers appropriate.

(7) Any person who asks the registration authority for a copy of a report prepared under subsection (5) shal be entitled to have one on payment of a reasonable fee determined by the registration authority; but nothing in this subsection prevents the registration authority from providing a copy free of charge when it considers it appropriate to do so.

(8) [. . .]

AMENDMENT
Subsection (8) was repealed by the Health and Social Care (Community Health and **5–019** Standards) Act 2003, s.196, Sch.14, Pt 2.

DEFINITIONS
  agency: s.4(9).   **5–020**
  establishment: s.4(8).
  registration authority: s.5.

GENERAL NOTE
This section authorises the registration authority inspector to remove any document or **5–021** other material which could be used as evidence of a possible breach of an obligation under Part 2 of the Act (subs.(1)), imposes a requirement to assist the inspector (subs.(2)), enables the inspector to take such measurements and photographs and to make such recordings as he considers necessary (subs.(2)), and gives the inspector a right to have access to, and to check the operation of, computers (subs.(3)). The registration authority is required to prepare a report after carrying out an inspection and send a copy of the report to the registered person (subs.(5)). This copy must be made available to a member of the public (subs.(6)), who may be required to pay a fee (subs.(7)).

SUBS.(1)
The effect of s.67(9) of the Police and Criminal Evidence Act 1984 is that where an **5–022** inspector, as part of an investigation into an alleged offence under this Act, considers that property should be seized under this provision, then the inspector must act in compliance with the relevant provisions of Code of Practice B issued under that Act. In these circumstances, a caution should be issued at the commencement of the inspection. Section 67(9) is considered in the Introduction to Part 6.

SUBS.(2)
  Recordings: Including tape recordings.   **5–023**

PART 6

OFFENCES

Apart from the offences considered in this Part, the Act also contains the following **6–001** offences:

(a) carrying on an establishment or agency without being registered (s.11);

(b) obstructing an inspection of an establishment or agency (s.31(9)(a)); and

(c) a failure to comply with the requirements of either s.31 or s.32 (s.31(9)(b)).

Section 67(9) of the Police and Criminal Evidence Act 1984 states that persons "other than police officers who are charged with the duty of investigating offences or charging offenders shall in the discharge of that duty have regard to any relevant provisions of [the Codes of Practice issued under s.60(1)(a) and s.66 of that Act]." Officers of the CSCI and the CHAI come within the ambit of s.67(9) when they are engaged in investigating a possible offence under the Care Standards Act (*Dudley MBC v Debenhams plc* (1994) 158 J.P.N. 746, DC). This means, inter alia, that an inspector who has grounds to suspect that an offence under the Act (or the regulations made under it) might have been committed issue a caution before interviewing the suspect. The wording of the caution is:

> "You do not have to say anything. But it may harm your defence if you do not mention when questioned something which you later rely on in court. Anything you say may be given in evidence" (Code C, para.10(5)).

If a suspect is interviewed without a caution being administered, any evidence obtained during the course of the interview may be excluded by the court by virtue of s.78 of the 1984 Act.

Code C contains general provisions regarding the interviewing of suspects. Codes B and **6–002** E are relevant to the work of officers of the Commissions in so far as they refer to the searching of premises and the tape recording of interviews with suspects.

As an alternative to issuing proceedings under this Act, the Commissions could consider issuing a formal written caution which, if accepted by the person concerned, (a) will influence the Commissions in their decision whether or not to institute proceedings if the person should offend again; and (b) may be cited in any subsequent court proceedings if the person is found guilty of an offence. According to the Home Office National Standards for Cautioning, the purposes of a formal caution are:

(i) to deal quickly and simply with less serious offenders;

(ii) to divert them from unnecessary appearances in the criminal courts; and

(iii) to reduce the chances of re-offending.

A formal caution can only be administered:

(i) is there is evidence of guilt sufficient to give a realistic prospect of conviction;

(ii) if the offender admits the offence; and

(iii) the offender understands the significance of a caution and gives written consent to being cautioned.

Part I of the Sexual Offences Act 2003 creates the following offences relating to care workers who care for persons with a mental disorder: sexual activity with a person with a mental disorder (s.38); causing or inciting sexual activity (s.39); sexual activity in the presence of a person with a mental disorder (s.40); and causing a person with a mental disorder to watch a sexual act (s.41).

Failure to comply with conditions

24. If a person registered in respect of an establishment or agency fails, without **6–003** reasonable excuse, to comply with any condition for the time being in force by virtue of this Part in respect of the establishment or agency, he shall be guilty of an offence and liable on summary conviction to a fine not exceeding level 5 on the standard scale.

DEFINITIONS **6–004**
agency: s.4(9).
establishment: s.4(8).

GENERAL NOTE
Where the conditions of registration are not adhered to without reasonable excuse, the **6–005** registration authority may prosecute.
Person: Or company (s.30).

Contravention of regulations

25.—(1) Regulations under this Part may provide that a contravention of or fail- **6–006** ure to comply with any specified provision of the regulations shall be an offence.

(2) A person guilty of an offence under the regulations shall be liable on sum- mary conviction to a fine not exceeding level 4 on the standard scale.

DEFINITION **6–007**
regulations: s.121(1).

GENERAL NOTE
The relevant regulations state that if a regulation is breached, the breach of which is an **6–008** offence, providers will be given a notice setting out:

- the regulation breached;
- how the service is considered deficient;
- what must be done to remedy the deficiency;
- a time scale within which the deficiency must be remedied.

If the deficiency is not remedied, a prosecution may follow.
It is not an offence to contravene the National Minimum Standards.

SUBS.(1)
Regulations: See the National Care Standards Commission (Registration) Regulations **6–009** 2001 (SI 2001/3969), reg.11.

SUBS.(2) **6–010**
Person: Or company (s.30).

False descriptions of establishments and agencies

26.—(1) A person who, with intent to deceive any person— **6–011**

(a) applies any name to premises in England or Wales; or

(b) in any way describes such premises or holds such premises out, so as to indicate, or reasonably be understood to indicate, that the premises are an establishment, or an agency, of a particular description shall be liable on summary conviction to a fine not exceeding level 5 on the standard scale unless registration has been effected under this Part in respect of the premises as an establishment or agency of that description.

(2) References to premises in subsection (1) shall be taken to include references to an undertaking or organisation.

(3) No person shall, with intent to deceive any person, in any way describe or hold out an establishment or agency as able to provide any service or do any thing the provision or doing of which would contravene a condition for the time being in force by virtue of this Part in respect of the establishment or agency.

(4) A person who contravenes subsection (3) shall be liable on summary conviction to a fine not exceeding level 5 on the standard scale.

DEFINITIONS

6–012 agency: s.4(9).
establishment: s.4(8).

GENERAL NOTE

6–013 This section makes it an offence for a person who, with intent to deceive any person, describes unregistered premises so as to indicate that the premises are an establishment or agency. It is also an offence under this section to describe an establishment or agency as being able to provide a service which is not permitted by the registration conditions (subs.(3)). For offences committed by companies, see s.30.

SUBS.(1)

6–014 *A person:* Or company (s.30).

To deceive: Is to induce a person to believe that a thing is true which is false, or to believe a thing to be false which is true, contrary to what the person practising the deceit believes to be the case (*Re London and Globe Finance Corporation Ltd* [1903] 1 Ch. 728 at 732, *per* Buckley J., as modified by the observation of Lord Radcliffe in *Welham v DPP* [1961] A.C. 103 at 126, 127).

Describes: Either in the name that is given to the business, in publicity material, or in oral communication.

False statements in applications

6–015 **27.**—(1) Any person who, in an application for registration under this Part or for the variation of any condition in force in relation to his registration, knowingly makes a statement which is false or misleading in a material respect shall be guilty of an offence.

(2) A person guilty of an offence under this section shall be liable on summary conviction to a fine not exceeding level 4 on the standard scale.

GENERAL NOTE
SUBS.(1)

6–016 *Person:* Or company (s.30).

False: This term is defined for the purposes of the Forgery and Counterfeiting Act 1981 in s.9 of that Act. An entry or statement may be false on account of what it omits, even though the statement or entry itself is literally true (*R. v Lord Kylsant* [1932] 1 K.B. 442).

Failure to display certificate of registration

28.—(1) A certificate of registration issued under this Part in respect of any **6–017** establishment or agency shall be kept affixed in a conspicuous place in the establishment or at the agency.

(2) If default is made in complying with subsection (1), any person registered in respect of the establishment or agency shall be guilty of an offence and liable on summary conviction to a fine not exceeding level 2 on the standard scale.

DEFINITIONS

    establishment: s.4(8).   **6–018**

    agency: s.4(9).

GENERAL NOTE

    This section makes no provision for daily fines.   **6–019**

SUBS.(2)

    Person: Or company (s.30).   **6–020**

Proceedings for offences

29.—(1) Proceedings in respect of an offence under this Part or regulations **6–021** made under it shall not, without the written consent of the Attorney General, be taken by any person other than—

  (a) [the CHAI or the CSCI (as appropriate)] or, in relation to any functions of [either the CHAI or the CSCI] which the Secretary of State is by virtue of sections 113 for the time being discharging, the Secretary of State; or

  (b) the Assembly.

(2) Proceedings for an offence under this Part or regulations made under it may be brought within a period of six months from the date on which evidence sufficient in the opinion of the prosecutor to warrant the proceedings came to his knowledge; but no such proceedings shall be brought by virtue of this subsection more than three years after the commission of the offence.

AMENDMENTS

    The words in square brackets in subs.(1) were substituted by the Health and Social Care **6–022** (Community Health and Standards) Act 2003, s.147, Sch.9, Pt 2, para.22.

DEFINITIONS   **6–023**

    Assembly: s.5.

    regulations: s.121(1).

    CHAI: s.121(13).

    CSCI: s.121(13).

GENERAL NOTE

    This section provides that proceedings in respect of offences under this Part or regu- **6–024** lations made under it shall not, without the written consent of the Attorney General, be taken by any person other than the Commission (or, in the context of his default powers, the Secretary of State) or the Assembly.

Subs.(2)

6–025   There is a six-month time limit for the prosecution of summary offences, but the registration authority may not be able to bring a prosecution within that time scale because it may only find evidence of the offence more than six months after it has been committed. This provision allows prosecutions to be brought within six months of the evidence coming to light as long as the prosecution is brought within three years after the commission of the offence.

Offences by bodies corporate

6–026   **30.**—(1) This section applies where any offence under this Part or regulations made under it is committed by a body corporate.

(2) If the offence is proved to have been committed with the consent or connivance of, or to be attributable to any neglect on the part of—

(a) any director, manager, or secretary of the body corporate; or

(b) any person who was purporting to act in any such capacity,

he (as well as the body corporate) shall be guilty of the offence and shall be liable to be proceeded against and punished accordingly.

(3) The reference in subsection (2) to a director, manager or secretary of a body corporate includes a reference—

(a) to any other similar officer of the body; and

(b) where the body is a local authority, to any officer or member of the authority.

DEFINITIONS

6–027   local authority: s.121(1).
regulations: s.121(1).

GENERAL NOTE

6–028   This section states that if an offence under this Part is committed by a company, not only the company itself, but also any employee of the company to whom the offence is attributable shall be liable to a penalty. The same principle applies to local authorities (subs.(3)).

PART 7

CARE STANDARDS TRIBUNAL

The Care Standards Tribunal was established under s.9 of the Protection of Children Act **7–001** 1999 and handles appeals provided for under a range of legislation, including appeals under the Act. The constitution of the Tribunal is to be found in the Schedule to the 1999 Act. The Tribunal's powers extend to England and Wales only. It is an independent judicial body whose members are appointed by the Lord Chancellor (Sch.1, para.2 of the 1999 Act). The Tribunal has a judicial President, currently Judge David Pearl, who is responsible for the legal management of the Tribunal, giving guidance on practice and procedure, for the training of Tribunal members and for certain responsibilities specified in the Protection of Children and Vulnerable Adults and Care Standards Tribunal Regulations 2002. The President is also responsible for appointing members to the Tribunal that will hear each appeal. Each Tribunal will consist of a legally qualified chairman and two laypersons (Sch.1, para.1(2) of the 1999 Act). The chairmen must have a seven-year general qualification within the meaning of s.71 of the Courts and Legal Services Act 1990 (*ibid.*, para.2(2)). The requirements for membership of the lay panel are set out in reg.3 of the 2002 Regulations.

The Tribunal's jurisdiction for hearing appeals under the Act is to be found in s.21. The procedure of the Tribunal is governed by the 2002 regulations.

An appeal of a decision of the Tribunal on a point of law can be made to the High Court: see s.9(6) of the 1999 Act. The Tribunal is not a party to the proceedings on an appeal. The Tribunal is subject to the supervision of the Council on Tribunals (Tribunal and Inquiries Act 1992, Sch.1, para.36B).

In *Re A Care Home (Guidance Note)* [2002] 32 N.C., the Tribunal said that on a "strict reading" of s.21(5) of the 2000 Act "it is clear that there is no express power [for the Tribunal] to publish guidance". Nevertheless, the Tribunal proceeded to offer guidance on the correct approach to the transfer of conditions and categories from the regime under the 1984 Act to 2000 Act: see the note on s.11.

The address of the Tribunal is 18 Pocock St, London SE1 0BV, tel: 020 7960 0660; fax: 020 7960 0662; email: *CST@CST.gsi.gov.uk*. The Tribunal, which has an informative website at *www.carestandardstribunal.gov.uk*, has published "A guide to the appeals process and procedures of the Tribunal" to assist appellants. The guide, which is available from the Tribunal secretariat and is on the Tribunal's website, contains appeal forms and provides advice on time limits for the submission of documents.

Appeals to the Tribunal

7–002   **21.**—(1) An appeal against—

(a) a decision of the registration authority under this Part; or

(b) an order made by a justice of the peace under section 20,

shall lie to the Tribunal.

(2) No appeal against a decision or order may be brought by a person more than 28 days after service on him of notice of the decision or order.

(3) On an appeal against a decision of the registration authority the Tribunal may confirm the decision or direct that it shall not have effect.

(4) On an appeal against an order made by a justice of the peace the Tribunal may confirm the order or direct that it shall cease to have effect.

(5) The Tribunal shall also have power on an appeal against a decision or order—

(a) to vary any condition for the time bieng in force in respect of the establishment or agency to which the appeal relates;

(b) to direct that any such condition shall cease to have effect; or

(c) to direct that any such condition as it thinks fit shall have effect in respect of the establishment or agency.

DEFINITIONS

7–003   registration authority: s.5.
          the Tribunal: s.121(1).

GENERAL NOTE

7–004   This section provides for an appeal against a decision of the registration authority or a justice of the peace under the Act and identifies the powers of the appellate body. The appeal is to the Care Standards Tribunal. An appeal must be submitted within 28 days of the receipt of a notice of the decision of registration authority or order of the magistrates. The proceedings of the Tribunal are governed by the Protection of Children and Vulnerable Adults and Care Standards Tribunal Regulations 2002 (SI 2002/816).

This Act is silent on the issue of which party has the burden of proof. The general principle of the law of evidence is that the burden of proof should lies upon the party who substantially asserts the affirmative of the issue, *i.e.* "he who asserts must prove" (*Constantine Line v Imperial Smelting Corporation* [1942] A.C. 154). This principle was applied by the Tribunal in *Affirmative Futures Ltd v NCSC* [2002] 101–111 N.C. The standard of proof is one of a balance of probability. In *Brown and Brown (High Ridge Children's Home) v NCSC* [2002] 83 N.C., the Tribunal applied the standard set out in the following passage from Lord Nicholl's speech in *Re H (Minors) (Sexual Abuse) (Standard of Proof)* [1996] 1 All E.R. 1 at 16, 17:

"When assessing the probabilities the court will have in mind as a factor, to whatever extent is appropriate in the particular case, that the more serious the allegation the less likely it is that the event occurred and, hence, the stronger should be the evidence before the court concludes that the allegation is established on the balance of probability.
. . .

The more improbable the event, the stronger must be the evidence that it did not occur before, on the balance of probability, its occurrence will be established."

An appeal is a re-hearing. The Tribunal can therefore admit evidence that has previously **7–005** been overlooked or which relates to events that occurred after the decision of the registration authority or the justice of the peace (*Lyons v East Sussex County Council, The Times*, July 27, 1987, Farquharson J.; also see *Her Majesty's Chief Inspector of Schools v Spicer* [2004] EWHC 440 (Admin)) if this is deemed by the Tribunal to be fair. The post-decision events that the Tribunal can consider include the manner in which the registered person has responded to the decision. The Tribunal has said that its role is not to review the decision of the registration authority or justice of the peace; rather it is engaged in a total examination of all the evidence. It conducts a merits appeal, not a judicial review (*Appiah-Anane v NCSC* [2002] 96 NC).

In *WH v NCSC* [2003] 176 N.C., the Tribunal dismissed an appeal against the cancellation of a children's home. Due to its concern about the welfare of two of the residents of the home, the Tribunal asked that enquiries be made. Having considered the responses that it received, the Tribunal declared itself satisfied "that the agreement that has been reached between the parties is appropriate and that there is no risk that children would remain in an unregistered home". The Tribunal then proceeded to "incorporate the agreement" into its decision. It is submitted that the Tribunal has no jurisdiction either to incorporate such an agreement into its decision, to enforce such an agreement or to revisit its decision in the event of the agreement not being honoured.

The question of whether there has been a breach of s.11 of this Act is a matter within the jurisdiction of the tribunal when considering an appeal under this section because falling foul of s.11 would, by way of regulations made under s.22, be relevant to questions of fitness, integrity and good character (*The London Cosmetic Laser Centre Ltd v CHAI* [2004] 278 EA, para.13).

An appeal can be brought even though the establishment or agency is no longer functioning (*Alternative Futures and others v National Care Standards Commission and Sefton MBC* [2002] EWHC 3032 (Admin), following *Kowlessur v Suffolk Health Authority* [2002] C/2000/2662, CA, noted under s.15(1)(b)). It is uncertain whether an appeal can be brought if the establishment or agency is no longer available for use by the applicant because, for example, it has been sold. In *Sanjivi v East Kent Health Authority* (2001) 59 B.M.L.R. 115, Hallett J. held that the definition of "nursing home" in the 1984 Act which refers to "premises used, or intended to be used" for the purpose of nursing precluded an applicant from bringing an appeal if the premises were no longer available to her to be used. It is submitted that *Sanjivi* should not be applied to the Act as a deprivation of a right of appeal from a decision that has the effect of depriving the applicant of a licence to conduct a business is arguably a violation of the applicant's rights under Art.6 of the European Convention on Human Rights (*Bentham v Netherlands* (1986) 8 E.H.R.R. 1).

The discretion of the High Court to order judicial review before an applicant has exhausted the alternative remedy of an appeal to the Tribunal under this Act should be exercised with the greatest circumspection (*R. (on the application of M) v London Borough of Bromley* [2002] EWCA Civ 1113). In any event, the Administrative Court should be slow to interfere with the decision of a Tribunal, such as the Care Standards Tribunal, where its members are selected because of their particular expertise and in reality the issue is how it dealt with matters of fact (*Secretary of State for Health v C* [2002] EWHC 1381 (Admin), *per* Scott Baker J. at para.50).

SUBS.(1)

An appeal: The right of appeal lies in the person against whom the registration authority or **7–006** justice of the peace made its decision. An appeal against a decision of the registration authority is commenced by completing Form B1. Form B2 must be used if the appeal is against an order of the justice of the peace under s.20. These forms are available from the website of the Care Standards Tribunal.

There is no provision for restoration of the registration pending an appeal to the Tribunal from a decision of a justice of the peace under s.20.

Order. . . under s.20: The Tribunal should not confirm the order of the justice of the peace if it finds that the appellant is not a fit person to be concerned in carrying on an establishment but fails to find that the criterion in s.20(1)(b) is satisfied (*Lyons v East Sussex County Council*, above).

Subs.(2)

7–007   *No appeal:* There is no opportunity to appeal after the 28-day period set out in this provision have expired.

Subss.(3), (4)

7–008   *Confirm the decision/order or direct that it shall not have effect:* The Tribunal has no power to allow an appeal in part only.

Subs.(5)

Condition: See the notes to s.13(3).

THE PROTECTION OF CHILDREN AND VULNERABLE ADULTS AND CARE STANDARDS TRIBUNAL REGULATIONS 2002

(SI 2002/816)

Dated March 25, 2002, and made by the Secretary of State for Health under the Protection of Children Act 1999, s.9(2) to (4), Sch. para.2(4).

Abbreviation

7–009 Handbook: *The Care Standard Tribunal Members Handbook.*

7–010   Arrangements of Regulations

PART I

Introductory

REG.

1. Citation, commencement and extent

PART II

Constitution

2. Powers and functions exercisable by the President and Secretary
3. Requirements for membership of lay panel

PART III

Appeals, Determinations and Applications for Leave

4. Procedure for appeals, determinations and applications for leave

PART IV

Case Management

5. Appointment of Tribunal
6. Directions

PART V

HEARING

PART VI

DECISION

PART VII

SUPPLEMENTARY

PART VIII

REVOCATION OF REGULATIONS

SCHEDULES

PART I

INTRODUCTORY

Citation, commencement and interpretation

7–011   **1.**—(1) These Regulations may be cited as the Protection of Children and Vulnerable Adults and Care Standards Tribunal Regulations 2002 and shall come into force—

   (a) for the purposes of—

      (i) an appeal under section 86(1)(a) or (b) of the 2000 Act;

     (ii) an application for leave to appeal under section 86(1)(b) of the 2000 Act;

    (iii) a determination, or an application for leave for a determination, under section 86(2) of the 2000 Act,

      on the first day on which sections 80 to 93 of the 2000 Act are in force;

   (b) for all other purposes, on 1st April 2002.

   (2) In these Regulations—

"the 1989 Act" means the Children Act 1989;

["the 1998 Act" means the School Standards and Framework Act 1998;]

"the 1999 Act" means the Protection of Children Act 1999;

"the 2000 Act" means the Care Standards Act 2000;

["the 2002 Act" means the Education Act 2002;]

"case" in Parts IV and VI means—

   (a) an appeal under section 21 of the 2000 Act;
   (b) an appeal under section 79M of the 1989 Act;
   (c) an appeal under section 65A of the 1989 Act;
   (d) an appeal under section 4(1)(a) or (b) of the 1999 Act;
   (e) a determination under section 4(2) of the 1999 Act;
   (f) an appeal under the Education Regulations;
   (g) an appeal under section 86(1)(a) or (b) of the 2000 Act; [...]
   (h) a determination under section 86(2) of the 2000 Act;
  [(i) an appeal under section 68 of the 2000 Act; [...]
   (j) an appeal under the Suspension Regulations;] [...]
   (k) an appeal under paragraph 10(1A) of Schedule 26 to the 1998 Act;] [or
   (l) an appeal under section 166 of the 2002 Act including an application for, or consideration by the Tribunal of the making of an order under section 166(5);]

"application for leave" means an application to the Tribunal—

   (a) for leave to appeal under section 4(1)(b) of the 1999 Act or section 86(1)(b) of the 2000 Act;

(b) for leave for a determination by the Tribunal under section 4(2) of the 1999 Act or section 86(2) of the 2000 Act;

"appropriate authority" means in relation to an appeal under section 65A of the 1989 Act the [Commission for Social Care Inspection] or the Assembly;

"the Assembly" means the National Assembly for Wales;

"the Chief Inspector" means Her Majesty's Chief Inspector of Schools in England;

"the clerk" means, in relation to a hearing before the Tribunal, the person appointed by the Secretary to act as clerk to the Tribunal;

"the Commission" means the [Commission for Social Care Inspection or the Commission for Healthcare Audit and Inspection];

"costs order" shall be construed in accordance with regulation 24;

["Council" means in relation to England, the General Social Care Council or in relation to Wales, the Care Council for Wales;]

"county court" has the same meaning as in the County Courts Act 1984;

"document" means information recorded in writing or in any other form;

"the Education Regulations" means the Education (Restriction of Employment) Regulations 2000;

"an institution within the further education sector" shall be construed in accordance with section 4(3) of the Education Act 1996;

"local authority" has the same meaning as in section 105 of the 1989 Act;

"local education authority" shall be construed in accordance with section 12 of the Education Act 1996;

"nominated chairman" means the chairman appointed by the President in accordance with regulation 5 to determine a case or an application for leave;

"a party" means either the applicant or the respondent;

"parties" means the applicant and the respondent;

"the POCA list" means the list kept under section 1 of the 1999 Act;

"the POVA list" means the list kept under section 81 of the 2000 Act;

"records" means the records of the Tribunal;

"registration authority" means—

(a) in relation to an appeal under section 21 of the 2000 Act, the [Commission for Healthcare Audit and Inspection or the Commission for Social Care Inspection] or the Assembly; [...]
(b) in relation to an appeal under section 79M of the 1989 Act, the Chief Inspector or the Assembly;
[(c) in relation to an appeal under section 166 of the 2002 Act, the Secretary of State for Education and Skills or the Assembly;]

"relevant programme" means a programme included in a programme service within the meaning of the Broadcasting Act 1990;

"relevant social work" has the same meaning as in section 55(4) of the 2000 Act;

"the respondent" means—

(a) in relation to an appeal under section 21 of the 2000 Act, the registration authority;

(b) in relation to an appeal under section 79M of the 1989 Act, the registration authority;

(c) in relation to an appeal under section 65A of the 1989 Act, the appropriate authority;

(e) in relation to an appeal, an application for leave or a determination under section 4 of the 1999 Act, the Secretary of State for Health;

(f) in relation to an appeal under the Education Regulations, the Secretary of State for Education and Skills or the National Assembly for Wales;

(g) in relation to an appeal, an application for leave or a determination under section 86 of the 2000 Act, the Secretary of State for Health;

[(h) in relation to an appeal under section 68 of the 2000 Act, the Council;

(i) in relation to an appeal under the Suspension Regulations, the Chief Inspector;]

[(j) in relation to an appeal under paragraph 10(1A) of Schedule 26 to the 1998 Act, the Chief Inspector;]

[(k) in relation to an appeal under section 166 of the 2002 Act, the registration authority.]

"residential family centre" has the same meaning as in section 4(2) of the 2000 Act;

"school" has the same meaning as in section 4 of the Education Act 1996;

"the Secretary" means the person for the time being acting as the Secretary to the Tribunal;

["the Suspension Regulations" means the Child Minding and Day Care (Suspension of Registration) (England) Regulations 2003;]

"vulnerable adult" means a person who is not a child and who—

(a) suffers from mental disorder within the meaning of the Mental Health Act 1983, or otherwise has a significant impairment of intelligence and social functioning; or

(b) has a physical disability or is suffering from a physical disorder;

"working day" means any day other than a Saturday, a Sunday, Christmas Day, Good Friday or a day which is a bank holiday within the meaning of the Banking and Financial Dealings Act 1971.

(3) In these Regulations, a reference—

(a) to a numbered regulation is to the regulation in these Regulations bearing that number;

(b) in a regulation to a numbered paragraph is to the paragraph of that regulation bearing that number;

(c) to a numbered Schedule, is to a Schedule in these Regulations bearing that number;

(d) in a paragraph to a numbered or lettered sub-paragraph is to the sub-paragraph of that paragraph bearing that number or letter.

AMENDMENTS

The amendments to this regulation were made by SI 2003/626, reg.2, SI 2003/1060, **7–012**
reg.2, SI 2003/2043, reg.3 and SI 2004/664, art.2, Sch.1, para.7.

GENERAL NOTE
PARA.(2)
The secretary: Note reg.2(2).   **7–013**
Vulnerable adult: Mental disorder is defined in s.1(2) of the Mental Health Act 1983 as
meaning "mental illness, arrested or incomplete development of mind, psychopathic dis-
order and any other disorder or disability of mind".

PART II

CONSTITUTION

Powers and functions exercisable by the President and Secretary

2.—(1) Anything which must or may be done by the President (except under **7–014**
regulation 5(1), (2), (4) or (5) or 25(4)), may be done by a member of the chairmen's panel authorised by the President.

(2) Anything which must or may be done by the Secretary may be done by a
member of the Tribunal's staff authorised by the Secretary.

Requirements for membership of lay panel

3.—(1) A person may be appointed a member of the lay panel if he satisfies the **7–015**
requirements of—

(a) paragraph (2);

(b) paragraphs (3) and (4); or

(c) paragraph (5).

(2) The requirements of this paragraph are—

(a) experience in the provision of services—

(i) which must or may be provided by local authorities under the 1989 Act
[or the Adoption Act 1976] or which are similar to such services;
(ii) for vulnerable adults; or
(iii) in a residential family centre; and

(b) experience in relevant social work.

(3) The requirements of this paragraph are—

(a) experience in the provision of services by a Health Authority, a Special Health Authority, a National Health Service trust[, an NHS foundation trust] or a Primary Care Trust;

(b) experience in the provision of education in a school or in an institution within the further education sector; or

(c) experience of being employed by a local education authority in connection with the exercise of its functions under Part I of the Education Act 1996.

(4) The requirements of this paragraph are—

(a) experience in the conduct of disciplinary investigations;

(b) experience as a member of an Area Child Protection Committee, or similar experience;

(c) experience of taking part in child protection conferences or in child protection review conferences, or similar experience; or

(d) experience in negotiating the conditions of service of employees.

(5) The requirements of this paragraph are—

(a) experience in carrying out inspections under Part II of the 2000 Act;

(b) experience in carrying out inspections under the Registered Homes Act 1984;

(c) experience in carrying out inspections under the 1989 Act [or the Adoption Act 1976];

(d) experience in managing an establishment or agency under Part II of the 2000 Act;

(e) experience in managing a children's home under the 1989 Act;

[(ee) experience in managing an adoption society approved under the Adoption Act 1976;]

(f) experience in managing a nursing home, mental nursing home or residential care home under the Registered Homes Act 1984;

(g) experience in managing the provision of local authority social services;

(h) that the person is a registered nurse or registered medical practitioner who has experience of the provision of health care services;

(i) experience in managing or inspecting child minding and day care provision for children under 8 years of age; or

(j) experience in a professional, managerial or supervisory position in the provision of early childhood education[, child minding or day care] or child development.

AMENDMENTS

7–016   The amendments to this regulation were made by SI 2003/1060, reg.3 and by SI 2004/696, art.3(4), Sch.4.

the 1989 Act: reg.1(2).   **7–017**
vulnerable adult: reg.1(2).
residential family centre: reg.1(2).
relevant social work: reg.1(2).
an institution within the further education sector: reg.1(2).
local education authority: reg.1(2).
2000 Act: reg.1(2).
local authority: reg.1(2).

PART III

APPEALS, DETERMINATIONS AND APPLICATIONS FOR LEAVE

Procedure for appeals, determinations and applications for leave
   4.—(1) In the case of an appeal under section 21 of the 2000 Act, the procedure **7–018**
set out in Schedule 1 shall apply.
   (2) In the case of an appeal under section 79M of the 1989 Act, the procedure
set out in Schedule 2 shall apply.
   (3) In the case of an appeal under section 65A of the 1989 Act, the procedure set
out in Schedule 3 shall apply.
   (4) In the case of—

(a) an application for leave under section 4(1)(b) or (2) of the 1999 Act;

(b) an appeal under section 4(1)(a) of the 1999 Act against a decision to include
     an individual in the POCA list;

(c) an appeal under section 4(1)(b) of the 1999 Act against a decision not to
     remove an individual from the POCA list under section 1(3) of that Act;

(d) a determination under section 4(2) of the 1999 Act as to whether an individ-
     ual should be included in the POCA list;

(e) an appeal under regulation 13 of the Education Regulations against a
     decision to give a direction under regulation 5 of those Regulations; or

(f) an appeal under regulation 13 of the Education Regulations against a
     decision not to revoke or vary such a direction,

the procedure set out in Schedule 4 shall apply.
   (5) In the case of—

(a) an application for leave to the Tribunal under section 86(1)(b) or (2) of the
     2000 Act;

(b) an appeal under section 86(1)(a) of the 2000 Act against a decision to
     include an individual in the POVA list;

(c) an appeal under section 86(1)(b) of the 2000 Act against a decision not to
     remove an individual from the POVA list; or

(d) a determination under section 86(2) of the 2000 Act as to whether an indi-
     vidual should be included in the POVA list,

the procedure set out in Schedule 5 shall apply.

[(6) In the case of an appeal under section 68 of the 2000 Act against a decision of the Council under Part IV of the 2000 Act, the procedure set out in Schedule 6 shall apply.

(7) In the case of—

(a) an appeal under regulation 8(1)(a) of the Suspension Regulations against a decision to suspend the registration of a person acting as a child minder or providing day care; or

(b) an appeal under regulation 8(1)(b) of the Suspension Regulations against a refusal to lift the suspension of such registration,

the procedure set out in Schedule 7 shall apply.]

[(8) In the case of an appeal under paragraph 10(1A) of Schedule 26 to the 1998 Act against a decision of the Chief Inspector, the procedure set out in Schedule 8 shall apply.]

[(9) In the case of an appeal under section 166 of the 2002 Act (including in relation to the making of an order under section 166(5)), the procedure set out in Schedule 9 shall apply.]

AMENDMENTS

7–019   The amendments to this regulation were made by SI 2003/626, reg.3, SI 2003/1060, reg.4 and SI 2003/2043, reg.3.

DEFINITIONS

7–020   application for leave: reg.1(2).
the 1999 Act: reg.1(2).
the 2000 Act: reg.1(2).
the POVA list: reg.1(2).
the 2002 Act: reg.1(2).

PART IV

CASE MANAGEMENT

Appointment of Tribunal

7–021   **5.**—(1) The President shall, at such time as he considers it appropriate to do so, nominate a chairman (who may be himself) and two members of the lay panel to determine the case.

(2) The President shall, at such time as he considers it appropriate to do so, nominate a chairman (who may be himself) to determine an application for leave.

(3) The President or the nominated chairman may determine any application made in relation to the case or any application for leave.

(4) The President may at any time before the hearing (or, if the case is to be determined without an oral hearing, before the case is determined) nominate from the appropriate panel another person in substitution for the chairman or other member previously nominated.

(5) The President shall nominate members of the lay panel who appear to him to have experience and qualifications relevant to the subject matter of the case.

DEFINITION

7–022   application for leave: reg.1(2).

  Lay panel: See r.3.   **7–023**

Directions

6.—[(Z1) This regulation shall not apply in the case of an appeal under the   **7–024**
Suspension Regulations [or in relation to an application for an order under
s.166(5) of the 2002 Act pursuant to paragraph 7(1) of Schedule 9].]

(1) If either party has requested that there shall be a preliminary hearing, or if
the President or the nominated chairman considers that a preliminary hearing is
necessary, the President or the nominated chairman, as the case may be, shall
fix a date for the preliminary hearing, as soon as possible after the expiry of the
5 working days referred to [in paragraph 6 of Schedule 1, 2, 3, 6, 8 or 9] or paragraph 9 of Schedule 4 or 5, as the case may be.

(2) At the preliminary hearing, or if a preliminary hearing is not to be held, as
soon as possible after, and in any event not later than 10 working days after, the
expiry of the 5 working days referred to in paragraph (1) the President or the nominated chairman—

(a) shall give directions as to the dates by which any document, witness state-
     ment or other material upon which any party is intending to rely shall be
     sent to the Tribunal, and, if the President or the nominated chairman con-
     siders it appropriate, to the other party;

(b) may give any other direction in exercise of his powers under this Part which
     he considers appropriate; and

(c) shall, where the applicant has requested that the case be determined without
     an oral hearing, give a direction as to the date, which shall be not less than
     10 working days after the last date on which he has directed that any docu-
     ment, witness statement or other evidence be sent to the Tribunal, by which
     the parties shall send any written representations regarding their appeal to
     the Tribunal.

(3) The President or the nominated chairman may direct that exchange of witness statements or other material shall be simultaneous or sequential, as he
considers appropriate.

(4) The Secretary shall notify the parties as soon as possible in writing of any
directions the President or the nominated chairman gives in writing under paragraphs (2) and (3) above.

(5) The Secretary shall notify the parties as soon as possible, and in any event
not less than 5 working days before the hearing of the date, time and place of any
preliminary hearing.

(6) The parties may be represented or assisted at any preliminary hearing by any
person.

AMENDMENTS
  The amendments to this regulation were made by SI 2003/626, reg.2, SI 2003/1060,   **7–025**
reg.5 and SI 2003/2043, reg.4.

DEFINITIONS
  the 2002 Act: reg.1(2).   **7–026**

party: reg.1(2).
nominated chairman: reg.1(2).
working days: reg.1(2).
document: reg.1(2).
the Secretary: reg.1(2).
parties: reg.1(2).

GENERAL NOTE

7–027   This regulation provides the tribunal with extensive powers to give directions to the parties before the hearing. The directions can be varied and further directions can be made reg.9. A sanction for non compliance with a direction is provided for in reg.10.

Among the matters that may be the subject of directions the directions "will set a timetable for the sending of witness statements (reg.14) and other documents (reg.11)" and "will direct whether exchange of such material be simultaneous or sequential" (Handbook, para.3.2).

PARA.(1)

7–028   *Five working days:* There would appear to be no reason why this time limit could not be shortened with the agreement of both parties. This has happened in practice (Handbook, para.2.7).

PARA.(2)(C)

7–029   The Handbook, at para.8.3, recommends that a no hearing appeal takes place in private.

[Directions: appeals under the Suspension Regulations

7–030   **6A.**—(1) This regulation shall apply in the case of an appeal under the Suspension Regulations [and in the case of an application for an order under section 166(5) of the 2002 Act].

(2) The President or the nominated chairman may, if he considers it necessary or expedient (and whether at the request of either party or otherwise)—

(a)   give directions as to the dates by which any document, witness statement or other material upon which any party is intending to rely shall be sent to the Tribunal, and, if the President or the nominated chairman considers it appropriate, to the other party;

(b)   give any other direction in exercise of his powers under this Part;

(c)   where the applicant has requested that the case be determined without an oral hearing, give a direction as to the date by which the parties shall send any written representations, regarding the appeal, to the Tribunal.

(3) The President or the nominated chairman may direct that exchange of witness statements or other material shall be simultaneous or sequential, as he considers appropriate.

(4) The Secretary shall notify the parties as soon as possible in writing of any directions the President or the nominated chairman gives in writing under paragraphs (2) and (3).]

AMENDMENT

7–031   This regulation was inserted by SI 2003/626 reg.5. The amendment to para.(1) was made by SI 2003/2043, reg.5.

Suspension Regulations: reg.1(2).   **7–032**
the 2002 Act: reg.1(2).
party: reg.1(2).
document: reg.1(2).
nominated chairman: reg.1(2).
the Secretary: reg.1(2).

Fixing and notification of hearing

7.—[(Z1) This regulation shall not apply in relation an application for an order   **7–033**
under section 166(5) of the 2002 Act.]

(1) The Secretary must, in consultation with the President or the nominated
chairman, fix a date for the hearing of the case unless the applicant has requested
in writing that the case be determined without a hearing.

(2) [Except in the case of an appeal under the Suspension Regulations, the date]
fixed for the hearing shall be the earliest practicable date having regard to any
directions which have been made by the President or the nominated chairman
with regard to the preparation of evidence but shall be no sooner than 15 working
days after the latest date on which the President or the nominated chairman has
directed that the evidence of the parties (including the statements of any witnesses
or experts) shall be filed or exchanged.

[(2A) In the case of an appeal under the Suspension Regulations, the date fixed
for the hearing shall be the earliest practicable date having regard to any directions
which have been made by the President or the nominated chairman with regard to
the preparation of evidence but shall be not later than 10 working days after the
date on which the Secretary receives the written response from the respondent
under paragraph 3 of Schedule 7.]

(3) [Except in the case of an appeal under the Suspension Regulations, the
Secretary] must inform the parties in writing of the date, time and place of the
hearing no less than 20 working days before the date fixed for the hearing.

[(3A) In the case of an appeal under the Suspension Regulations, the Secretary
must inform the parties in writing of the date, time and place of the hearing—

(a) subject to sub-paragraph (b), by no later than 5 working days before the date
fixed for the hearing, or by such later date as the parties may agree;

(b) where it appears to the President or the nominated chairman that it is necessary or expedient for the parties to be informed of the hearing at a date later
than 5 working days before the date fixed for the hearing, by such date as the
President or the nominated chairman may direct.]

(4) The Secretary may, in consultation with the President or the nominated
chairman, alter the place of the hearing and, if he does, he must without delay
inform the parties in writing of the alteration.

(5) Subject to paragraph (6), the President or the nominated chairman may
adjourn the hearing, either on the application of either party or on his own
initiative.

(6) The President or the nominated chairman shall not adjourn the hearing
unless satisfied that refusing the adjournment would prevent the just disposal of
the case.

(7) If the President or the nominated chairman adjourns the hearing, then the Secretary must, without delay, inform the parties in writing of the date, time and place at which the hearing will be resumed.

AMENDMENTS

7–034   The amendments to this regulation were made by SI 2003/626, reg.6 and SI 2003/2043, reg.6.

DEFINITIONS

7–035   the 2002 Act: reg.1(2).
the Secretary: reg.1(2).
Suspension Regulations: reg.1(2).
working days: reg.1(2).
nominated chairman: reg.1(2).
parties: reg.1(2).
party: reg.1(2).

GENERAL NOTE

7–036   In *Woodbine Villa v NCSC* [2002] 116 N.C., the President said that when considering an application for an adjournment he had "to look at the history of the matter, the interests of both parties and . . . of any residents" (para.6).

7–037 *PARA.(1)*
Without a hearing: There is no power vested in the tribunal to insist on an oral hearing when the appellant asks for the matter to be determined without one (*B v Secretary of State* [2002] 51 P.C.).

7–038 *PARA.(6)*
This paragraph contains a presumption against an adjournment. In *Havard v Hampshire County Council* (Decn. No.377), a case under the 1984 Act, the Registered Homes Tribunal suggested that the following three tests should apply when a tribunal is considering an adjournment due to the non-attendance at the hearing of the appellant: did the appellant have notice of the hearing; is the appellant able to understand the nature of the process; and is the appellant prevented by disability, illness or other cause from attending the hearing. Regulation 20(4) authorises the tribunal to hear an appeal in the absence of a party.

Multiple appeals

7–039   **8.**—(1) Subject to paragraphs (2) and (3), where two or more cases relate to the same person, establishment or agency, the President or the nominated chairman may, on the application of either party or on his own initiative, direct that such cases shall be heard together if he considers it appropriate to do so.

(2) Where a person ("the applicant") has by virtue of section 92(1) and (2) of the 2000 Act been included in the POVA list pursuant to a reference under section 2, 2A, or 2D of the 1999 Act or as a result of being named in a relevant inquiry within the meaning of section 2B of that Act, then subject to paragraph (4) any appeal against inclusion in the POVA list shall be joined with any appeal against inclusion in the POCA list and in that event the appeal against inclusion in the POCA list shall be heard first.

(3) Where a person ("the applicant") has by virtue of section 2C of the 1999 Act been included in the POCA list pursuant to a reference made under section 82, 83 or 84 of the 2000 Act or as a result of being named in a relevant inquiry within the meaning of section 85 of that Act, then subject to paragraph (4) any

appeal against inclusion in the POCA list shall be joined with any appeal against inclusion in the POVA list and in that event the appeal against inclusion in the POVA list shall be heard first.

(4) The applicant may request the President or the nominated chairman in writing to give a direction that the appeals referred to in paragraph (2) or (3) shall be heard separately.

(5) Before making any direction under paragraph (1) the President or the nominated chairman shall—

(a) where the direction which he proposes to give is at the request of either party, give the other party the opportunity [to make—

    (i) in the case of an appeal under the Suspension Regulations, oral representations at the commencement of the hearing; or

    (ii) in any other case, written representations]

  ; or

(b) where the direction which he proposes to give is on his own initiative, give both parties the opportunity [to make—

    (i) in the case of an appeal under the Suspension Regulations, oral representations at the commencment of the hearing; or

    (ii) in any other case, written representations].

(6) In considering whether to give a direction under paragraph (1), the President or the nominated chairman shall take into account the following matters—

[(a) any representations made by either party under paragraph (5);]

(b) the increased cost of hearing the cases together or separately; and

(c) any unreasonable delay in hearing any case which would be caused by hearing the appeals together or separately.

(7) In considering whether to give a direction under paragraph (4) the President or the nominated chairman shall take into account the following matters—

(a) any representations from the applicant which show he would be significantly disadvantaged if the appeals were to be heard together;

(b) the increased cost of hearing the appeals together or separately; and

(c) any unreasonable delay in hearing either appeal which would be caused by hearing the appeals together or separately,

and shall give a direction that the appeals be heard separately where he is satisfied that it would be unfair in all the circumstances to hear the appeals together.

AMENDMENTS
  The amendments to this paragraph were made by SI 2003/626, reg.7.   **7–040**

DEFINITIONS
  nominated chairman: reg.1(2).   **7–041**
  2000 Act: reg.1(2).

the POVA list: reg.1(2).
the 1999 Act: reg.1(2).
the POCA list: reg.1(2).
the 1999 Act: reg.1(2).
party: reg.1(2).

7–042   This regulation enables the tribunal to direct that cases be heard together if they relate to the same person, establishment or agency.

Further directions
7–043   **9.**—(1) The President or the nominated chairman may at any time on the application of either party or on his own initiative, vary any direction which he has given or give any further direction in exercise of any of his powers under this Part as he considers appropriate.

(2) Before making any further direction, or varying any direction under paragraph (1)—

(a)   the President or the nominated chairman shall, where the variation or further direction which he proposes to give—

(i) is at the request of either party, give the other party the opportunity to make written representations; or
(ii) is on his own initiative, give both parties the opportunity to make written representations;

(b)   [except in relation to an application for an order under section 166(5) of the 2002 Act] the President or the nominated chairman may direct that there shall be a preliminary hearing in relation to any proposed variation or further direction if he considers it appropriate or if a preliminary hearing has been requested by either party.

DEFINITIONS
7–044   nominated chairman: reg.1(2).
party: reg.1(2).
the 2002 Act: reg.1(2).

GENERAL NOTE
7–045   This regulation enables a direction that has been made under reg.6 to be varied and for further directions to be made. A sanction for non compliance with a direction is provided for in reg.10.

Unless orders
7–046   **10.**—(1) The President or the nominated chairman may at any time make an order to the effect that, unless the party to whom the order is addressed takes a step specified in the order within the period specified in the order, the case may be determined in favour of the other party.

(2) The Secretary shall give written notification of the order to the party to whom it is addressed and to the other party and shall inform him of the effect of paragraph (3).

(3) If a party fails to comply with an order addressed to him under this regulation, the President or the nominated chairman may determine the case in favour of the other party.

DEFINITIONS

nominated chairman: reg.1(2).   **7–047**
party: reg.1(2).
the Secretary: reg.1(2).

GENERAL NOTE

This rule provides for a power to enforce any order which is made in a directions hearing   **7–048**
by providing the tribunal with a discretion to determine the appeal in favour of the non-
defaulting party. The Handbook states that the power "is a draconian measure, and the
application of reg.10(1) must be proportionate" (para.3.5).

Copies of documents

11.—(1) The President or the nominated chairman may give a direction as to   **7–049**
the number of copies of relevant material, which each party must send to the
Tribunal and relevant material means, all documents, witness statements and
other material on which the parties intend to rely or which they have been ordered
by the President or the nominated chairman to send to the Secretary under this
Part.

(2) The President or the nominated chairman may, if he considers it appropriate
to do so, direct the form and order in which relevant material shall be supplied to
the Tribunal.

DEFINITIONS

nominated chairman: reg.1(2).   **7–050**
document: reg.1(2).
parties: reg.1(2).

Disclosure of information and documents

12.—(1) Subject to paragraphs (3) to (5), the President or the nominated chair-   **7–051**
man may give directions—

(a) requiring a party to send to the Secretary any document or other material
    which he considers may assist the Tribunal in determining the case and
    which that party is able to send, and the Secretary shall take such steps as
    the President or the nominated chairman may direct, to supply copies of
    any information or document obtained under this paragraph to the other
    party;

(b) granting to a party the right to inspect and take copies of any document or
    other material which it is in the power of the other party to disclose, and
    appointing the date, time and place at which any such inspection and copy-
    ing is to be done.

(2) Subject to paragraphs (3) to (5), the President or the nominated chairman
may give a direction on the application of either party, requiring a person who
is not a party to the proceedings to disclose any document or other material to
the party making the application, if he is satisfied that—

(a) the documents or other material sought are likely to support the applicant's case or adversely affect the case of the other party;

(b) it is within the power of the person subject to the direction to disclose any document or other material; and

(c) disclosure is necessary for the fair determination of the case.

(3) It shall be a condition of the supply of any document or material under paragraph (1) or (2) that a party shall use it only for the purpose of the proceedings.

(4) Paragraphs (1) and (2) do not apply in relation to any document or material which the party could not be compelled to produce in legal proceedings in a county court.

(5) Before making a direction under paragraph (1) or (2), the President or the nominated chairman shall take into account the need to protect any matter which relates to intimate personal or financial circumstances, is commercially sensitive, or was communicated or obtained in confidence.

DEFINITIONS

7–052   nominated chairman: reg.1(2).
party: reg.1(2).
document: reg.1(2).
county court: reg.1(2).

GENERAL NOTE

7–053   This regulation enables the tribunal to direct (1) a party to send a document to the tribunal; (2) a party to disclose a document to the other party; and (3) a person who is not a party to disclose a document to a party.

7–054   PARA.(1)(A)
Which that party is able to send: The tribunal has no power to direct a party to disclose any document or other material which is not in the possession or control of that party.

7–055   PARA.(4)
Examples of such documents include communications between solicitor and client and documents prepared in contemplation of the proceedings.

Expert evidence

7–056   **13.**—(1) The President or the nominated chairman may, if he thinks that any question arises in relation to the case on which it would be desirable for the Tribunal to have the assistance of an expert, appoint a person having appropriate qualifications to enquire into and report on the matter.

(2) The Secretary must supply the parties with a copy of any written report received under paragraph (1) in advance of the hearing (or, if the case is to be determined without an oral hearing, before the case is determined).

(3) If the President or the nominated chairman sees fit, he may direct that the expert shall attend the hearing, and give evidence.

(4) The Tribunal shall pay such reasonable fees as the President or the nominated chairman may determine to any person appointed under this regulation.

DEFINITIONS

7–057   nominated chairman: reg.1(2).
working days: reg.1(2).

the Secretary: reg.1(2).
parties: reg.1(2).

GENERAL NOTE
This rule enable the chairman, where he or she considers it desirable, to have an expert **7–058**
appointed to assist the tribunal. It is suggested that the terms of reference of the expert
should be discussed with the legal representatives of the parties. The tribunal's power
under this provision does not preclude a party from calling its own expert witness.

Evidence of witnesses

14.—(1) The President or the nominated chairman may direct that the parties **7–059**
send to each other by the date specified in the direction a copy of a witness statement in respect of each witness on whose evidence he wishes to rely.

(2) A witness statement must contain the words "I believe that the facts stated
in this witness statement are true", and be signed by the person who makes it.

(3) The President or the nominated chairman (before the hearing or, if the case
is to be determined without an oral hearing, before the case is determined) or the
Tribunal may direct that a document or the evidence of any witness other than the
applicant shall be excluded from consideration because—

(a) it would be unfair in all the circumstances to consider it;

(b) the party wishing to rely on the document or evidence has failed to submit
the document, or witness statement containing it, in compliance with any
direction; or

(c) it would not assist the Tribunal in determining the case.

(4) Instead of excluding evidence under this regulation the President or the
nominated chairman or the Tribunal may permit it to be considered on such
terms as he or it thinks fit, including, subject to regulation 24, the making of a
costs order.

(5) The President or the nominated chairman may direct that a witness (other
than the applicant) shall not give oral evidence.

DEFINITIONS
    nominated chairman: reg.1(2).   **7–060**
    parties: reg.1(2).
    document: reg.1(2).
    costs order: reg.1(2).

GENERAL NOTE
This regulation enables the tribunal to direct that the parties exchange witness state- **7–061**
ments. It also provides the tribunal with a power to exclude a document or the evidence
of a witness from consideration by the tribunal. As an alternative to excluding the document
or evidence, the tribunal could permit it to be considered subject to such terms as are considered to be fit, including the making of a costs order.

Withholding medical report from disclosure in exceptional circumstances

15.—(1) This regulation applies where the respondent wishes the Tribunal, in **7–062**
determining the case, to consider a medical report and the President or the nominated chairman is satisfied—

(a) that disclosure to the applicant of all or any part of the contents of the report would be so harmful to his health or welfare that it would be wrong to disclose it to him; and

(b) that in all the circumstances it would not be unfair if the report or that part of it is considered by the Tribunal.

(2) The President or the nominated chairman may appoint a person having appropriate skills or experience to—

(a) assess whether disclosure of the report to the applicant would be harmful to the applicant's health or welfare; and

(b) report on the matter to the President or the nominated chairman.

(3) The President or the nominated chairman may direct that—

(a) the report may be considered by the Tribunal; and

(b) all or any part of its contents must not be disclosed to the applicant.

DEFINITION

7–063   nominated chairman: reg.1(2).

GENERAL NOTE

7–064   It is difficult to envisage circumstances where the tribunal would wish to exercise its power under this provision to order the non-disclosure of a medical report to the applicant. The rule is silent as to whether a medical report which is withheld should be disclosed to the applicant's legal adviser.

Summoning of witnesses

7–065   **16.**—(1) The President or the nominated chairman may, on the application of either party or on his own initiative, issue a summons requiring any person—

(a) to attend as a witness at the hearing, at the date, time and place set out in the summons; and

(b) to answer any questions or produce any documents or other material in his possession or under his control which relate to any matter in question in the case.

(2) The summons must—

(a) explain that it is an offence under section 9(5)(c) of the 1999 Act to fail, without reasonable excuse, to comply with it; and

(b) explain the right to apply under this regulation to have it varied or set aside.

(3) A person summoned under this regulation may apply in writing to the Secretary for the summons to be varied or set aside by the President or the nominated chairman, and—

(a) the President or the nominated chairman may do so if he sees fit; and

(b) the Secretary must notify him and the parties in writing of the decision.

(4) No person shall be required to attend, answer questions or produce any document in obedience to a summons issued under this regulation unless—

(a) he has been given at least 5 working days' notice of the hearing [or has consented to a shorter period of notice]; and

(b) the necessary expenses of his attendance are paid or tendered to him by the party who requested his attendance or by the Tribunal, as the President or the nominated chairman shall direct.

(5) No person shall be required under this regulation to give any evidence or produce any document or other material that he could not be required to produce in legal proceedings in a county court.

AMENDMENT
The amendment to this paragraph was made by SI 2003/626, reg.8.   **7–066**

DEFINITIONS
   nominated chairman: reg.1(2).   **7–067**
   party: reg.1(2).
   document: reg.1(2).
   the 1999 Act: reg.1(2).
   the Secretary: reg.1(2).
   parties: reg.1(2).
   working days': reg.1(2).
   county court: reg.1(2).

GENERAL NOTE
This regulation enables the tribunal to issue a summons requiring a person to attend as a **7–068**
witness and to answer questions or to produce a document. It is an offence under s.9(5)(c) of
the Protection of Children Act 1999 to fail to comply with the summons.

SUBS.(2)(A)   **7–069**
Offence: Which, on conviction, can lead to a fine not exceeding level 3 on the standard
scale.

Child and vulnerable adult witnesses
   17.—(1) A child shall only give evidence in person where—   **7–070**

(a) the President or the nominated chairman has given the parties an opportunity to make written representations before the hearing or representations at the hearing; and

(b) having regard to all the available evidence, and the representations of the parties, the President or the nominated chairman considers that the welfare of the child will not be prejudiced by so doing.

(2) If he directs that a child shall give evidence in person, the President or the nominated chairman shall—

(a) secure that any arrangements he considers appropriate (such as the use of a video link) are made to safeguard the welfare of the child; and

(b) appoint for the purpose of the hearing a person with appropriate skills or experience in facilitating the giving of evidence by children.

(3) Where the President or the nominated chairman believes that it might not be in the best interests of a vulnerable adult for the vulnerable adult to give oral evidence to the Tribunal, the President or the nominated chairman shall—

(a) give the parties the opportunity to make written representations before the hearing or representations at the hearing; and

(b) having regard to all the available evidence, including any written representations made by the parties consider whether it would prejudice the vulnerable adult's welfare to give oral evidence to the Tribunal—

(i) in any circumstances; or
(ii) otherwise than in accordance with paragraph (5).

(4) If the President or the nominated chairman considers that—

(a) it would prejudice the vulnerable adult's welfare to give oral evidence to the Tribunal in any circumstances, he shall direct that the vulnerable adult shall not do so; or

(b) it would prejudice the vulnerable adult's welfare to give oral evidence to the Tribunal otherwise than in accordance with paragraph (5) he shall direct that paragraph (5) shall apply in relation to the vulnerable adult.

(5) If he directs that this paragraph shall apply in relation to the vulnerable adult, the President or the nominated chairman shall—

(a) secure that any arrangements he considers appropriate (such as the use of a video link) are made to safeguard the welfare of the vulnerable adult; and

(b) appoint for the purpose of the hearing a person with appropriate skills or experience in facilitating the giving of evidence by vulnerable adults.

(6) The President or the nominated chairman shall pay such fees as he may determine to any person appointed under this regulation.

DEFINITIONS

7–071   nominated chairman: reg.1(2).
parties: reg.1(2).
vulnerable adult: reg.1(2).

GENERAL NOTE

7–072   This regulation enables the tribunal to direct that a child or a vulnerable adult shall not give evidence in the proceedings and provides for safeguards to be put in place if a witness in either category does give evidence. The Handbook states that in "approaching the issue of child witnesses, it is suggested that it will be appropriate for the tribunal to adopt relevant provisions of the Home Office guidance entitled "Achieving Best Evidence in Criminal

Proceedings: Guidance for Vulnerable or Intimidated Witnesses, including Children"
(para.5.11).

PARA.(1)
The welfare of the child is the sole criterion for determining whether a child should give **7–073**
evidence. If the child does give evidence, only the tribunal or a person appointed under
para.(2) can question the child (reg.22(3)).

PARA.(2)
The tribunal must decide whether the potential witness is a "vulnerable adult" bearing in **7–074**
mind the definition contained in regulation 1(2). Although the Handbook states at para.5.8
that the tribunal should not reach such a decision without first having considered medical
evidence, this is unduly restrictive as in some situations the person's legal status will provide the tribunal with the necessary evidence, for example a person who is subject to
guardianship under the Mental Health Act 1983.

PARA.(5)
This provision prevents the appellant or his or her legal representative from cross-exam- **7–075**
ining the witness. For a suggested approach to deal with this situation, see the note on
reg.22(3).

Restricted reporting orders

18.—(1) If it appears appropriate to do so, the President or the nominated **7–076**
chairman (or, at the hearing, the Tribunal) may make a restricted reporting order.

(2) A restricted reporting order is an order prohibiting the publication (including by electronic means) in a written publication available to the public, or the
inclusion in a relevant programme for reception in England and Wales, of any
matter likely to lead members of the public to identify the applicant, any child,
any vulnerable adult or any other person who the President or the nominated
chairman or the Tribunal considers should not be identified.

(3) An order that may be made under this regulation may be made in respect of a
limited period and may be varied or revoked by the President or the nominated
chairman before the hearing (or by the Tribunal at the hearing).

DEFINITIONS
    nominated chairman: reg.1(2). **7–077**
    relevant programme: reg.1(2).
    vulnerable adult: reg.1(2).

GENERAL NOTE
    This regulation enables the tribunal to make an order which prohibits the publication of **7–078**
any matter likely to lead the public to identify the applicant, any child, any vulnerable adult
or any other person who the tribunal considers should not be identified. Reference to the
individuals identified in this rule could be made in an anonymised form as long as this
would not lead to their identifiation.

Exclusion of press and public

19.—(1) Where paragraph (2) applies, the President or the nominated chairman **7–079**
(or, at the hearing, the Tribunal) may on his (or its) own initiative, or on a written
request by either party that the hearing or any part of it should be conducted in
private, direct that—

(a) any member of the public specified in the direction;

(b) members of the public generally; or

(c) members of the press and members of the public,

be excluded from all or part of the hearing.

(2) This paragraph applies where the President or the nominated chairman (or, at the hearing, the Tribunal) is satisfied that a direction under paragraph (1) is necessary in order to—

(a) safeguard the welfare of any child or vulnerable adult;

(b) protect a person's private life; or

(c) avoid the risk of injustice in any legal proceedings.

DEFINITIONS
7–080   nominated chairman: reg.1(2).
party: reg.1(2).
vulnerable adult: reg.1(2).

GENERAL NOTE
7–081   This regulation, which enables the press and public to be excluded from the tribunal hearing, provides an exception to the general rule set out in reg.21. Certain persons are entitled by reg.21(2) to attend a private hearing. A direction under this regulation should not be made if the matter could be deal with appropriately by an order being made under reg.18.

PART V

HEARING

Procedure at the hearing
7–082   **20.**—(1) The Tribunal may regulate its own procedure.

(2) At the beginning of the hearing the chairman must explain the order of proceedings which the Tribunal proposes to adopt.

(3) The parties may be represented or assisted at the hearing by any person.

(4) If either party fails to attend or be represented at the hearing, the Tribunal may hear and determine the case in that party's absence.

DEFINITION
7–083   parties: reg.1(2).

GENERAL NOTE
7–084   This regulation enables the tribunal to regulate its own procedure. This is subject to the imperative that the procedure must comply with the rules of natural justice. It also provides for the parties to be assisted at the hearing by either legal or non-legal representatives and for the hearing to proceed if either party or their representative fails to attend.

PARA.(2)
7–085   The tribunal has taken the view that the party upon whom rests the burden of proof begins the case (Handbook, para.9.4).

Hearing to be in public

21.—(1) The hearing must be in public except in so far as any person is exclu- **7–086**
ded under regulation 19.

(2) Whether or not the hearing is held in public—

(a) a member of the Council on Tribunals;

(b) the President;

(c) the clerk; and

(d) any person whom the President or the nominated chairman permits to be present in order to assist the Tribunal,

are entitled to attend the hearing.

(3) Whether or not the hearing is held in public—

(a) a member of the Council on Tribunals; and

(b) the President,

may remain present during the Tribunal's deliberations, but must not take part in the deliberations.

DEFINITIONS
   the clerk: reg.1(2).   **7–087**
   nominated chairman: reg.1(2).

Evidence

22.—(1) The Tribunal may consider any evidence, whether or not such evi- **7–088**
dence would be admissible in a court of law.

(2) The applicant has the right to give evidence at the hearing in person, and any other witness may do so unless the President or the nominated chairman has directed otherwise.

(3) No child may be asked any question except by the Tribunal or a person appointed under regulation 17(2).

(4) Where a direction has been made under regulation 17 that paragraph (5) of that regulation shall apply to any vulnerable adult, the vulnerable adult may not be asked any question except by the Tribunal or a person appointed under regulation 17(5).

(5) The Tribunal may require any witness to give evidence on oath or affir-mation which may be administered for the purpose by the chairman or the clerk.

DEFINITIONS
   nominated chairman: reg.1(2).   **7–089**
   vulnerable adult: reg.1(2).
   the clerk: reg.1(2).

GENERAL NOTE
   This regulation enables the tribunal to hear hearsay evidence, restricts the mode of ques- **7–090**
tioning for child and, where the tribunal has made a determination under reg.17, vulnerable adult witnesses and provides for witnesses to give evidence on oath or affirmation.

7–091   This provision, which precludes a child from being cross-examined however mature the child might be, gives no discretion to the tribunal. This is unfortunate, especially where the evidence of child is central to the issue before the tribunal. In such a situation either the appellant or his or her legal representative could suggest questions that the tribunal should put to the child. A failure by the tribunal to put the suggested questions to the child would risk contravening the appellant's rights under Article 6 of the European Convention on Human Rights.

Child: Is a person under the age of 18 years of age: see s.121(1) of the Act.

PART VI

Decision

The decision

7–092   **23.**—(1) The Tribunal's decision may be taken by a majority and the decision shall record whether it was unanimous or taken by a majority.

(2) The decision may be made and announced at the end of the hearing or reserved, and in any event, whether there has been a hearing or not, the decision must be recorded without delay in a document signed and dated by the chairman (or if as a result of his death or incapacity he is unable to sign, or if he ceases to be a member of the chairman's panel, by another member of the Tribunal).

(3) The document mentioned in paragraph (2) must also state—

(a) the reasons for the decision; and

(b) what, if any, order the Tribunal has made as a result of its decision.

(4) The Secretary must, as soon as reasonably possible, send to each party a copy of the document mentioned in paragraph (2) and [(except where the decision relates to the making of an order under section 166(5) of the 2002 Act)] a notice explaining to the parties any right of appeal which they may have against the Tribunal's decision and the right to apply for a review of the Tribunal's decision.

(5) Where the appeal was against an order made by a justice of the peace under section 20 of the 2000 Act or section 79K of the 1989 Act, the Secretary must, as soon as reasonably practicable, send a copy of the document mentioned in paragraph (2) to the justice of the peace who made the order.

(6) Except where a decision is announced at the end of the hearing, the decision shall be treated as having been made on the day on which a copy of the document mentioned in paragraph (2) is sent to the applicant.

(7) The decision shall be entered in the records.

Amendment
7–093   The amendment to this regulation was made by SI 2003/2043, reg.8.

Definitions
7–094   document: reg.1(2).
parties: reg.1(2).
the 2002 Act: reg.1(2).
the 2000 Act: reg.1(2).
the1989 Act: reg.1(2).
records: reg.1(2).

GENERAL NOTE
The decision of the tribunal is not confined to either allowing or dismissing an appeal: **7–095**
the tribunal also has the powers set out in s.21(5) of the 2000 Act. The decision can either be
given at the end of the hearing or reserved and reasons must be given for the decision. Also
see the notes to s.21.

PARA.(2)
Death or incapacity: If the death or incapacity of the chairman occurs after the conclusion **7–096**
of the hearing but before the document has been completed, a fresh tribunal should be constituted (*R. v Department of Health Ex p. Bhaugeerutty*, CO 2454–97, *The Times*, May 1,
1998).

PARA.(3)
Reasons: In *R. (on the application of W) v National Care Standards Commission* [2003] **7–097**
EWHC 621 (Admin), para.36, MacKay J. extracted a number "broad propositions" from
the following cases on the quality of the reasons given by the tribunal: *Elliott v Southwark
Borough Council* [1976] 1 W.L.R. 449, *Meek v City of Birmingham District Council* [1987]
I.R.L.R. 250, *Martin v Glynwed Distribution Limited* [1983] I.R.L.R. 1198, and *Harrison v
Cornwall County Council* 90 L.G.R. 81. They are:

"First, [the] tribunal is bound to give not just its decision but proper reasons for it.
Secondly, those reasons, to be proper reasons, should enable the losing party to understand why he or she has lost. Thirdly, where it has been necessary to resolve 'basic
findings of fact' those should be expressed in a summary way, but one that is clear
and comprehensible to someone with knowledge of the case. Fourthly, in reaching
each such finding of fact the tribunal does not have to give a complete account of the
evidence relating to it or the submissions made on either side of it or a recitation of every-
thing it has considered. It does not have to descend to the level of detail which would be
appropriate to be found in the judgment of a court of record governed by the formal rules
of evidence. Fifthly, the findings of fact should be such as to be capable of rationally supporting the eventual final decision, in this case the question—unfit or not?"

PARA.(4)
As soon as reasonably possible: The working time scale that has been adopted by the tribunal **7–098**
for the delivery of the decision to the parties is ten working days from the date of the hearing (Handbook, para.11.6).

Costs

24.—(1) Subject to regulation 31 and to paragraph (2) below, if in the opinion **7–099**
of the Tribunal a party has acted unreasonably in bringing or conducting the proceedings, it may make an order (a "costs order") requiring that party ("the paying
party") to make a payment to the other party ("the receiving party") to cover
costs incurred by the receiving party.

(2) Before making a costs order against a party, the Tribunal must—

(a) invite the receiving party to provide to the Tribunal a schedule of costs
incurred by him in respect of the proceedings; and

(b) invite representations from the paying party and consider any representations he makes, consider whether he is able to comply with such an order
and consider any relevant written information which he has provided.

(3) When making a costs order, the Tribunal must—

(a) order the payment of any sum which the parties have agreed should be paid;

(b) order the payment of any sum which it considers appropriate having considered any representations the parties may make; or

(c) order the payment of the whole or part of the costs incurred by the receiving party in connection with the proceedings as assessed.

(4) Any costs required by an order under this regulation to be assessed may be assessed in a county court according to such rules applicable to proceedings in a county court as shall be directed in the order.

(5) A costs order may, by leave of a county court, be enforced in the same manner as a judgment or order of that court to the same effect.

DEFINITIONS

7–100   party: reg.1(2).
parties: reg.1(2).
county court: reg.1(2).

GENERAL NOTE

7–101   The nature of the costs regime under this regulation was examined by the President in *Fun Camps Ltd v OFSTED* [2003] 124 E.Y. His Honour held that:

(1) The test of unreasonableness is a high one.

(2) The burden is the party alleging unreasonableness to satisfy the tribunal to that standard that the other party has acted unreasonably.

(3) The conduct of both parties as a whole is relevant, and this includes matters prior to the initiation of the proceedings.

(4) If no findings of fact have been made, the Tribunal cannot deal with allegations that may or may not be true.

(5) Costs can only be awarded from the date when the proceedings start.

(6) The individual directors of a Limited Company should only be the subject of a costs order where (a) the company is a façade or sham, (b) where the company is involved in an impropriety, and (c) where it is necessary to do so in the interests of justice (*Trustor AB v Smallbone*, March 16, 2001, applied).

The presumption in favour of a no costs order which is created by this regulation can be rebutted by proof that the paying party acted unreasonably. Litigants in person are not to be judged by the standards of experienced lawyers and a litigant could not be held to have acted unreasonably merely because he or she decided not to retain the services of a lawyer. A party will not be held to have acted unreasonably in bringing proceedings merely because he or she has persisted with a case which is ultimately rejected. Further, it is unlikely that a party acting in person would be held to have acted unreasonably in bringing proceedings merely because he or she pursued an appeal which, with the benefit of hindsight or greater insight, was seen to be obviously unmeritorious. Costs order are more likely to be made where a party has acted unreasonably in conducting the proceedings, in particular by failing to comply with directions or "unless orders". However, inadequate written or oral presentations of cases by parties acting without the benefit of professional assistance are unlikely to be characterised as unreasonable (*Woodbine Villa v NCSC* [2002] 116 N.C., para.50 *et seq.*).

As costs can only be awarded against a "party", this rule has no application to a case where in fact there is no appeal before the tribunal as the purported decision was a nullity (*Re an appeal by Ram and Ram* [2002] 100 E.Y.).

PARA.(1)

The Tribunal: Neither the President nor the nominated chairman can make a costs order. **7–102**

PARA.(2)

The Handbook, at para.12.3, suggests that "the tribunal deal with costs applications by **7–103** way of written representations". This approach was endorsed by the tribunal in *Walkes v HM Chief Inspector of Schools* [2003] 212 E.Y. S.U.S., at para.86. In this case the tribunal said that the effect of this paragraph is that, if the tribunal considers that the paying party would not be able to comply with a costs order, it should not, in the exercise of its discretion, make such an order" (para.45).

Schedule: In *Coventry Homes (MHC) Ltd v NCSC* [2002] 17 N.C., the chairman of the tribunal said at para.17:

"In future cases Chairmen will be greatly assisted by a Schedule showing what activities have been undertaken by which personnel, broken down into the various stages of the proceedings for example; interlocutory preparation, attendance at directions hearing, preparation for final hearing etc. In this way those challenging an order can do so by reference to specific sums at different stages of the proceedings."

Review of the Tribunal's decision

25.—[(Z1) This regulation shall not apply in relation to an application for an **7–104** order under section 166(5) of the 2002 Act.]

(1) A party may apply to the President for the Tribunal's decision to be reviewed on the grounds that—

(a) it was wrongly made as a result of an error on the part of the Tribunal staff;

(b) a party, who was entitled to be heard at a hearing but failed to appear or to be represented, had good and sufficient reason for failing to appear; or

(c) there was an obvious error in the decision.

(2) An application under this regulation must—

(a) be made not later than ten working days after the date on which the decision was sent to the party applying for the Tribunal's decision to be reviewed; and

(b) must be in writing stating the grounds in full.

(3) An application under this regulation may be refused by the President, or by the chairman of the Tribunal which decided the case, if in his opinion it has no reasonable prospect of success.

(4) Unless an application under this regulation is refused under paragraph (3), it shall be determined, after the parties have had an opportunity to be heard, by the Tribunal which decided the case or, where that is not practicable, by another Tribunal appointed by the President.

(5) The Tribunal may on its own initiative propose to review its decision on any of the grounds referred to in paragraph (1) above, in which case—

(a) the Secretary shall serve notice on the parties not later than ten working days after the date on which the decision was sent to them; and

(b) the parties shall have an opportunity to be heard.

(6) If, on the application of a party or on its own initiative the Tribunal is satisfied as to any of the grounds referred to in paragraph (1)—

(a) it shall order that the whole or a specified part of the decision be reviewed; and

(b) it may give directions to be complied with before or after the hearing of the review.

(7) The power to give directions under paragraph (6) includes a power to give a direction requiring a party to provide such particulars, evidence or statements as may reasonably be required for the determination of the review.

AMENDMENT

7–105   The amendment to this regulation was made by SI 2003/2043, reg.9.

DEFINITIONS

7–106   party: reg.1(2).
the Secretary: reg.1(2).
working days: reg.1(2).
parties: reg.1(2).

GENERAL NOTE

7–107   This regulation enables a party to apply to the President for the tribunal's decision to be reviewed on specific grounds. The tribunal may on its own initiative review its decision if one or more of the grounds are satisfied and the parties have been given an opportunity to be heard. The powers of the tribunal subsequent to a review are set out in reg.25. The Handbook states that there are four phases to a review:

"First, the application; secondly, a preliminary 'screening' of the review application by the chairman; thirdly, the application for the review (determined by the full tribunal); finally, the review itself" (para.14.1).

PARA.(1)(A)

7–108   *Tribunal staff:* Not the tribunal itself (*Her Majesty's Chief Inspector of Schools v Spicer* [2004] EWHC 440 (Admin), para.49).

PARA.(1)(C)

7–109   *Obvious error in the decision:* Such an error does not include an error of law, including a failure to give adequate reasons or defective reasoning (*Her Majesty's Chief Inspector of Schools v Spicer*, above).

PARA.(2)(A)

7–110   *Sent:* The ten-working-day limit may be extended under reg.35.

Powers of Tribunal on review

7–111   **26.**—[(Z1) This regulation shall not apply in relation to an application for an order under s.166(5) of the 2002 Act.]

(1) The Tribunal may, having reviewed all or part of a decision—

(a) set aside or vary the decision by certificate signed by the chairman (or if as a result of his death or incapacity he is unable to sign, or if he ceases to be a member of the chairmen's panel, by another member of the Tribunal); and

(b) substitute such other decision as it thinks fit or order a rehearing before the same or a differently constituted Tribunal.

(2) If any decision is set aside or varied (whether as a result of a review or by order of the High Court), the Secretary shall alter the relevant entry in the records to conform to the chairman's certificate or the order of the High Court and shall notify the parties accordingly.

(3) Any decision of the Tribunal under this regulation may be taken by a majority and the decision shall record whether it was unanimous or taken by a majority.

AMENDMENT

The amendment to this regulation was made by SI 2003/2043, reg.10.　　**7–112**

DEFINITIONS

the Secretary: reg.1(2).　　**7–113**
parties: reg.1(2).

GENERAL NOTE

This regulation provides the tribunal with extensive powers after having reviewed a **7–114** decision under reg.25. It can set aside or vary the decision, substitute a fresh decision or order a rehearing. The tribunal can also decide not to exercise its discretion under this regulation in which case the original decision stands.

Publication

27.—(1) The President must make such arrangements as he considers appropri- **7–115** ate for the publication of Tribunal decisions.

(2) Decisions may be published electronically.

(3) The decision may be published in an edited form, or subject to any deletions, if the President or the nominated chairman considers it appears appropriate bearing in mind—

(a) the need to safeguard the welfare of any child or vulnerable adult;

(b) the need to protect the private life of any person;

(c) any representations on the matter which either party has provided in writing;

(d) the effect of any subsisting restricted reporting order; and

(e) the effect of any direction under regulation 15.

DEFINITIONS

nominated chairman: reg.1(2).　　**7–116**
vulnerable adult: reg.1(2).
party: reg.2(1).

GENERAL NOTE
7–117   This regulation provides for the publication of tribunal decisions. Every decision must be published, although the decision could be edited or published in an anonymised form if one or more of the criteria in para.(3) are satisfied.

PART VII

SUPPLEMENTARY

Method of sending documents

7–118   **28.**—(1) Any document may be sent to the Secretary by post, by fax, electronically or through a document exchange, unless the President or the nominated chairman directs otherwise.

(2) Any notice or document which these Regulations authorise or require the Secretary to send to a party shall be sent—

(a) by first-class post to the address given for the purpose by that party in accordance with these Regulations;

(b) by fax or electronically to a number or address given by that party for the purpose; or

(c) where the party has given for the purpose an address which includes a numbered box number at a document exchange, by leaving the notice or document addressed to that numbered box at that document exchange or at a document exchange which transmits documents on every working day to that exchange.

(3) If a notice or document cannot be sent to a party in accordance with paragraph (2), the President or the nominated chairman may dispense with service of it or direct that it be served on that party in such manner as he thinks appropriate.

(4) Any notice or document sent by the Secretary to a party in accordance with these Regulations shall be taken to have been received—

(a) if sent by post and not returned, on the second working day after it was posted;

(b) if sent by fax or electronically, unless the Secretary has been notified that the transmission has been unsuccessful, on the next working day after it was sent;

(c) if left at a document exchange in accordance with paragraph (2), on the second working day after it was left; and

(d) if served in accordance with a direction under paragraph (3), on the next working day after it was so served.

DEFINITIONS
7–119   document: reg.1(2).
the Secretary: reg.1(2).
nominated chairman: reg.1(2).
party: reg.1(2).
working day: reg.1(2).

Irregularities

29.—(1) An irregularity resulting from failure to comply with any provision of these Regulations or any direction given in accordance with them before the Tribunal has reached its decision shall not of itself render the proceedings void. **7–120**

(2) Where any irregularity comes to the attention of the President or the nominated chairman (before the hearing) or the Tribunal he or it may and, if it appears that any person may have been prejudiced by the irregularity, shall, before reaching a decision, give such directions as he or it thinks just to cure or waive the irregularity.

(3) Clerical mistakes in any document recording the decision of the Tribunal or a direction or decision of the President or the nominated chairman, or errors arising in such documents from accidental slips or omissions, may at any time be corrected by the chairman or, as the case may be, the President, or nominated chairman by means of a certificate signed by him.

(4) The Secretary shall as soon as practicable where a document is corrected in accordance with paragraph (3) send the parties a copy of any corrected document together with reasons for the decision to correct the document.

DEFINITIONS

nominated chairman: reg.1(2). **7–121**
document: reg.1(2).
parties: reg.1(2).

GENERAL NOTE

This regulation states that an irregularity resulting from a failure to comply with these **7–122** regulations or with a direction does not of itself void the proceedings. It also provides for the correction of clerical errors.

Application on behalf of person under a disability

30.—(1) A person may, by writing to the Secretary, request authorisation by the **7–123** President or the nominated chairman to make any application to the Tribunal on behalf of any person who is prevented by mental or physical infirmity from acting on his own behalf.

(2) A person acting in accordance with an authorisation under this regulation may on behalf of the other person take any step or do anything which that person is required or permitted to do under these Regulations, subject to any conditions which the President or the nominated chairman may impose.

DEFINITIONS

the Secretary: reg.1(2). **7–124**
nominated chairman: reg.1(2).

Death of applicant

31. If the applicant dies, before the case or application for leave is determined, **7–125** the President or the nominated chairman may—

(a) strike out the case or application for leave in so far as it relates to that individual without making a costs order;

(b) appoint such person as he thinks fit to proceed with the appeal in the place of the deceased applicant.

DEFINITIONS
7–126   application for leave: reg.1(2).
nominated chairman: reg.1(2).
costs order: reg.1(2).

Amendment of appeal, application for leave or response

7–127   **32.**—(1) The applicant may amend the reasons he gives in support of the case or application for leave as the case may be, but only with the leave of the President or the nominated chairman (or at the hearing, with the leave of the Tribunal).

(2) The respondent may amend the reasons he gives for opposing the applicant's case or application for leave, as the case may be, but only with the leave of the President or the nominated chairman (or at the hearing, with the leave of the Tribunal).

(3) Where the President, the nominated chairman or Tribunal gives leave to either party to amend the reasons given in support of his case, he may do so on such terms as he thinks fit (including, subject to regulation 24, the making of a costs order).

DEFINITIONS
7–128   application for leave: reg.1(2).
nominated chairman: reg.1(2).
costs order: reg.1(2).

Withdrawal of proceedings or opposition to proceedings

7–129   **33.**—(1) If the applicant at any time notifies the Secretary in writing, or states at a hearing, that he no longer wishes to pursue the proceedings, the President or the nominated chairman (or at the hearing, the Tribunal) must dismiss the proceedings, and may, subject to regulation 24(2) and (3) make a costs order.

(2) If the respondent notifies the Secretary in writing, or states at a hearing, that he does not oppose or no longer opposes the proceedings, the President (or at the hearing, the Tribunal)—

(a) must without delay determine the case or, as the case may be, the application for leave in the applicant's favour;

(b) subject to regulation 24(2) and (3) may make a costs order; and

(c) must consider making one.

DEFINITIONS
7–130   the Secretary: reg.1(2).
nominated chairman: reg.1(2).
costs order: reg.1(2).
respondent: reg.1(2).

GENERAL NOTE
7–131   This regulation is concerned with the situation where the appeal is withdrawn, or the respondent withdraws its opposition to the appeal prior to the prior to the decision of the tribunal.

The test of unreasonableness set out in reg.24(1) applies to a costs order made under this regulation (*Fun Camps Ltd v OFSTED* [2003] 124 E.Y.).

This is the only provision that imposes a duty on the tribunal to allow the appeal. **7–132**
Note that the tribunal must consider making a costs order if the respondent withdraws its opposition to the appeal. A similar obligation is not placed on the tribunal under para.(1).

Proof of documents and certification of decisions

34.—(1) A document purporting to be issued by the Secretary shall be taken to **7–133** have been so issued, unless the contrary is proved.

(2) A document purporting to be certified by the Secretary to be a true copy of a document containing—

(a) a decision of the Tribunal; or

(b) an order of the President or the nominated chairman or of the Tribunal,

shall be sufficient evidence of the matters contained in it, unless the contrary is proved.

DEFINITIONS
document: reg.1(2). **7–134**
the Secretary: reg.1(2).
nominated chairman: reg.1(2).

Time

35.—(1) The President or the nominated chairman may extend any time limit **7–135** mentioned in these Regulations if in the circumstances—

(a) it would be unreasonable to expect it to be, or to have been, complied with; and

(b) it would be unfair not to extend it.

(2) Where the time prescribed by these Regulations, or specified in any direction given by the President or the nominated chairman, for taking any step expires on a day which is not a working day, the step must be treated as having been done in time if it is done on the next working day.

[(3) This regulation does not apply to the time limits provided for the initiating of an appeal mentioned in paragraph 1 of [Schedule 2, 6, 7, 8 or 9].

AMENDMENT
Paragraph (3) was substituted by SI 2003/626, reg.9, SI 2003/1060, reg.6 and SI 2003/ **7–136** 2043, reg.11.

DEFINITIONS
nominated chairman: reg.1(2). **7–137**
working day: reg.1(2).
vulnerable adult: reg.1(2).

GENERAL NOTE
This regulation enables any time limit set out in these regulations to be extended by the **7–138** tribunal. The time limit for initiating an appeal is set out in s.21(2) of the Act and therefore cannot be extended by the tribunal.

When exercising its discretion under this provision, the tribunal will err on the side of caution in circumstances where the consequences for the appellant will be draconian (*Hawkes v Secretary of State* [2004] 243 P.C. at para.23; also see *Davis v Secretary of State* [2002] 13 P.C.).

PART VIII

MISCELLANEOUS

Revocation

7–139   **36.**—(1) The Protection of Children Act Tribunal Regulations 2000 ("the 2000 Regulations") are hereby revoked.

(2) Any application or appeal which—

(a) was made to the Tribunal under the 2000 Regulations before 1st April 2002; and

(b) the Tribunal has not determined before that date,

shall for the purposes of these Regulations be treated as having been made to the Tribunal under these Regulations.

(3) Any direction or notice given, or thing done, by the Tribunal before 1st April 2002 shall for the purposes of these Regulations be treated as having been given or done by the Tribunal under these Regulations.

Regulation 4(1)   SCHEDULE 1

APPEAL UNDER SECTION 21 OF THE 2000 ACT AGAINST A DECISION OF THE REGISTRATION AUTHORITY OR AN ORDER OF A JUSTICE OF THE PEACE

Initiating an appeal

7–140   **1.**—(1) A person who wishes to appeal to the Tribunal under section 21 of the 2000 Act against a decision of the registration authority under Part II of the 2000 Act, or an order made by a justice of the peace under section 20 of that Act, must do so by application in writing to the Secretary.

(2) An application under this paragraph may be made on the application form available from the Secretary.

(3) An application under this paragraph must—

(a) give the applicant's name and full postal address, if the applicant is an individual his date of birth and, if the applicant is a company, the address of its registered office;

(b) give the name, address and profession of the person (if any) representing the applicant;

(c) give the address within the United Kingdom to which the Secretary should send documents concerning the appeal;

(d) give, where these are available, the applicant's telephone number, fax number and e-mail address and those of the applicant's representative;

(e) identify the decision or order against which the appeal is brought and give particulars of—

(i) whether the appeal is against a refusal of registration, an imposition or variation of conditions of registration, a refusal to remove or vary any condition, or a cancellation of registration;

(ii) whether the appeal is against a decision of the registration authority or an order made by a justice of the peace;

(iii) where the appeal is in respect of a cancellation of registration, whether the establishment or agency in respect of which the appeal is made remains open and, in the case of an establishment, the number of residents in that establishment;

(f) give a short statement of the grounds of appeal; and

(g) be signed and dated by the applicant.

GENERAL NOTE

The Care Standard Tribunal has drafted a series of appeal forms for use in appeals under **7–141** this Schedule:

B1: The application form for Sch.1 appeals.

B2: Appeals against Orders of a J.P.

B4: The response form from the respondent.

B5: Further information from the applicant.

B6: Further information from the respondent.

Acknowledgement and notification of application

2.—(1) On receiving an application, made within the period for bringing an appeal speci- **7–142** fied in section 21 of the 2000 Act, the Secretary must—

(a) immediately send an acknowledgement of its receipt to the applicant; and

(b) enter particulars of the appeal, and the date of its receipt in the records and send a copy of it, together with any documents supplied by the applicant in support of it, to the respondent.

(2) If in the Secretary's opinion there is an obvious error in the application—

(a) he may correct it;

(b) he must notify the applicant in writing that he has done so; and

(c) unless, within five working days of receipt of notification under head (b) of this sub-paragraph the applicant notifies the Secretary in writing that he objects to the correction, the application shall be amended accordingly.

Response to application

3.—(1) The Secretary must send the information provided by the applicant under para- **7–143** graph 1 to the respondent together with a request that it respond to the application within 20 working days of receiving it.

(2) If the respondent fails to respond as requested, it shall not be entitled to take any further part in the proceedings.

(3) The response must—

(a) acknowledge that the respondent has received a copy of the application;

(b) indicate whether or not the respondent opposes it, and if it does, give the reasons why it opposes the application;

(c) provide the following information and documents—

(i) the name, address and profession of the person (if any) representing the respondent and whether the Secretary should send documents concerning the appeal to the representative rather than to the respondent; and

(ii) in the case of an appeal under section 21(1)(a) of the 2000 Act, a copy of the written notice of the decision (which is the subject of the appeal) served under section 19(3) of that Act, and the reasons for the decision; or

(iii) in the case of an appeal under section 21(1)(b) of the 2000 Act, a copy of the order made by the justice of the peace.

(4) The Secretary must without delay send to the applicant a copy of the response and the information and documents provided with it.

Misconceived appeals etc.

7–144   **4.**—(1) The President or the nominated chairman may at any time strike out the appeal on the grounds that—

(a) it is made otherwise than in accordance with paragraph 1;

(b) it is outside the jurisdiction of the Tribunal or is otherwise misconceived; or

(c) it is frivolous or vexatious.

(2) Before striking out an appeal under this paragraph, the President or the nominated chairman must—

(a) invite the parties to make representations on the matter within such period as he may direct;

(b) if within the period specified in the direction the applicant so requests in writing, afford the parties an opportunity to make oral representations;

(c) consider any representations the parties may make.

General Note

7–145   In order to determine whether an appeal is misconceived, the pleaded documents must be examined to ascertain whether they disclose any grounds of appeal relevant to the decision taken by the registration authority (*Woodbine Villa v NCSC* [2002] 116 N.C.) or whether the registration authority has reached a decision that could be appealed (*Chorley Nursing Home v NCSC* [2003] 125 N.C.).

In *Aliyu v OFSTED* [2004] 254 E.Y., the President described the strike out procedure as a "draconian provision . . . and, at the present time, there is no internal appeal or review procedure . . . The only remedy against a successful strike out would be to judicially review the decision" (para.15). In this case, the President advised himself that he had a responsibility to ensure that his decision was in conformity with Art.6 of the European Convention of Human Rights, and said that the terms of reg.29 encouraged him "to interpret the regulations in such a way that there is available to the President a margin of flexibility so as to ensure compliance with the . . . Convention" (paras 14, 16). On applying this approach, the President held that it would be "wholly disproportionate" to strike out the appeal in a situation where an incorrect application form was submitted within the 28-day time limit. The President has no jurisdiction to extend the time limit for submitting an appeal (reg.35(3)).

7–146   This paragraph does not provide the President or nominated chairman with the power to make a costs order after striking out an appeal (*Woodbine Villa v NCSC* [2002] 116 N.C., para.43). The tribunal has jurisdiction to make a costs order under reg.24.

Further information to be sent by the applicant and respondent

7–147   **5.**—(1) As soon as the respondent has provided the information set out in paragraph 3, the Secretary must write to each party requesting that he send to the Secretary within 15 working days after the date on which he receives the Secretary's letter the following information—

(a) the name of any witness whose evidence the party wishes the Tribunal to consider (and whether the party may wish the Tribunal to consider additional witness evidence from a witness whose name is not yet known) and the nature of that evidence;

(b) whether the party wishes the President or the nominated chairman to give any directions or exercise any of his powers under Part IV of these Regulations;

(c) whether the party wishes there to be a preliminary hearing with regard to directions;

(d) a provisional estimate of the time the party considers will be required to present his case;

(e) the earliest date by which the party considers he would be able to prepare his case for hearing; and

(f) in the case of the applicant, whether he wishes his appeal to be determined without a hearing.

(2) Once the Secretary has received the information referred to in sub-paragraph (1) from both parties, he must without delay send a copy of the information supplied by the applicant to the respondent and that supplied by the respondent to the applicant.

GENERAL NOTE
PARA.5(1)(F)
There is no power vested in the tribunal to insist on an oral hearing when the appellant **7–148** asks for the matter to be determined without one (*B v Secretary of State* [2002] 51 P.C.).

Changes to further information supplied to the Tribunal
6.—(1) Either party, within 5 working days of receiving the further information in **7–149** respect of the other party from the Secretary, may ask the Secretary in writing to amend or add to any of the information given under paragraph 5(1).
(2) If the Secretary receives any further information under sub-paragraph (1) from either party he must, without delay, send a copy of it to the other party.

DEFINITIONS
2000 Act: reg.1(2). **7–150**
registration authority: reg.1(2).
the Secretary: reg.1(2).
working days: reg.1(2).
respondent: reg.1(2).
nominated chairman: reg.1(2).
parties: reg.1(2).
party: reg.1(2).

ANNEX A

INTERPRETATION

The interpretation section of the Act is contained in s.121: **A–001**

General interpretation, etc.
121.—(1) In this Act— **A–002**

"adult" means a person who is not a child;

"appropriate Minister" means—

(a) in relation to England, Scotland or Northern Ireland, the Secretary of State;

(b) in relation to Wales, the Assembly;

and in relation to England and Wales means the Secretary of State and the Assembly acting jointly;

"child" means a person under the age of 18;

"community home" has the same meaning as in the 1989 Act;

"employment agency" and "employment business" have the same meanings as in the Employment Agencies Act 1973; but no business which is an employment business shall be taken to be an employment agency;

"enactment" includes an enactment comprised in subordinate legislation (within the meaning of the Interpretation Act 1978);

"to foster a child privately" has the same meaning as in the 1989 Act;

"harm"—

(a) in relation to an adult who is not mentally impaired, means ill-treatment or the impairment of health;

(b) in relation to an adult who is mentally impaired, or a child, means ill-treatment or the impairment of health or development;

"health service hospital" has the same meaning as in the National Health Service Act 1977;

"illness" includes any injury;

"independent school" has the same meaning as in the Education Act 1996;

"local authority" has the same meaning as in the 1989 Act;

"local authority foster parent" has the same meaning as in the 1989 Act;

"medical" includes surgical;

"mental disorder" means mental illness, arrested or incomplete development of mind, psychopathic disorder, and any other disorder or disability of mind;

"National Health Service body" means a National Health Service trust, [a Strategic Health Authority,] a Health Authority, a Special Health Authority[, a Primary Care Trust or a Local Health Board];

"parent", in relation to a child, includes any person who is not a parent of his but who has parental responsibility for him;

"parental responsibility" has the same meaning as in the 1989 Act;

"prescribed" means prescribed by regulations;

"proprietor", in relation to a school, has the same meaning as in the Education Act 1996;

"regulations" (except where provision is made for them to be made by the Secretary of State or the Assembly) means regulations made by the appropriate Minister;

"relative" has the same meaning as in the 1989 Act;

"school" has the same meaning as in the Education Act 1996;

"social services functions" means functions which are social services functions for the purposes of the Local Authority Social Services Act 1970;

"treatment" includes diagnosis;

"the Tribunal" means the tribunal established by section 9 of the 1999 Act;

"undertaking" includes any business or profession and—

    (a) in relation to a public or local authority, includes the exercise of any functions of that authority; and
    (b) in relation to any other body of persons, whether corporate or unincorporate, includes any of the activities of that body;

"voluntary organisation" has the same meaning as in the Adoption Act 1976.

(2) For the purposes of this Act—

  (a) a person is disabled if—

    (i) his sight, hearing or speech is substantially impaired;
    (ii) he has a mental disorder; or
    (iii) he is physically substantially disabled by any illness, any impairment present since birth, or otherwise;

  (b) an adult is mentally impaired if he is in a state of arrested or incomplete development of mind (including a significant impairment of intelligence and social functioning).

(3) In this Act, the expression "personal care" does not include any prescribed activity.

(4) For the purposes of this Act, the person who carries on a fostering agency falling within section 4(4)(b), or a voluntary adoption agency, is the voluntary organisation itself.

(5) References in this Act to a person who carries on an establishment or agency include references to a person who carries it on otherwise than for profit.

(6) For the purposes of this Act, a community home which is provided by a voluntary organisation shall be taken to be carried on by—

(a) the person who equips and maintains it; and

(b) if the appropriate Minister determines that the body of managers for the home, or a specified member of that body, is also to be treated as carrying on the home, that body or member.

(7) Where a community home is provided by a voluntary organisation, the appropriate Minister may determine that for the purposes of this Act the home is to be taken to be managed solely by—

(a) any specified member of the body of managers for the home; or

(b) any other specified person on whom functions are conferred under the home's instrument of management.

(8) A determination under subsection (6) or (7) may be made either generally or in relation to a particular home or class of homes.

(9) An establishment is not a care home for the purposes of this Act unless the care which it provides includes assistance with bodily functions where such assistance is required.

(10) References in this Act to a child's being looked after by a local authority shall be construed in accordance with section 22 of the 1989 Act.

(11) For the purposes of this Act an individual is made redundant if—

(a) he is dismissed; and

(b) for the purposes of the Employment Rights Act 1996 the dismissal is by reason of redundancy.

(12) Any register kept for the purposes of this Act may be kept by means of a computer.

(13) In this Act, the expressions listed in the left-hand column have the meaning given by, or are to be interpreted in accordance with, the provisions listed in the right-hand column.

Expression	*Provision of this Act*
1989 Act	Children Act 1989
1999 Act	Protection of Children Act 1999
Assembly	Section 5
Care home	Section 3
CCETSW	Section 70
[CHAI	Section 5A]
Children's home	Section 1
[. . .]	[. . .]
Commissioner	Section 72
Council, the English Council, the Welsh Council	Section 54
[CSCI	Section 5B]

Domiciliary care agency	Section 4
Fostering agency	Section 4
Hospital and independent hospital	Section 2
Independent clinic and independent medical agency	Section 2
Registration authority	Section 5
Residential family centre	Section 4
Voluntary adoption agency	Section 4

AMENDMENTS

A–003   The amendments to "National Heath Service body" in subs.(1) were made by the NHS Reform and Health Care Professional Act 2002, s.6(2), Sch.5, para.46 and the National Health Service Reform and Health Care Professions Act 2002 (Supplementary, Consequential etc. Provisions) Regulations 2002 (SI 2002/2469), reg.4, Sch.1, para.27. The references to CHAI and CSCI in subs.(13) were inserted by the Health and Social Care (Community Health and Standards) Act 2003, s.147, Sch.9, Pt 2, para.30 and the reference to the "Commission" was deleted by s.196, Sch.14, Pt 2 of that Act.

GENERAL NOTE

A–004   *SUBS.(9)*

Assistance with bodily functions: In *R. v National Insurance Commissioner Ex p. Secretary of State for Social Services* [1981] 2 All E.R. 738 CA at 741, Lord Denning M.R. defined "bodily functions" as including:

> "breathing, hearing, seeing, eating, drinking, walking, sitting, sleeping, getting in and out of bed, dressing, undressing, eliminating waste products and the like, all of which an ordinary person, who is not suffering from any disability, does for himself. But they do not include cooking, shopping or any other things which a wife or daughter does as part of her domestic duties; or generally which one of the household normally does for the rest of the family".

Subsequently the House of Lords in *Wooding v Secretary of State for Social Services* [1984] 1 All E.R. 593, confirmed this approach by holding that the phrase "bodily functions" is a restricted and precise term directed primarily to those functions which a fit person normally performs for himself. The use physical assistance is not necessarily required as the act of prompting or encouraging a person to perform a bodily function would probably come within the meaning of "assistance".

This provision should not be read to mean that where bodily assistance is provided or required then registration as a care home must follow.

ANNEX B

DEPARTMENT OF HEALTH GUIDANCE

Supported Housing and Care Homes—Guidance on Regulation

INTRODUCTION

This is guidance for councils with social services responsibilities in England, **B–001** issued as statutory guidance under section 7 of the Local Authority Social Services Act 1970. The guidance is also issued to the National Care Standards Commission under section 6(2)(b) of the Care Standards Act 2000.

The guidance will also be relevant to NHS Primary Care Trusts and councils with housing responsibilities concerned with joint planning and commissioning of supported housing models.

The guidance should be read in conjunction with the following documents:

- the conditions for use of *Supporting People* Grant, issued by the Office of the Deputy Prime Minister, available on the *Supporting People* Knowledge Web *www.spkweb.org.uk* under General Documents and Discussions—General Docs—Finance and Contracting—Financial Package Chapter 1. If you have any problems downloading the document, please call the SP Help line on 020 7944 2556 and

- the Department for Work & Pensions circular HB/CTB A47/2001 on the Transitional Housing Benefit Scheme, dated 31 October 2001, available on *http://www.dss.gov.uk/hbctb/index.htm*.

GUIDANCE

Summary
1. Government policy for community care aims to promote independence, while **B–002** protecting service users' safety. Promotion of independence implies recognition of individuals' own choices regarding housing, care, and support, including their choices in relation to risk and protection.
2. The new regulatory framework under the Care Standards Act, 2000 aims to ensure high standards of care and to protect vulnerable people, but the Act will not fundamentally change the definition of a care home as compared with the current legislation.
3. Transitional Housing Benefit and, from April 2003, the *Supporting People* grant are not in general payable for care homes. Their main aim is the promotion of independence through non-intensive, housing-related support in the community.
4. Government policy would support changes to care homes and their replacement with other provision in cases where assessments/care plans of the individuals in the scheme lead to changes that might promote greater independence. Government policy is to enable people to receive care and

support in their own home, where they wish and wherever possible. In some cases, the greater consistency of regulation applied by the National Care Standards Commission after April 2002 may lead to re-designation of care homes.

5. Government policy would not support inappropriate changes to care homes which do not promote genuine independence, but seek primarily to secure funding through Transitional Housing Benefit and *Supporting People*. Such changes risk removing necessary protection from vulnerable people and may be unlawful. They also risk future disruption to funding, if the National Care Standards Commission later decides that registration as a care home is required.

6. This guidance aims to explain in broad terms where registration as a care home is required and how to distinguish care homes from supported housing of various kinds. The distinction is not always a simple matter. Advice must be sought from the National Care Standards Commission, wherever a change to registration of a care home is contemplated.

7. This guidance applies both during the currency of Transitional Housing Benefit up to March 2003 and after the introduction of the *Supporting People* grant from April 2003.

Personal care

B–003   8. The Care Standards Act, 2000 did not include a definition of "personal care" (except that regulations may be made excluding prescribed activities from personal care). Its established, ordinary meaning includes four main types of care, which are:

- assistance with bodily functions such as feeding, bathing, and toileting

- care which falls just short of assistance with bodily functions, but still involving physical and intimate touching, including activities such as helping a person get out of a bath and helping them to get dressed

- non-physical care, such as advice, encouragement and supervision relating to the foregoing, such as prompting a person to take a bath and supervising them during this

- emotional and psychological support, including the promotion of social functioning, behaviour management, and assistance with cognitive functions

9. In summary, in relation to personal care, the requirement under the Care Standards Act for registration as a care home is only triggered where personal care is provided and, in addition, the most intensive kind of personal care (1st bullet) is available, when such assistance is required.

10. It is only the two more intensive kinds of personal care (1st and 2nd bullets), which trigger the requirement under the Care Standards Act for registration as a domiciliary care agency, although other kinds of personal care and support may also be provided by such an agency.

11. Non-physical care, emotional and psychological support do not of themselves trigger a requirement for registration with the National Care Standards Commission. Such care and support may be provided by various agencies

according to the context and the person's overall needs. In certain circumstances, these will be part of housing-related support, funded through Transitional Housing Benefit, or, from April 2003, *Supporting People*. Funding responsibilities for these types of care and support is further discussed in:

- the conditions for use of *Supporting People* Grant, issued by the Office of the Deputy Prime Minister, available on the *Supporting People* Knowledge Web under Emerging Policy/Administrative Guidance]— *www.spkweb. org.uk* and

- the Department for Work & Pensions circular HB/CTB A47/2001 on the Transitional Housing Benefit Scheme, available on *http://www.dss.gov.uk/ hbctb/index.htm.*

Care Homes

12. The Care Standards Act, 2000 specifies two elements to determine which **B–004** establishments must be registered as care homes from April 2002. This is, firstly, establishments that provide accommodation *together with* nursing or personal care (as described broadly at paragraph 8) for people who are or have been ill, who have or have had a mental disorder, who are disabled or infirm, or who are or have been dependent on alcohol or drugs (section 3 of the Act).

13. Secondly, to fall within the definition of a care home, an establishment must also meet the requirement in section 121(9) of the Act, which provides that an establishment is not a care home unless the care it provides includes assistance with bodily functions, where such assistance is required. This does not mean that personal care provided by a care home is limited to assistance with bodily functions, but that this type of assistance must be available and given, if required, for an establishment to be registrable as a care home. Such assistance with bodily functions need not be given ordinarily and regularly, to come within the definition of a care home. Such assistance might only be required occasionally, but, if that requirement cannot be met, there would be no eligibility for registration as a care home. This requirement replicates that in the Registered Homes Act 1984.

14. The definition of a care home in the Care Standards Act 2000 differs slightly from the definition in the Registered Homes Act 1984 in that it does not refer to the provision of board. The intention behind this change was to close the loophole whereby unscrupulous care homeowners could avoid registration by charging residents for their food on a pay-as-you-eat basis

15. Beyond this, there is no intention to extend regulation to new types of accommodation, which have not previously been required to register. The type of care provided in a home, which will trigger registration, is the same under the Care Standards Act as it was under the Registered Homes Act.

Domiciliary Care

16. Where an agency arranges to provide personal care (as described at paragraph **B–005** 9) to a person in their own home, it must register as a domiciliary care agency. A sole individual home care worker may provide paid, personal care to a

person in their own home, but will not need to register as a domiciliary care agency.

17. A domiciliary care agency is defined in section 4(3) of the Act as "an under-taking which consists of or includes arranging the provision of personal care in their own homes for persons who by reason of illness, infirmity or dis-ability are unable to provide it for themselves without assistance". The words "unable to provide it for themselves without assistance" mean that personal care—in this context—has a narrower application than in the con-text of a care home. It will include assistance with bodily functions and physical care, which fall just short of that assistance, such as helping a person to get dressed. But it could not, within this definition, extend to encourage-ment and emotional support, since this is not a form of personal care which a person could be said to be able or unable to provide for themselves.

18. Personal care delivered to people in their own homes will be regulated under the provisions in the Act covering domiciliary care agencies and the Domiciliary Care Agency Regulations. This will ensure that vulnerable people receiving personal care in their own homes get the protection they need.

Housing and care schemes and registration as a Care Home

B–006 19. Concerns have been raised about whether "very sheltered housing" or "extra care housing" for older people, or group homes (supported housing) for learning disabled people, or people with mental health problems, will be registrable as a care home. While it is not possible to say categorically that, any scheme describing itself as providing very sheltered housing, or extra care, or supported housing, will necessarily not be registrable as a care home, the following paragraphs aim to provide guidance on good prac-tice schemes. There is no intention to extend regulation to new types of accommodation, which have not previously been required to register. The type of care provided in a home, which will trigger registration, is the same under the Care Standards Act as it was under the Registered Homes Act.

Extra care or very sheltered housing for older people

B–007 20. Government policy strongly supports the promotion of independence for older people. Extra care housing models have an important and growing role to play, within the whole spectrum of housing and care options for people with various levels of need. One possible role for extra care housing is as an alternative option to residential care.

21. Good practice models of extra care housing provide a high degree of choice over everyday living. In contrast to care homes, a fundamental feature is that users live in their own self-contained dwelling, ie, with their own kitchen and bathroom and other features of an ordinary dwelling. This is often described as people having their "own front door". Service users also have housing rights, usually through a tenancy, which gives them greater control.

22. This form of housing may be built as either houses or flats and will often be in a group, with some communal facilities, such as a lounge, assisted bathing facility, laundry, hairdressing, and dining facility. In some schemes, a meals service may be provided, in others this may be arranged through social services.

23. There are different models for the provision of care and accommodation, which may be provided separately or by the same organisation, and may be managed in various ways. Each has its merits. The Department wishes to encourage the development of good practice models of extra care housing for older people, as one way of promoting partnership in the provision of care and housing and encouraging independent living for older people.

24. As part of a preventive, enabling (or re-enabling) philosophy, some extra care housing schemes have a mixed dependency population, of which a proportion would otherwise be in residential care, although it is not possible to be categorical about this. Flexibility in care should be built into schemes, so that, if a person's care needs change, their care plan will change accordingly. In some cases, people who move in may improve or recover, so that they no longer have a need for personal care. Unless this was part of the original care plan, eg, as part of intermediate care prior to returning to the person's permanent home, the person should not be asked to leave. They would have the right to refuse to leave, if asked, as they will have an assured tenancy, or in the case of private schemes a lease.

25. Many, but not all, schemes also focus on supporting other older people in the surrounding community, as well as those living in the scheme. This may, for example, be through provision of home care in older people's own homes outside the scheme or through day care.

26. As a matter of policy, the Department does not envisage good practice extra care housing of the kinds described here being registered as care homes. Provision of personal care within these schemes would usually be expected to lead to registration as a domiciliary care agency. Further advice below aims to help NCSC inspectors to distinguish good practice extra care housing schemes from other schemes which should properly be registered as care homes, and to explain the legal basis for making the distinction.

Housing and support for people with learning disabilities

27. The White Paper, *Valuing People* (2001) is underpinned by four key principles—Rights, Independence, Choice and Inclusion. The way in which housing, care and support are offered to people with learning disabilities should reflect this. **B–008**

28. The Government objective in this area of services is to develop person-centred services which enable people with learning disabilities and their families to have greater choice and control over where and how they live. Housing, care and support options should enhance opportunities for people with learning disabilities and their families to exercise choice and control in their lives.

29. People with learning disabilities with all levels of support need can live successfully in different types of housing. They can cope with the full range of tenures. Expanding the range and choice of housing care and support services is central to giving individuals more choice and control in their lives.

30. Widening the housing, care and support options available creates the potential for choice, but many people with learning disabilities will need advice and support to do this. This advice should include the strengths and weaknesses of different options within the context of the four key principles—Rights, Independence, Choice and Inclusion.

Meaning of establishment—Who provides the personal care and the accommodation?

B–009 31. As stated above and discussed further below, a care home must be an "establishment". Under section 3 of the Act, an establishment is a care home if it provides accommodation, *together with* nursing or personal care for certain categories of person. Note that section 3 says that an establishment is a care home if *it* (i.e. the establishment, not the provider) provides accommodation.

32. It must first be established whether, as a matter of fact, the establishment meets this definition. The factual situation would include the way the accommodation and care are provided. Whether accommodation and care are provided by separate individuals or companies is not necessarily the most important issue.

33. There must be a considerable range of permutations, depending upon the particular facts of each case. At one end of the spectrum will be where a person rents a flat and receives domiciliary care, where there is no connection between the landlord and the care agency. At the other end you could have two or more separate companies all engaged in running the *establishment*. The point is not whether a particular company provides accommodation or care, but rather whether it carries on an establishment which provides (through however many companies) accommodation together with nursing or personal care. **Where it is clear that the domiciliary care provisions do not apply,** separate provision of accommodation and care by different companies will not necessarily escape the conclusion that there is an establishment providing accommodation together with nursing or personal care. Once it has been found that, as a matter of fact, the establishment is a care home, it would then be necessary to consider who carries on or manages the care home.

Provision of personal care in a person's "own home"—Extra care or very sheltered housing

B–010 34. The underlying intention of the Care Standards Act provisions is that, whereas care homes involve a fully integrated package of accommodation and care, a person receiving domiciliary care would be expected to have a high degree of autonomy in relation to their accommodation, like that enjoyed by most persons living in ordinary housing with secure tenure. In the vast majority of "very sheltered housing" or "extra care" schemes, personal care is being provided to people in their own homes, whether they are an owner-occupier or a tenant. Where it is clearly the case that personal care is being provided in a person's own home, then registration as a domiciliary care agency of the person or body providing personal care is likely to be required. There will be no registration as a care home, irrespective of the level of personal care available.

35. What is meant by a person's "own home"? This is not defined in the Act and it should be given its ordinary meaning. If a person is an owner-occupier (freehold or leasehold) then there is unlikely to be any argument about it. If it is clear that they have an assured tenancy[1], this is a strong indication

---

[1] For local authority provided schemes and some Registered Social Landlord schemes, "secure tenancies" are equivalent to assured tenancies.

that they are living in their own home. Further advice on the distinction between assured tenancies and licences is included at Annex A.

36. A fundamental point is that whether a person has an assured tenancy or a licence is a question of fact in each case. There have been a number of court rulings which found that licences so described were in fact assured tenancies, and *vice versa*. In the case of extra care housing or supported housing, possession of an assured tenancy will generally mean that a person has a right to deny entry to other people, including any care workers, without this having an effect on their right to occupy the dwelling. There may be practical difficulties about exercising choices over personal care, meals, or laundry. For example, the commissioning of care may not allow for particular choices of care provider by a user. Nevertheless, the fact that the person's security of housing tenure would be unaffected by denying entry to a care worker, in the same way as for any person living in ordinary housing, is a crucial difference from most care home provision and a factor in their greater independence. It means that the person is genuinely living "in their own home".

Provision of personal care in a person's "own home"—Supported housing and group homes/shared accommodation

37. Can a person's "own home" be in shared accommodation? It is common for **B–011** supported housing to be shared accommodation, usually in small group homes, for learning disabled people, people with mental health problems, and for some other groups.

38. As noted in Annex A, it is legally possible to have an assured joint tenancy in shared housing. This may be joint tenancy as a group for the whole of the property. Alternatively, there will be individual tenancy of part of the dwelling, such as a bedroom, with access to common areas. Each of these may be properly assured tenancies.

39. As stated in paragraph 35, possession of an assured tenancy is a strong indication that personal care is being provided in a person's "own home". Particular issues arise in determining whether shared accommodation is supported housing, where registration of a domiciliary care agency is needed, or registration as a care home. It will be necessary to look beyond the question of whether there is an assured tenancy/tenancies in the shared accommodation.

40. The scale of any shared accommodation is a relevant issue to be taken into account in considering whether personal care is being provided in a person's "own home". The Domiciliary Care Regulations are designed for application where care is delivered in small scale, domestic settings, where it can reasonably be said that service users exercise a high degree of control. Where shared accommodation goes beyond a small, domestic scale, a higher level of organisation is needed in the delivery of care, users' own control of their environment and delivery of their care may be less, and the need for regulation of the delivery of care and of accommodation greater.

41. As general guidance, particular care will need to be exercised over shared accommodation for service users with highly intensive care needs, where the number of users is more than might be expected in a family or a domestic setting. Account should be taken, eg, of factors such as the mixture of care needs, or where residents include relatives or informal carers. But there will be cases where it is not realistic to regard shared accommodation larger than family or domestic scale as each person's "own home" in the terms of

the Act, despite the fact that each person may have an assured tenancy. The approach should be to assess all the facts involved in each case, rather than applying any rigid rule as to scale. In some cases, registration as a care home, rather than as a domiciliary care agency, might better reflect the reality of the situation.

Capacity

B–012 42. A service user's capacity may be relevant both to whether the person has an assured tenancy and to whether personal care can truly be said to be delivered in the person's "own home", particularly for shared accommodation. The approach to be adopted in relation to tenancies is summarised in Annex B, and is consistent with that set out in *"Making Decisions—the Government's proposals for making decisions on behalf of mentally incapacitated adults"*.[1]

43. This does not mean any generalised assumption that certain groups are incapable of exercising such rights. The aim should be to protect vulnerable persons, but not to inhibit self-determination. Due weight should always be given to the person's own wishes in relation to their care and accommodation, as part of a proper assessment of the person's needs and as part of an individual care plan. Even where users have a limited understanding of the detail of tenancies and contracts, no assumption should be made that they cannot be supported to achieve the maximum degree of rights, choice, inclusion, and independence

44. Assessing a user's ability to understand, to communicate their wishes, and to exercise control over the delivery of care in their own home should allow for the contribution of care workers, relatives or informal carers, who are actively involved in the user's care and can aid their understanding or ability to communicate.

Adult placements

B–013 45. Adult placement[2] provides short or long term accommodation and/or care and support normally to between one and three adults, placed through and supported by an adult placement scheme or by an adult placement carer approved by the scheme. Adult Placements may include:

- accommodation with personal care, or intermediate care, in the family home of an AP Carer registered under the Care Standards Act;

- housing with support administered under Supported Living;

- home based day services;

- respite care, where personal care is not provided; and

- extended family ("kinship") support in the community.

46. An Adult Placement Scheme, managed by a local authority or independent (profitmaking or non-profit-making) agency, is responsible for recruiting, assessing, training and supporting AP Carers; for taking referrals, matching

---

[1] Lord Chancellor's Department, October 1999
[2] See regulations 45–46 of the Care Home Regulations

and placing service users with AP Carers; and for supporting and monitoring the Placement.

47. In cases where personal care (including assistance with bodily functions, where this is required, as provided for care homes) is provided, AP Carers who are formally approved by an Adult Placement Scheme are the registered person under the Care Standards Act. They are registered in respect of their own home for the limited purpose of providing Adult Placements. Registration under the Care Standards Act means that the registered person (the AP Carer) will be responsible for complying with relevant legislative requirements. The Commission must take into account the National Minimum Standards when making decisions about registration. These will apply only to those placements that provide personal care.

48. Service users in Adult Placements may receive personal care and/or housing related support. Service users who have a licence agreement are able to claim Transitional Housing Benefit for housing-related support costs and, after April 2003, funding could be provided from *Supporting People.*

49. Adult Placement Schemes and Carers work in a highly flexible way and provide a wide range of different services. They are subject, therefore, to a number of different regulatory requirements. Adult Placement Schemes have to comply with:

- the Guidance issued by the Department of Health for Adult Placement Schemes

- the National Minimum Standards and regulations for Domiciliary Care Agencies

- Supporting People quality and monitoring requirements

50. AP Carers have to comply with:

- the National Minimum Standards and regulations for adult placements registered with the NCSC (if they provide accommodation and personal care)

- Supporting People quality and monitoring requirements.

Regulatory frameworks—How do these interrelate?

51. This guidance seeks to help decisions on whether schemes should be subject **B–014** to regulation as care homes, or other regulatory frameworks. In broad terms for care homes and adult placements, the National Minimum Standards for Older People, the National Minimum Standards for Younger Adults, the National Minimum Standards for Adult Placement, and the National Minimum Standards for young people aged 16 and 17 regulate the areas of:

(a) user choice, information, dignity, privacy, and involvement in assessment of needs

(b) proper management and administration, financial probity, staff supervision, and safe working practices

(c) complaints, user rights, and protection

(d) staffing, including staff complement, qualifications and training

(e) quality

(f) the environment, space, facilities and fittings, heating, hygiene and control of infection.

52. In broad terms also, the National Minimum Standards for Domiciliary Care cover areas (a) to (e) above. It is clearly not possible, or appropriate, to seek to regulate the environment (f) when care is delivered to a person's own home, when this will usually be ordinary housing in which the person has lived for many years. Within area (d), the National Minimum Standards for Domiciliary Care focus on requirements for proper assessment of each individual's need and development of an individual care plan, in consultation with the service user. A domiciliary care agency is expected to demonstrate its capacity to meet the assessed needs of individuals accepted by the agency (Standard 3). The Domiciliary Care Agency Regulations provide that, where an agency is acting otherwise than as an employment agency, then the registered person must (having regard to the nature of the agency and the number and needs of service users) ensure that at all times there is an appropriate number of suitably qualified, skilled, and experienced persons employed for the purposes of the agency.

53. The Housing Corporation regulates registered social landlords, generally known as housing associations. The key aims of the Housing Corporation's regulatory function are to ensure that housing associations are viable, properly governed, and properly managed. The Corporation's regulatory remit includes elements of (a), (b), (c), and (f).

54. Housing association stock, which falls under the Housing Corporation's regulatory control, may include sheltered housing, extra care housing, supported housing, and some registered care homes. The Housing Corporation seeks to minimise possible regulatory duplication by working with other regulators, including the National Care Standards Commission.

55. Extra care housing or supported housing, whether provided by housing associations or local authorities, may be fully or partly funded by the Supporting People programme from April 2003 and will be subject to Supporting People performance review mechanisms.

Changes to registered care homes

B–015 56. There are positive reasons why organisations might seek to change a care home and cease registration as a care home. This might be appropriate in circumstances where the assessments/care plans of the individuals in the scheme lead to changes that might promote greater independence. In some cases, the greater consistency of regulation applied by the National Care Standards Commission after April 2002 may lead to re-designation of care homes, which have previously been registered. Such changes should *only* occur where there has been a service review involving residents/tenants and it is clear that the requirements for registration no longer apply.

57. In the run up to Supporting People, due for implementation in April 2003, we are aware that some organisations have been advised to change their care homes. This has involved persuading their tenants/residents to claim Transitional Housing Benefit (THB) for housing related support costs, on

the basis that the services provided in the home is no longer a care home. Once a claim is made and approved, the housing related support costs, determined through THB, will be added to the Supporting People (SP) "pot". This "pot" is being calculated from THB claims (along with other funding sources) in the run up to April 2003 and will be transferred to local authorities, subject to schemes complying with Supporting People Grant conditions after April 2003. Local authorities will then take on the funding and administration of housing related support through a Supporting People Grant.

58. Government policy would not support inappropriate changes to care homes which do not genuinely promote the independence of users, but seek primarily to secure funding through Transitional Housing Benefit and *Supporting People*. Such changes risk removing necessary protection from vulnerable people and may be unlawful.

59. If there is any argument about whether an establishment is a care home or not, then the National Care Standards Commission will need to take a view. And, of course, the Commission's decision will be subject to appeal and may be tested in a Tribunal and ultimately a court of law

60. The Office of the Deputy Prime Minister issued a pre-consultation draft of Directions and Grant conditions for Supporting People on 10 June 2002, and will issue further elements of those directions and grant conditions at the same time as this guidance. These do not allow for funding of registered care homes from Supporting People funds, other than transitionally for care homes previously funded (in part) by Social Housing Management Grant. Any schemes found to be properly registrable as care homes will forfeit funding from Transitional Housing Benefit (up to March 2003) or from Supporting People Grant (from April 2003). Under section 11 of the Care Standards Act, the scheme provider will be committing an offence of carrying on or managing an establishment without being registered. We strongly recommend that providers take advice from the National Care Standards Commission, before changing the registration of any scheme under the Care Standards Act 2000.

61. The Care Standards Act 2000 and associated regulations recognise that in some circumstances an existing registered care home provider will wish to relinquish their registered status to seek to provide alternative forms of care or simply to cease trading. Regulation 15 of the NCSC (Registration) Regulations 2001 allows registered providers to apply for 'Voluntary Cancellation' of their registration. Such an application must be made at least 3 months before the proposed date when the registration as a care home will cease. Certain information must be supplied to the NCSC to satisfy the Commission that all necessary arrangements have been made to secure the appropriate relocation of service users. For further advice on the process to be applied advice must be sought from the NCSC.

Summary: To register as a care home or as a domiciliary care agency?

B–016 [This chart is for illustrative purposes only and should be read in conjunction with the detailed guidance. References are to paragraph numbers in the guidance.]

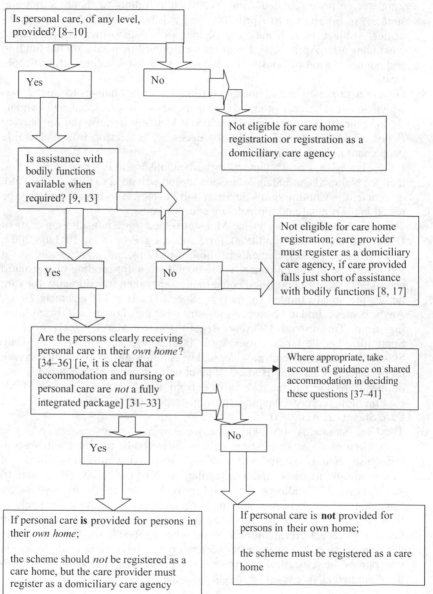

Is personal care, of any level, provided? [8–10]

Yes

No

Not eligible for care home registration or registration as a domiciliary care agency

Is assistance with bodily functions available when required? [9, 13]

Yes

No

Not eligible for care home registration; care provider must register as a domiciliary care agency, if care provided falls just short of assistance with bodily functions [8, 17]

Are the persons clearly receiving personal care in their *own home*? [34–36] [ie, it is clear that accommodation and nursing or personal care are *not* a fully integrated package] [31–33]

Where appropriate, take account of guidance on shared accommodation in deciding these questions [37–41]

Yes

No

If personal care **is** provided for persons in their *own home*;

the scheme should *not* be registered as a care home, but the care provider must register as a domiciliary care agency

If personal care is **not** provided for persons in their own home;

the scheme must be registered as a care home

ANNEX A

Assured Tenancies and Security of Tenure
(based on the Housing Corporation's Code of Practice on Tenure, October 1999)

Introduction
1. The Housing Corporation requires registered social landlords (housing as- **B–017** sociations) to give residents in supported housing the most secure form of tenancy compatible with the purpose of the housing. Implementation of the Code of Practice on Tenure is assessed as part of compliance with the performance standards for supported housing.
2. Supported housing includes:—

- Direct access hostels

- Group homes

- Purpose built self contained housing

- Foyers.

3. Supported housing can be provided in self contained or shared housing. It excludes general housing in which residents only receive care services from another agency (e.g. social services) and the housing association is not itself providing, or contracting to provide, further services.

Assured tenancies
4. Assured tenants have security of tenure and can only be asked to leave under **B–018** certain conditions, which are specified in law. (Section 2 of the Housing Act 1988) These will relate to issues such as non-payment of rent, nuisance, use of premises, damage, racial and other harassment etc.
5. A tenancy is a grant of interest in the land and a licence is merely permission to stay. According to the Housing Corporation's code the *conditions for a tenancy* as opposed to a licence are that:—

- There must be identifiable parties

- An area of occupation must be defined

- The arrangement must relate to a particular period or cycle of time, for example for 6 months, monthly or for life

- The occupier must have *exclusive possession* of at least a part of the premises and will usually pay a charge for occupancy (the rent).

6. *Exclusive occupation or use/Possession* is the right of an occupier to exclude others from the property, subject to certain restricted rights, which the landlord may reserve, for example, to enter to repair or review the condition of the property or to clean the premises.
7. It is legally possible to have an assured joint tenancy in *shared housing*. This may be joint tenancy as a group for the whole of the property. Alternatively, there will be individual tenancy of part of the dwelling, such as a bedroom, which amounts to exclusive occupation (reference to Street vs. Mountford

case) with access to common areas. Each of these may be assured tenancies. A third possibility for shared houses is for a landlord to contract with each individual occupier for a right to live in the property, but without specifying which part of it. Because each occupier has neither identifiable premises nor a jointness with other occupiers to make the arrangement a tenancy of the whole property, there is not sufficient exclusivity for the arrangement to be a tenancy, it is a *licence* to occupy.

8. This has been a contentious area of law, which ultimately only a court can decide. In the past, landlords would set up what they called "licence arrangements" with occupiers to get round some of the protections (security of tenure, and particularly rent) that tenants (not licensees) had. Sometimes this consisted only of putting the heading on the agreement, with the terms of occupation being exactly as for a tenancy. Many cases were brought, and the courts have become increasingly stringent in what they will accept as a licence: the default assumption is usually that an arrangement is a tenancy, and it is only where the reality of how it works points to it being "less" that would make it a licence.

9. Assured tenancies are fixed or periodic. Since the introduction of the Housing Act 1996 an assured shorthold tenancy can be fixed of periodic. In shorthold tenancies there will be a time limit on the tenancy and this might be appropriate in cases where there is short stay or temporary accommodation being offered. The Housing Corporation *recommends assured tenancies in cases where there is a home for life, permanent or long term accommodation and the conditions for a tenancy are met.* This applies to self contained and shared housing.

Secure tenancies

B–019 10. Under Part IV of the Housing Act 1985, local authorities (and historically, until the commencement of the Housing Act 1988, housing associations) are empowered to grant secure tenancies. Secure tenants have security of tenure and can only be asked to leave under certain conditions, which are specified in law, and enjoy the right to the quiet enjoyment of their home. These rights are closely analogous to those applying for assured tenancies. Secure tenancies and assured tenancies should be treated as interchangeable for the purposes of this guidance.

Licences

B–020 11. The conditions for the issuing of a licence as opposed to a tenancy are where the occupant does not have exclusive possession of any part of the premises. This could include:—

- Two or more unrelated people, each with their own occupancy agreement are required to share a bedroom

- *The Landlord or agent requires and actually does gain access to the resident's rooms for the purposes of administering care or protecting a resident's welfare*

- The Landlord or agent requires to and actually does move residents between rooms for the purposes of managing the accommodation efficiently.

12. Registration as a care home does not in itself confer the status of a licence. It is the issue of having unrestricted access to a person's room, which does. For example registration inspections of resident's rooms should be made with the consent of residents and would not constitute a genuine requirement for unrestricted access. In the case of assured tenancies, there will not be unrestricted access.

National Housing Federation guidance issued in October 1997 on tenancies

13. The National Housing Federation provides model assured tenancy agreements, which set down the requirements for a range of types of tenure in the light of the Housing Act 1996. In summary, the models set out the landlord's and the tenant's obligations. There are model agreements for self contained and shared supported housing. In the case of very sheltered housing the self contained assured tenancy model will be appropriate. In the case of group living the assured tenancy model for shared supported housing will be appropriate. **B–021**

14. Tenants have the right to occupy the premises without interruption or interference from the association for the duration of the tenancy (except for the obligation contained in the agreement to give access to the associations' employees or contractors. This is in relation to inspections to carry out repairs or other works to the premises.) This right to occupy is so long as the tenant complies with the terms of the agreement and has proper respect for the rights of other tenants and other persons in the neighbourhood.

ANNEX B

Capacity and Housing Tenancies
A summary of the position is: **B–022**

i. Generally there is a legal presumption that a person is capable until proved otherwise.

ii. The test of capacity should be functional, ie, take account of the particular activity and the complexity of the elements of the contract, not a blanket test that a person is incapable of understanding; buying a bus ticket or a house is not the same. This would look at the information available and its form. Normally if you have exclusive possession, pay rent, for a term (e.g. a week or month) the Courts will recognise a tenancy exists regardless of documents and the person's understanding of them.

iii. A contract will also still be binding if the landlord believed the tenant was capable of making it.

iv. The penalty, if there is one, for having a void contract falls entirely on the party (ie, landlord) to the contract that has capacity not on the vulnerable person who lacks capacity.

v. Common law also provides that, for goods and services which are 'necessaries', the supplier can recover the price even if the contract is technically unenforceable. This allows the grant of a tenancy with the safeguard that rent is recoverable.

vi. Furthermore, the Official Solicitor has confirmed in advice to a local authority that the grant of a tenancy would be proper even though capacity may be limited. The landlord would be bound by the Agreement and a claim could be pursued by a "next friend" even though its provisions might be unenforceable against the tenant.

Index

Cancellation—*cont.*
registration—*cont.*
relevant offences, 3–024, 3–025
responsibility, 3–026
urgent procedure, 3–001, 3–026, 3–053—
3–061
Care homes, 1–013
absence, notice of, 4–14, 4–142
accommodation, 1–031, 1–037
adult placements, 4–164—4–116
carers, 4–168—4–170
short-term break for service user, 4–171—
4–173
alcohol or drug dependence, 1–031, 1–043
appointment of manager, 4–051
assessment of service users, 4–074—4–077
board, 1–033
changes, notice of, 4–145—4–147
children,
additional information and documents to be
obtained, 4–189
application of regulations to, 4–123
fitness of workers, 4–132
matters to be monitored, 4–190
offences, 4–136
registered person, 4–126
review of quality and care, 4–135
separate provision, 4–127
staff disciplinary procedure, 4–133
statement of purpose, 4–125
welfare and protection, 4–130, 4–131
complaints, 4–107—4–109
compliance with regulations, 4–162, 4–163
conduct,
assessment of service users, 4–074—4–077
complaints, 4–107—4–109
facilities and services, 4–081—4–085
fitness of workers, 4–094—4–099
health and welfare of service
users, 4–063—4–066
records, 4–086—4–093
restrictions on acting for service
user, 4–104
service user's plan, 4–078—4–080
staff views, 4–104—4–106
court holding establishment to be, effect
of, 1–034
Criminal Records Bureau checks, 4–098,
4–176—4–178
death,
notification of, 4–138—4–141
registered person, 4–155, 4–156
definition, 1–01, 1–031—1–044
disabled persons, 1–031, 1–042
establishment, 1–031, 1–037
European Convention on Human
Rights, 1–034
excepted establishments, 4–024—4–027
exclusions from definition, 1–031, 1–044
facilities and services, 4–081—4–085
fees, 4–036—4–040

Care homes—*cont.*
financial position, 4–117—4–119
fitness,
premises, 4–110—4–113
registered manager, 4–054
registered provider, 4–044—4–050
workers, 4–094—4–099
health and welfare of service users, 4–063—
4–066
requirements, 4–067—4–073
hospital premises not, 1–013
illness, notification of, 4–138—4–141
infirmity, 1–040
liquidation, 4–152—4–154
local authority residential homes, 1–033
management,
financial position, 4–117—4–119
review of quality and care, 4–114—4–116
visits by registered provider, 4–120—
4–122
manager,
appointment, 4–051—4–053
fitness, 4–054—4–056
information and documents, 4–176—
4–178
meeting criteria for, effect of, 1–037
mental disorder, persons with, 1–031, 1–041
NHS residential care homes, 1–033
non-overnight accommodation, 1–037
notice,
absence, 4–142, 4–143
changes, 4–145—4–147
termination of accommodation, 4–148—
4–150
notification of death, illness and other
events, 4–138—4–141
notification of offences, 4–060—4–062
number of residents, 1–031, 1–039
nursing care, 1–031, 1–038
nursing homes, 1–033
offences, 4–157—4–160
notification, 4–060—4–062
older people, 1–034
personal care, 1–031, 1–039
premises,
fitness, 4–110—4–113
provider, 1–031, 1–038
records, 4–086—4–093, 4–179—4–187
registered persons,
appointment of manager, 4–051
children, 4–126
death, 4–155, 4–156
fitness of registered manager, 4–054—
4–056
fitness of registered provider, 4–044—
4–050
general requirements, 4–057—4–059
interviews, 4–056
notification of offences, 4–060—4–062
registers, 3–126
registration, 3–121

314

Index